"Nash and White bring to life union women who helped to drive—and drew strength from—the women's movement. Fierce, visionary, and willing to challenge their own unions, they fought for equal pay, childcare, reproductive rights, parental leave, harassment-free workplaces, affirmative action, gender and racial equality, 2SLGBTQ+ rights, and union rights legislation—winning the support of male allies along the way. With solidarity and love, their struggles transformed their union, reshaped the labour movement, and sparked broader societal change, leaving a legacy to inspire new generations of feminist activists."

Barb MacQuarrie, community director (retired), Center for Research and Education on Violence Against Women and Children, Faculty of Education, Western University

"*Women United* is a fascinating, meticulously researched, insiders' account of how women gained their place in unions and advanced women's rights from equal pay to affirmative action to gender-based violence. Its insights into the strategies and tactics of mobilizing quickly and leveraging allies within and beyond, without sugar coating the challenges of navigating male-dominated environments, is invaluable. As Peggy Nash reminds us: 'Your belief in building a better world will see you through the tough times. When you have to fight to make change, remember you are also making history.'"

Wendy Cukier, Diversity Institute, Toronto Metropolitan University; co-founder of the Coalition for Gun Control

"This extraordinary book is a powerful testament to the strength and resilience of women in the labour movement. Nash and White weave together a complex tapestry of history, personal story, and sharp analysis, and in doing so, show how women have shaped labour in Canada and continue to redefine the meaning of solidarity. At a time when workers' rights are under attack, this powerful rallying cry reminds us that women have long been the unsung heroes at the heart of progress and are wholly deserving of respect in workplaces, in unions, and in history."

Lana Payne, national president of Unifor

Women United

Women United

Stories of Women's Struggles for Equality in the Canadian Auto Workers Union

Peggy Nash
& Julie White

First published in 2025 by
Between the Lines
401 Richmond Street West, Studio 281
Toronto, Ontario · M5V 3A8 · Canada
www.btlbooks.com

Library and Archives Canada Cataloguing in Publication
Title: Women united : stories of women's struggles for equality in the Canadian Auto Workers Union / Peggy Nash and Julie White.
Names: Nash, Peggy, 1951- | White, Julie, author.
Description: Includes bibliographical references and index.
Identifiers: Canadiana (print) 20250237121 | Canadiana (ebook) 20250237172 | ISBN 9781771136839 (softcover) | ISBN 9781771136846 (EPUB)
Subjects: LCSH: Women labor union members—Canada—History. | LCSH: Labor union members—Canada—History. | LCSH: CAW-Canada—History. | LCSH: Women in the labor movement—Canada—History. | LCSH: Labor movement—Canada—History.
Classification: LCC HD6079.2.C3 N37 2025 | DDC 331.4/780971—dc23

Cover and text design by DEEVE

Printed in Canada

We acknowledge for their financial support of our publishing activities: the Government of Canada; the Canada Council for the Arts; and the Government of Ontario through the Ontario Arts Council, the Ontario Book Publishers Tax Credit program, and Ontario Creates.

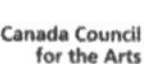

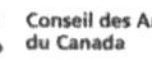

This book is dedicated to the resilience of those women activists who have come before and those that will come after.

The value of our interviews took on new meaning when two of the women we spoke with subsequently passed away. We want to pay special tribute to former CAW Local 88 President Cathy Austin and former CAW Local 240 president and later national representative Colette Hooson. These two women were courageous in challenging the status quo and blazed trails for others to follow.

Another world is not only possible, she is on her way. On a quiet day, I can hear her breathing.

—Arundhati Roy

Contents

Preface xi

Prologue: The Win—A Woman President xv

PART I: How Women of the UAW/CAW Made It Their Union

Chapter One
UAW, A Woman's Place Is in the Union, 1935–1978 3

Chapter Two
Union Women Winning Victories, 1978–1985 33

Chapter Three
CAW Mergers Building a Sisterhood, 1985–1995 65

Chapter Four
Tragedy and Transformation, 1990–1995 103

Chapter Five
Women on the March, 1995–2000 135

PART II: CAW Women Diversifying Their Union

Chapter Six
Contradictory Progress, 2000–2014 173

Chapter Seven
The Privilege and the Price of Change 215

Epilogue: The Future Looks Feminist, Lana Payne, President 255

Afterword: Advice for New Activists 269

Biographies of Interviewees 275

Notes 287

Index 291

Preface

History is usually written about leaders. When we looked at the history of our union, the Canadian Auto Workers (CAW), we saw that women were mostly absent. Similarly in the histories of the women's movements, labour women are mostly absent, at least women from industrial, male-dominated unions.

We didn't feel absent, we the women of the CAW, originally the United Auto Workers Canada (UAW-Canada) and now Unifor. We organized, we educated, we initiated programs, we negotiated, we fought for change, and we united. The union elected, in 2022, its first woman president. She is standing on the shoulders of a long line of feminist activists in this tough, remarkable organization.

This is the story of some women in this one union, the UAW/CAW, 1985 to 2013. We offer our experiences to younger activists in any union or any community. We hope they can learn from our lessons, just as we learned from the women who came before us. They left us a powerful legacy that we have built on, and we pass one on to those who come next.

This book is dedicated to the contributions of women to the making of a union. So many of women's contributions to the union went unremarked upon or were ignored. We have begun correcting that here.

This is not a CAW book or a Unifor book. This is an initiative of the authors, and we have been free to write as we wish, to not only applaud the union but also to be critical.

We limited our attention to the UAW/CAW, to what we know and lived in our local unions and later at the national level. We did not devote our time to the former CEP (Communications, Energy and Paperworkers Union of Canada), another important story in Unifor's formation. That history is for the feminists in that union to record, and we hope they are able to do that.

So who are we, Peggy Nash and Julie White, the authors behind the telling of this story? We met as colleagues in the CAW and, for a time, we worked closely together. While our paths in the union took different directions, our commitment to honouring the work of women in our union brought us back together once again to embark on this project. Every aspect of it reflects our combined effort—from developing the structure and themes through conducting the interviews to shaping the narrative. This book is a joint project by the two of us in every sense. While one of us may have taken the lead in putting words to the page, the ideas and direction throughout the book are shared.

In telling this story, we chose to use the third person rather than "we," particularly when expressing our own experiences. Using "I" felt limiting and did not reflect the collaborative nature of our work, and "we" felt awkward in the telling of our individual stories. So instead, we've chosen to use third person throughout, except for our quotes, which we have treated in the same way as those of the other women we interviewed.

And we interviewed many women. Thank you to the many women who gave their time in interviews for this book. What you achieved is a rich labour history that has until now not been celebrated or even properly documented. Labour history is about regular people who just go to work every day to earn a living, and who decide to step forward and lead. You are inspiring, and we hope that your stories will spur others to similarly rise to the challenge.

There are so many more women we could have interviewed, women who made valuable contributions, who were underappreciated or ignored, women in their local unions who could never break through the barriers they faced. We encourage you to document those stories. They are all valuable. In writing this book, we realize that we have just touched the surface and there is much more work to be done. We hope others take up that challenge.

The text, the selection of quotes from the over fifty hours of interviews, the opinions, and conclusions are all signed off by the two of us.

We especially thank Wendy Cuthbertson and Pam Sugiman for their extensive and detailed published research into UAW/CAW history. We also thank Wendy Cuthbertson and Jane

Armstrong for reading draft text and for their editing advice. Kim Crump helped with research, and Trinh Lai of CAW/Unifor, thank you for giving us access to important history. Thanks to Toronto Metropolitan University for their ongoing support. Huge thanks to all the folks at Between the Lines publishing, Amanda Crocker and our amazing editor Mary Newberry, who made this work so much more enjoyable. It was with Mary's assistance that the book really took shape, and she never let us take the easy way out. Vince Pietropaolo was our photography consultant and gave us invaluable assistance. Any errors or omissions rest with the authors alone.

And thanks to our families: we thank you for putting up with us during this project. What we thought would take about a year took three times as long. Sometimes we got a bit snarly.

Most importantly this book is dedicated to the women of the union. The union made you strong, but you made the union so much stronger. This is your book.

In sisterhood and solidarity,
Peggy Nash and Julie White

Prologue

The Win—A Woman President

The air was taut with the fever of competition. Every moment was a chance to win someone over. Each candidate was frantic to shore up supporters and hoover up the few uncommitted delegates who remained on the sidelines. Every vote could make the difference. Months of jostling and wooing of union members was culminating in one single day's voting.

Union conventions are meetings of hundreds of elected leaders and staff who gather in giant, dimly lit halls of grey urban hotels for mostly routine proceedings. The occasionally fiery speaker or compelling debate is interspersed with stretches of reports, motions, procedural wrangling, and speeches from the floor by the delegates before a resolution, the outcome of which was often never in doubt.

Even at conventions where the union held elections for the top positions, there was limited excitement as the outcome was usually predictable. Since the earliest days of this union, the sitting president, in consultation with key advisers and other leaders in the union, would pronounce on his, always "his," recommended successor. Once endorsed by the union's national executive board, a body of top local leaders, that person's election was pretty much guaranteed. Occasionally opponents would run against the official choice, but their vote would be swamped by the tidal wave of votes in favour of the "official" candidate.

This election was different. The union was Unifor, the largest private-sector Canadian union with 320,000 members. In August 2022, heated competition for the top union offices electrified every interaction, from the order of agenda items to who was huddled in hushed voices with whom outside the main hall. Those supporting the same candidate recognized each other with a knowing eye. However, if they were supporting an opposing candidate, even former friends eyed each other with suspicion. Unable to persuade someone to change their support, colleagues stared straight ahead while passing in a hallway, as though eye contact would contaminate their fervent support for their chosen candidate. Relationships were stretched paper thin.

All candidates were confident in their victory. Scott Doherty, a senior negotiator in the union, tapped for succession by the former President Jerry Dias. Doherty's campaign was based on his bargaining experience and his leadership roles in the union. In normal times, with the president's endorsement, he would be the successor. That had been the practice since the earliest days of the union.

However, Dias's term had ended under a dubious cloud when he committed an ethical breach by inappropriately accepting money from a supplier who sold goods to the union. Nevertheless, he maintained support with sections of the union, and there was loyalty to his chosen candidate.

Lana Payne was the union's national secretary treasurer. When the issue of the ethical breach was brought to her attention, she refused to accept the tendency to minimize the issue, given the clear break in trust. Instead she sought legal advice and held an independent investigation. This confirmed that Dias had acted inappropriately, and he abruptly retired before the end of his term. Payne took over as acting president for the duration. She was concerned that Dias persisted in recommending Doherty as his successor; she believed he should have recused himself because of the investigation into his actions.

Some had suggested that the issues with Dias should have been kept in house so as not to taint the union's reputation. Payne was concerned that not being transparent about the investigation would end up tainting the union even more as the facts would eventually bubble up to the light of day. She believed that the union needed to be completely transparent and needed to transform how it operated to increase accountability and ethical practices. Concerned that nothing was going to change, and prompted by a growing number of local leaders, she decided to jump into the race herself and run for the presidency.

Former staff member Laurell Ritchie sums it up this way:

> I was thrilled when I heard the first rumours that she was going to be running and encouraged her to stay the course, not in spite of the existential crisis for the Union but because of it. I always assumed that she would want to run for president one day. But I'm equally sure that this was not the timing or the circumstances that she would have had in mind. I know in my heart that this must have been a few months of living hell for a lot of people inside that building, no truer than for the person in charge of watching the books, the national secretary treasurer, and that was Lana's job.
>
> I think a lesser person would have just looked the other way, which was the advice that many were giving, either in hindsight or in the moment. But one of the things about Lana, she has a strong moral compass, and that would not have lent itself to looking the other way. She has a deep sense of responsibility. She's got the fortitude. She's got the strength of character and a kind of generosity that doesn't always exist with leaders.

The third candidate was a skilled trades leader from Windsor, Dave Cassidy. He was the president of the large Local 444 representing workers at many workplaces including at Stellantis, Caesars and other casinos, and auto parts companies. He ran as a rank-and-file leader. He vowed to stay close to the membership and to give a strong voice to the auto sector, the historic base of the union.

All three candidates were running strong campaigns; all three believed that they would win.

After fierce and unprecedented campaigning, voting day arrived. Months of effort by the candidates trying to prove themselves as the best choice culminated with an electronic vote, the results of which would be flashed almost immediately on the convention screens. The voting ended. Everyone held their breath.

Suddenly a thunder of cheering and applause exploded through the giant hall when the vote was announced. There would be an immediate runoff, but it was clear that Payne was in the lead and would win. After the second vote, people were on their feet, with enthusiastic applause and shouts of joy. The woman at the centre of it, Lana Payne was wearing a jacket in her signature purple. She calmly rose to her feet, beaming, her arms raised in victory. She seemed both exhilarated in her success and fully confident in the outcome, mentally preparing, ten steps ahead for what would follow.

Payne has high praise for her campaign strategist and key organizer Roxanne Dubois, a Franco-Ontarian, who was a community activist and student organizer, skills she brought to the union. They had executed an effective strategy. "She was brilliant and left no stone unturned," says Payne. "We had created this almost-like-family in the campaign, so when we won, you're feeling everyone's joy. And I remember looking over at Roxanne, and the joy, she was so excited she couldn't sit down."

Payne made her way through a crowd of joyous excitement and hugs by well-wishers to the microphone where she pronounced her acceptance of the results. Payne's speech harkened back to

Lana Payne wins the Unifor presidency. Photo: Unifor.

Barack Obama's speech where he spoke about blue states or red states. "There is only the United States of America," he thundered.

"Starting today," Payne began, "there are no campaigns. There is no us and them. There is only Unifor."

She then signalled a new path for the union, tapping into the desire for recovery after the pandemic and the need to turn the page on missteps by past leadership, to chart a path for a better future.

> We can have a fighting, democratic transparent union. We can build this union stronger. And we will. All of us together. We can confront power, we can build working-class power across our union, from the bottom up. And we will, all of us together. We can dismantle sexism and racism. We can build love and unity, and true solidarity across our union and with all workers. And we will. All of us together.
>
> We can bring our union to more and more workers because we know every worker deserves the power of our union. We can be principled and smart in our fights and we will be. We will empower our local bargaining committees. We will build union power when we do.

The desire to capture the rare moment of political change in the union is signalled in the need to not only move on from the past ethical problems but also to rekindle the fire of building working-class power that is part of the union's origin. It is as though Payne felt that personal aggrandizement and greed have somehow poisoned the union, allowing it to stray from its principles. Now she was determined to set the union back on track, returning to the primary goal of defending workers' interests by challenging power. That goal she believes would be achieved through trusting the membership and building their power.

The applause for her victory was not universal. The other two candidates believed they would be the ones celebrating on the podium that day, and their supporters were naturally disappointed. It would take concerted effort to heal wounds and knit the union back together.

Payne's win however was not only a win by one candidate over others. It was the first time in the organization's history that a woman had secured the top spot, the presidency. This was not just any organization. The union now called Unifor, with its roots in the Communications, Energy and Paperworkers Union (CEP) and in the CAW and the US-based UAW, is known for being high profile, progressive, and socially engaged. It was also known as an industrial union made up predominantly of men, with a tough, combative culture at the bargaining table. So where did this woman come from?

PART I

How Women of the UAW/CAW Made It Their Union

Chapter One

UAW, A Woman's Place Is in the Union, 1935-1978

Margery Ferguson, 1940s

In the 1940s, Margery Ferguson was an officer in the Canadian region of the UAW (United Auto Workers) Local 439 at the Massey-Harris plant in Toronto where she wrote a local union newspaper column for women, "A Woman's Place Is In the Union." Ferguson was elected financial secretary of her local and was a delegate to the UAW council, a key leadership group in the union. She was the first woman to give a committee report there.[1]

A feminist, she advocated not only for full equal rights for women but also for the special needs of women, which she saw were overlooked by the male leadership. She compared the problems women faced to racism, both within the context of the working class. Ferguson anticipated second wave feminism's affirmative action programs by advocating for equal representation of women in leadership on committees. She also called for women's committees to be set up in every local union so that women could give attention to issues often otherwise ignored, such as the goal of equal pay.

Local union newspapers tried to give visibility to women members during the war years, especially when they were elected to union positions. For example, when UAW Local 199 in St. Catharines elected a woman to the bargaining committee at McKinnon Industries, they reported "We feel this is one of the best ways to build up the union for we have a lot of female workers in the plant."[2]

Pressured by their women members who wanted their needs taken up by the union, the UAW initially took up the goal of equal pay as a way to recruit more women into the union. By June 1942 there were more than 1000 women working at the McKinnon works in St. Catharines. The local union found it hard to encourage women to join the union, an action that was voluntary. By August later that year, Local 199 in St. Catharines submitted a resolution to the area council, supported by the Ford Windsor Local 200, and passed a resolution supporting equal pay.

Locals also encouraged women to be part of the union's activities, including social and recreational. "Some such occasions of sociability were women-only. The UAW held sessions at its union schools especially for women workers. Women-only meetings and groups were organized, sometimes at the recommendation of women activists. UAW Locals 673 or 112 at De Havilland, for example, set up a women's council to encourage women to become active in the union, and the council invited women from neighbouring locals to attend its meetings to further extend (women's) aims.'"[3]

At De Havilland Aircraft, women pushed to incorporate their goals into the union. They set up a women's group that advocated for childcare and pregnancy provisions, clean restrooms, and equal pay, and these proposals were adopted by the union.

In addition, women relatives of UAW members established women's auxiliaries, which were a support network for members, especially during strikes. In the war years, the auxiliaries took on a more political stance and argued for women's equality. Some local auxiliaries linked up with the women's movement of the time.

All these initial spaces and structures for women would plant seeds that would flourish in the future of the union.

Organizing, Mid-Nineteenth Century

For centuries, workers have organized themselves to increase their power with employers. The earliest craft unions in the United Kingdom, Europe, and North America based their power on their skill and their craftsmanship. With the era of mechanization in the early nineteenth century, these efforts intensified. Workers would join unions to pressure their employers to improve their conditions at work, and if they achieved their goal, they would disband their organization and continue to work. There was no legal right to form a union in Canada until 1872 with the passage of the Trade Unions Act, and workers who struggled for improvements were often arrested and jailed.

By the mid-nineteenth century, mass organizing in Canada spread to mines, forests, and textile factories. The idea of a union for unskilled workers as well as those with skills began to spread as the goal of a nine-hour workday took hold.

After the First World War, with the horrific loss of life, mass organizing, inspired by revolutionary 1872 movements in Russia and elsewhere, spurred hundreds of thousands of Canadian workers to join unions, culminating in the Winnipeg General Strike of 1919. In addition to higher wages and better working conditions, a key demand of the strike was the goal of union security—the right to be represented by a union in the workplace.

A bloody crackdown by police eventually broke the general strike without workers winning their goals, but their efforts inspired others. A recession in 1921 cooled militancy, and union representation fell. The Great Depression of the 1930s did eventually lead to more organizing of the unemployed. In 1935, US President Roosevelt passed the National Labour Relations Act, or Wagner Act, which formally recognized the right of workers to organize and bargain collectively. This, along with his New Deal, passed later in the 1930s to kickstart the economy, gave massive impetus for US workers to organize into unions.

Change in Canada came more slowly. The economic depression of the 1930s left people desperate for work to support themselves and their families.

It was the Second World War, with its massive government investments in industry that gave Canadian workers a renewed interest in unions. Unemployment during the war years dropped from double digits to almost zero. Union membership doubled to 25 per cent of the non-agricultural workforce during the war. More than a million women were recruited into the paid workforce to replace the men who had gone off to fight—women like Margery Ferguson, who opens this chapter.

These women who united to influence a male-dominated, industrial union to establish constitutional rights for women in their organization.

Women in Labour Activism during WWII

Labour historian Wendy Cuthbertson's 2012 study of labour activism during WWII, *Labour Goes to War: The CIO and the Construction of a New Social Order, 1939–1945*, noted how the culture of the war years helped with union organizing drives back home.

> Workers remembered Canada's callous treatment of Great War veterans and its ruthless repression of working-class organizations during that period. They had just suffered through the insecurity of the Great Depression, the blame for which most placed at the foot of business. The fact of war and the very nature of the enemy—the tyranny and racism of Nazism in particular—produced wartime discourses about such fundamental concepts as democracy, human rights, the obligations and rights of citizenship, and social equity.[4]

To keep the economy running and to boost the war effort, women were recruited into the paid workforce in droves. They built aircraft and military vehicles; they drove trucks and other heavy equipment. With secure jobs during the war years, workers' confidence rose and they joined unions to push for a better deal from employers. Incomes improved with negotiated union contracts. There were hundreds of strikes during the war years, and key strikes by auto workers, steelworkers, and women's clothing workers would manage to secure a stable place in the workforce.

The Congress of Industrial Organizations (CIO) was a group of unions that broke away from the American Federation of Labor (AFL) and formed a central labour organization to which unions became affiliated. Unlike the skilled workers normally in unions at that time, they were dedicated to organizing unskilled industrial workers from the mid-1930s to 1955. Until the CIO, mass organizing of unskilled workers in industries like auto, steel, and rubber had been organized around their craft or skill. With innovative organizing techniques like sit-down strikes and blockages, they had broken through with some key union recognition strikes in the auto and steel industries. For example, in 1937, the auto workers won a momentous forty-four-day sit-down strike at General Motors in Flint Michigan.

CIO unions in Canada, such as the UAW and the United Steelworkers of America (USWA), were formed as Canadian sections of US-based parent unions. Greater resources and a sense of larger solidarity was important during these formative years. The fascinating details of the history of the CIO is well-documented.[5] For our purposes, we note that in 1955 during the communist purges of the McCarthy era in the US, when key UAW leader Walter Reuther was the head of CIO, they agreed to reunite with the AFL to form the AFL-CIO. The differences between the two organizations had narrowed, as industrial unions had become firmly established.

In Canada, where more than four thousand workers in Oshawa, members of the UAW, fought and won a strike for union recognition, they formed the Canadian Congress of Labour (CCL), having been expelled from the trades-based Trades and Labour Congress (TLC), which was the voice of skilled workers. Similar anti-communist purges preceded the formation of the Canadian Labour Congress in 1956, which united the CCL and the TLC.

The CIO early on had pledged belief in full sexual and racial equality, and during the war turned its attention to appealing to women workers. The goal of equal pay for equal work became a key incentive for women to join. Organizing campaigns in several unions revolved around the goal of equal pay, and sometimes strike action backed up this goal.

Equal pay was not a new concept. There had been a demand for it since the 1880s. Men were concerned that lower wages for women would exert downward pressure on their wages. But it was during the war years, when women worked alongside men in industry, that the concept just seemed fair. Also, it was an important incentive for women to sign a union card.

While some argued for more women's involvement in unions to prevent cheap labour, many saw that it was about uniting women in the labour movement to advance women's equality. "Union feminists . . . championed the inclusion of women in the life of the union."[6]

Union and Labour Movement Structure

> When the union's inspiration through the workers'
> blood shall run,
> There can be no power greater anywhere beneath the sun;
> Yet what force on earth is weaker than the feeble
> strength of one,
> But the union makes us strong.
> —"Solidarity Forever," by Ralph Chaplin, 1915

Here it's useful to explain how unions work. There are different kinds of unions, and there is no one structure for all. To complicate matters, unions evolve so that a structure from one era, will change over time.

When workers understand they are at a disadvantage as individuals trying to improve their working conditions, they may join together to press their employer for improvements. They can try to do this informally, but the employer may disregard or delay making changes. Workers may decide to form a union, which is protected by law. If a majority (or whatever percentage is required by law) of the workers sign a card pledging support, they can try to form a union. In some provinces, having a majority or a certain percentage of workers sign cards is enough for the province to declare automatic certification of the union. This is called *card check certification*. However, in most jurisdictions, there is a second step. The workers are required to vote for the union in a vote organized by the government.

If the union is certified, the workers then elect a committee of their peers to negotiate with their employer on their behalf. This is called *collective bargaining*. The core work of a union is to negotiate a collective agreement for its members and, once that is achieved, to enforce that agreement throughout the life of the contract. Most collective agreements last from two to five years.

Once the collective agreement is negotiated, workers begin to pay *union dues*. This is a small amount of money that they pay every month to the union to pay for their representation during the agreement. These dues are tax deductible.

To enforce the agreement, the membership elects *representatives* in the workplace. These *reps* are often called *stewards*. If a worker has a complaint with management, they can go to their steward who will advise them and act on their behalf.

The workplace then becomes a unit—called a *bargaining unit*—that negotiates with the employer. A single unit may not have the resources needed to effectively represent its members. For example, they might need advice about negotiating pensions, benefits, health and safety, economics, and so forth. This drives bargaining units to come together to form larger organizations.

In the early years, the UAW was an international union, and Canada was seen as a region, officially recognized as region 7 of the union. The head of the union in Canada was called the Canadian director. The director would be supported by one or more assistants who would, if needed, represent them in collective bargaining or in leadership meetings. Eventually, in the post-war period, the UAW's Canadian region was affiliated with the central labour bodies in Canada, such as the Canadian Labour Congress, the Ontario Federation of Labour, other provincial federations, and local labour councils. Local unions would elect delegates to attend meetings or conventions of these central labour bodies.

Inside the UAW, there were local unions, each headed by a local president and a local financial secretary and other local union officials. A local union could represent one large bargaining unit that would bargain with one employer, such as an auto or aerospace company. Or it could be a collection of local employers representing, for example, auto parts companies.

The union's constitution would guide accountability for elected leaders and members, representation at bigger meetings such as conventions, and structures within the union. For example, in the UAW's Canadian region in the early days, there was a council of all locals that would come together periodically to debate and decide on issues facing the Canadian membership. This body was called the Canadian council. The Canadian council had its own bylaws and structures. All UAW regions had their own councils.

The council became an important body for leadership accountability. For example, when UAW-Canada, led by Canadian Director Bob White, wanted to separate from the US union, the key decision-making body was the Canadian council, which brought together elected leaders from across the union. White called this body the parliament of the union. In 1985, the Canadians did break away from the UAW to form the Canadian Auto Workers (CAW) and merged with many other Canadian unions. In 2013, the CAW and the Canadian Energy and Paperworkers Union joined together to form Unifor.

The UAW/CAW's structure was very much as just described.[7] In theory, the membership holds the power with the various levels of leadership, from local to national, carrying the membership's needs to the top. In practice the day-to-day decisions of the union are made by the national president in consultation with the national executive board. The CAW became a hierarchical union where the national officers, especially the president, held a great deal of power.

Nonetheless, the Canadian council is of particular importance to the history of women's struggles for equality in the CAW. It was here that women's committees made a breakthrough, and policies about childcare and harassment were first discussed.

Thirty-seven Women and the Ford Wildcat Strike,1942

The push for equal pay for women in the UAW came to a dramatic head as workers from Local 200 held a wildcat strike at Ford of Canada, in Windsor, Ontario. The plant was producing military vehicles. A wildcat strike is one where it is the workers themselves who decide to strike without the sanction of the union's leadership. That was the case at the massive Ford complex in 1942. In November that year, 13,500 workers walked off the job, protesting lower pay for women, thereby shutting down the plant's production of military vehicles. What is remarkable is that the union had signed its first ever contract with Ford as recently as January of 1942, after a bitter strike over how union dues were collected.

Of the November wildcat strike over equal pay for the newly hired women, Cuthbertson says: "At the centre of this storm? Thirty-seven women, who made up less than one-third of one per cent of Ford's Windsor workforce, and who were probably as astonished by their power to bring the corporation to a standstill as they were stunned by their national notoriety."[8]

In April 1942, they had been the first women ever hired by

Ford for clerical work previously done by men. Ford claimed it couldn't find any men for the jobs.

At the Canadian council meeting in August of that year, the union passed a resolution committing to the goal of equal pay for equal work.

Equal pay for equal work was already the law in Michigan, and women were working there at the Ford parent company. But there was no such law in Ontario. However, the Canadian National Labour Board, in September 1942, ruled in favour of equal pay for relatively equal work.

With a government mediator, the workers at Ford agreed to return to work without penalty after six days, while a referee worked on a plan for the thirty-seven women and the equal pay issue. Nothing prevented the company from giving the women equal pay; however, it resisted, saying that it would be too costly. The union argued that the women were strictly doing clerical work previously done by men and were therefore entitled to be on the seniority list and treated like the men. Instead, an arbitrator sided with the company. The women would stay out of the plant and lose the right to unionize.

The following year the company again wanted to bring women into the plant at a lower wage, which the union resisted. The outcome for the thirty-seven women who had sparked the protest was not good. They were laid off and out of a job. However, the publicity around the equal pay strike spurred women to join the paid workforce. Union membership exploded under the banner of Equal Pay for Equal Work. At the time, many women were making half the wages men made, fifty cents to the dollar. Women were not working for pocket money or "pin money" as, notoriously, many years later, women's earnings were referred to in an effort to justify lack of equality (see chapter 3). Women needed to support themselves and their children. They joined the workforce in droves and they wanted equal pay. Unions had been slow to respond, but if they wanted to organize women, they needed to address women's concerns.

By the time the Canadian council passed its equal pay resolution in 1943, it framed the issue as no longer just a measure to prevent the undercutting of male wages but as a basic human right, and it moved up high on the union's list of priorities with the government.

Companies continued to resist. As late as 1944, Phoebe Blair, chair of the bargaining committee at UAW Local 192 in Tilbury, Ontario, reported that the company was refusing equal pay and threatened their jobs if they did not accept.[9] The labour board's decision in favour of equal pay in September 1942 was of little help to women.

UAW's Formation of Women's Council, 1944

But it was also in 1944 at its constitutional convention that the UAW passed an amendment to its constitution mandating the creation of a women's department at its Detroit headquarters, the formation of a women's group in every region of the UAW (including Canada), and the creating of women's committees in every local union with women members. This was a groundbreaking initiative that allowed the next generation of feminists and human rights activists to build on these constitutional structures to advance women's rights and, ultimately, to fight against racism and for 2SLGBTQ+ rights.

Putting amendments into practice, however, took time. It was not until 1973 that the UAW Canadian director Dennis McDermott established a UAW Canadian women's advisory council of local union women to advise him on women's issues. This was disbanded in 1981 by then-Canadian Director Bob White to form the union's Canadian UAW council women's committee, composed of elected women delegates, giving women a collective voice in the union's parliament.[10]

Women in the UAW Constitution

During the war years, unions had framed their efforts in organizing and equal pay as part of a broader push for democracy and human rights, mirroring the rhetoric of Allied war aims. Their organizing was in tune with public support for the war effort and thus support for the role of women during the war. "We're not Nazis. We don't see women as second-class citizens," reported the UAW, the Steelworkers, the United Electrical Workers, and other CIO unions in their publications.

However, workers reflected society at large. Sexism and racism were entrenched. The portrayal of women's traditional roles often clashed and co-existed with the goal of achieving equality in the workplace.

Despite all this organizing and recruiting of women, the industrial unions making up the CIO had very few women leaders. Only one woman was hired to work for the UAW in Canada during this period and no other woman would be hired again as a union staff representative until the 1970s. Coming from the Local 636 executive in Woodstock, Ontario, Ruth Thompson was the sole woman, hired temporarily to collect dues from members at Metallic Roofing in Toronto. A plant of mostly women, they were difficult to convince to pay dues, perhaps because of their low pay and the failure of the union to achieve equal pay for them.[11]

Officially women were full partners in the union movement, but old attitudes die hard. Informally, especially at the local union level, life was more difficult with sexism and bias still entrenched. There was a boys' club that still saw women as outsiders. Men argued that women weren't pulling their weight and were hard to organize, never recognizing that they still had to keep the house clean, the kids looked after, and dinner on the table, nor that they were still paid less than men. They had less time and less money to become activists.

> Despite cultural biases against women's equality and the lack of support for women on the part of many unionists, the CIO's championing of women's rights aligned with wartime public support for women in the workplace (if only "for the duration"), so that, during the war, the CIO was able to make gains with regard to such issues as equal pay for equal work for women.[12]

The 1944 UAW amendment to its constitution mandating local union women's committees, a national and regional women's department, and an annual women's conference were groundbreaking. While these structures may have been subdued during the 1950s, their establishment persisted after the war, becoming significant tools for future feminist initiatives.

Even toward the war's end in 1944, when the UAW asked its

women members about their post-war goals, and despite massive propaganda pushing a return to the domestic sphere, fully 74 per cent of them wanted to keep building aircraft. Mostly, this didn't happen. Many plants resorted to sex-based seniority systems, even in places where such discrimination was prohibited on other human rights grounds such as race or colour.

Women may have been more absent in the paid workforce than they would have liked, but their presence in union's constitutions kept them present. The union, overall, was committed to gender equality as a human right and thereby contributed greatly to the post-war public support for democracy and equality that led to the passage of Ontario's 1951 Equal Pay Act, the first of its kind in the British Commonwealth. Cuthbertson argues that this was a direct result of the big industrial unions battling together, through the CIO, for equal pay in the manufacturing heartland of Ontario. Their efforts contributed to the broad public support for equal pay, as high as 78 per cent of the wartime Canadian population according to a Gallup poll.

Even though most industrial workplaces once again became male dominated, "the war had shown women a larger world they could inhabit, one with more vocational choice, greater financial security and independence, the chance to work outside the home after marriage, and the opportunity to lead. The CIO's campaign for equal pay, which hundreds of thousands of working women would have contributed to, expanded their sense of their rights and their proper due."[13]

The war years and the push to organize women had led unions to champion women's rights, especially the right to equal pay. This influx of women during the war years pushed the UAW to create unique structures for women members such as local union women's committees and annual women's conferences. These structures persisted during the retrenchment of the post-war years and laid the foundation in the union for second wave feminism. They would serve as a solid foundation for the Canadians in later years when they separated from the US union and set off on their own path.

The Rand Formula: Collecting Union Fees by Checkoff, 1946

Unions struggled to maintain their organization even when they were recognized by the employer. Union workplace representatives, or stewards, would need to canvass each member every month to ask them to voluntarily pay their union dues. This kept the stewards in close contact with their members, but this work was time consuming and left unions on an insecure financial footing. Unions demanded not only union recognition but union security, that is, a requirement that the employer automatically deduct dues from each worker's pay and remit the dues monthly to the union. This goal was at the heart of many strikes including those of three thousand shipyard workers in Halifax in 1944, eleven thousand Ford Motor Company workers in Windsor in 1945, and two thousand steelworkers at Stelco in 1946 in Hamilton. There was no strike pay, so the strikers had to appeal to the community and to other unions for support.

The 1945 Ford strike over union security dragged on for months, lasting ninety-nine days, but there was huge community support. Union solidarity extended to joining in a blockade of the Ford facility with parked cars. The strike was finally settled with an agreement to accept an arbitration decision by Justice Ivan Rand. In January 1946, Justice Rand decided that, even if workers did not want to belong, all workers benefited from the union. So, he ruled that all workers had to pay union dues by a system that became known as dues checkoff. Checkoff is a monthly amount deducted by the employer from the pay of each worker to send to the union for its administration. It is called the union security clause because it provides secure income for the union to represent its members. In exchange, the union had to agree that there would be no strikes or walkouts during the life of the collective agreement. This was a key victory for workers and their unions, and many employers went on to recognize this ruling.

This Rand formula created the opportunity for workers to better organize into unions knowing that their union had a secure financial footing. It allowed the union to compensate leaders and hire staff. This union security was the underpinning for workers, through their unions, to negotiate a larger piece of the economic pie. Sharing in the post-war prosperity of Canada meant workers could gain more of the fruits of their labour.

But it was not the law. The Rand formula was an agreement

reached through contract arbitration, and it applied strictly to that one labour dispute at Ford of Canada. While many employers voluntarily agreed to adopt that formula and thereby create security for unions, it was not mandatory.

In Quebec, almost twenty years later, it would take a twenty-month strike, strikebreakers, and terrible unwarranted police brutality, before United Aircraft, now named Pratt and Whitney, would recognize the union and agree to dues checkoff. The Parti Quebecois government elected the next year in 1977, would enshrine dues checkoff in law. They also brought in Canada's first anti-scab law, whereby the employer was barred from trying to break a strike by bringing in outside replacement, or scab, labour.

Women Post-War, 1950s

After the war, the number of women members in UAW-Canada dropped to about 10 per cent, but the union remained committed to human rights, anti-racism, and equal treatment for women, much of which was now entrenched in the UAW's constitution.

The structures the union built in the war years also persisted. The UAW continued to hold annual women's conferences. Every year, UAW women leaders from the United States would come to speak to the Canadian women and bring a feminist message.

Bev McCloskey: Power of the Women's Committees

In Canada, there were pioneers like Bev McCloskey of UAW Local 222 at General Motors in Oshawa. Hired at GMC in 1949 at age twenty, she took part in a twenty-two-day wildcat strike later that year that turned her into a lifelong social activist. Such strikes, in defiance of the union leadership and their employer, were common in many industries in the 1940s, as workers fought for better wages, benefits, and working conditions.[14]

In the 1950s McCloskey became the recording secretary for the local union, the only position women held at that time. She kept that position for seventeen years. She also continuously held several elected positions through her years of employment at GM: committeeperson, alternate committeeperson, acting district committeeperson, along with her work on many standing committees.

Bev was first exposed to the idea of a women's committee

Bev McCloskey elected as recording secretary, 1956, on the UAW Local 222 executive, seated next to President Cliff Pilkey. Photo: UAW.

when she was a delegate to an international UAW convention in the United States. Upon returning to Canada, she actively began signing women up, co-founding, in September of 1968, the first women's committee in the Canadian region. The committee successfully led the fight against sex-segregated seniority lists by pressuring the Ontario government to amend the human rights code (see full story below). She and the women's committee later took up the fight against sexist photos, or pinups, in the workplace, attaching stickers that read "This Insults Women." By 1983, her campaign to the union and the company was successful, and the pinups came down. In 1999 the Sisterhood Room at the CAW Family Education Centre was named in honour of the Local 222 women's committee to recognize McCloskey and the committee's pioneering work to advance women's equality.

Women's Committee Victory over Seniority List, 1970

The post-war period was a time of labour-movement strength and progress. Struggles such as the GM 148-day strike led to better wages, new benefits, and more rights in the workplace. This period of economic expansion, although with periodic downturns, created an unprecedented prosperity. But prosperity was not equally shared. Racism excluded many Indigenous and Black workers from the higher-paid jobs. And sexism was at the heart of union security where women were placed on separate seniority lists, which meant they were laid off before the (even junior) men while doing the same work.

In the post-war period, the auto industry remained central to the Canadian economy. It created thousands of jobs and, thanks to union contracts, maintained its status of high pay and good benefits. However, women's employment in the auto industry had dropped significantly. For example, at McKinnon Industries in St. Catharines (later to become General Motors), women's employment fell from a wartime high of 1,200 to just 170 in 1966, according to Pam Sugiman's 1992 article "'That Wall's Comin' Down': Gendered Strategies of Worker Resistance in the UAW Canadian Region 1963–1970."

The industry was highly segregated with men's and women's seniority lists or women segregated to trim or parts work. Lower wages for women were linked to prevailing thinking of the male breadwinner who needed to earn a family wage.

After the Canada-US Auto Pact of 1965 was agreed to, auto companies began shifting their production to take advantage of the new agreement. In 1968 General Motors Canada decided to close the cutting and sewing department in Oshawa, where hundreds of women worked making trim for the GMC vehicles. The company wanted to consolidate the work with a sister plant in Windsor, Ontario, some 430 km away. The women were offered a few alternative jobs in Oshawa, but most faced transfer to the Windsor plant or layoff. The transfer was impossible for most because it meant uprooting families and cutting family and community ties.

What the women were not offered was jobs in the giant vehicle assembly facility, since the men who worked there had a separate seniority list embedded in the union's negotiated collective agreement. So a woman with twenty years seniority in the trim plant would lose her job while a five-year male employee would keep his. The men's jobs were off limits to the women. The unfairness and discrimination were clear.

The seven members of the UAW Local 222 Women's Committee, including co-founder Bev McCloskey, faced with massive job losses, decided to take the issue head on by fighting against discrimination. Merging the men's and women's seniority lists would disadvantage many of the men, so it was unpopular. The local union leadership found it difficult to side with the women, and they resisted.

The campaign waged by the Local 222 women's committee spread beyond the workplace. Second wave feminism was blossoming. It was twenty years after Simone de Beauvoir wrote *The Second Sex*, five years after Betty Friedan published her book *The Feminine Mystique*, and two years after she co-founded and was elected as the first president of the National Organization for Women (NOW). Journalist Gloria Steinem published an article, "After Black Power, Women's Liberation." Second wave feminism was bubbling in reaction to the post-war women-belong-in-the-home narrative. Women wanted an equal partnership with men, including in the workplace.

The UAW had introduced a women's department in 1944, which focused on all labour issues related to women. By the late 1960s, as the United States passed laws to improve women's rights, the US union established national and regional bodies and passed other measures to advance women's rights. For example, they issued policy statements opposing women's discrimination. The implementation, however, was uneven and not widely felt in Ontario.

A few Canadian women did attend the annual UAW women's conferences in the United States and drew inspiration from them. There they found the links between trade unionism and feminism. Local 222 formed their own women's committee in 1968 and began their campaign to agitate to eliminate discrimination in seniority.

As committee member Maurie Shorten said, quoted in the *Oshaworker* in 1968: "Most women work for the same reasons men do, because they need to … Of all the women workers in March 1968, 70 percent were single, widowed, separate or married to men whose income was less than $5,000 a year. Whether women should or should not work is no longer a question for debate."

The women did not get much support from their union. Grievances were dropped. Opposition was discouraged. Bev McCloskey said that the women fought as hard with the union as they did with the company. They decided to fight to get their rights enshrined in law by pushing to amend the Ontario Human Rights Code to include sex and marital status as prohibited grounds for discrimination.

Women united with the broader women's movement, marching in the International Women's Day marches and pressuring local politicians, among whom was a member of provincial parliament named Cliff Pilkey, a former president of Local 222. Pilkey understood that merging seniority lists would be extremely difficult for local union leaders who wanted re-election. But in the broader societal context, extending no discrimination laws to women caught the mood of the times. Pilkey ran with it, submitted a bill in the Ontario Legislature, and it passed in December 1970. For the first time, Canadian women would be protected from discriminatory treatment and by law.

There would be one seniority list. The word "female" was removed in contract negotiations, soon after the law was passed, and seniority lists were merged. Bev McCloskey and the women of local 222 had achieved their goal for all the women of the province. (See also "Pay Equity" in chapter 7.)

Lorna Moses and Edith Johnson: First Women on Staff, 1975

It wasn't until 1975 that women were again hired onto union staff in Canada. Lorna Moses, a member of the Tyendinaga Mohawk nation, was a member of the UAW Local 1834 in Belleville. Moses was the first woman hired in the union's organizing department, and it was she who organized the women at Fleck Manufacturing.

Edith Johnson

Joining Moses was Edith Johnson, an activist and financial secretary from Local 27 in London, Ontario. She was hired by the UAW-Canada to be responsible for women and retirees. Johnson was a feminist who had attended UAW women's conferences in the

United States. She understood the power of women's organizing and she worked with local unions to help connect women members and build local women's committees.

Edith was hired by 3M in London in 1964, and men in the plant encouraged her to become active in the union since few women went to union meetings in those days. She says the men weren't as "macho" as men in other big UAW locals, but rather they were "thoughtful and intelligent." Also, national staff reps who serviced Local 27, Bob Nickerson and Al Seymour, encouraged the involvement of more women members.

Edith Johnson speaking about abortion at an OFL convention. Photo: UAW.

As she rose up the ranks of the local union, Johnson encouraged other women to become active in the Local 27 women's committee, something she continued when she was named to the national staff and responsible for women's programs.

The following year, after Johnson and Moses joined the staff, a twenty-eight-year-old Wendy Cuthbertson left the Ontario NDP's caucus staff to join the UAW's national staff in the communications department. It was a steep learning curve for her, but her feminist and social democratic values were aligned with those of the union. There she was usually treated with respect.

The UAW-Canada Director Dennis McDermott had been a committed anti-racism activist in his local union, and he set a tone about the importance of human rights. It was still challenging for the three women to join a staff of sixty to seventy men.

Lorna Moses

Lorna Moses first got involved in her union to deal with workplace issues. "I had been working at a different plant, seeing how things evolved and how nothing really got done, and people that had grievances and problems never really got looked after properly. I thought, I guess you better put your money where your mouth is or not."

In 1961, Moses started work at Northern Electric (later known as Northern Telecom and later Nortel) in Belleville, Ontario, working on the assembly line making power supply units for Bell Canada. Three-quarters of the 1,600 workers were women. By this time, they had had an employee association for about seven years, but it was ineffective, not resolving the issues workers faced in the plant. They had no pension plan and few rights. Some of the women put up with it, but she could not.

A member of the Tyendinaga Mohawk nation, Moses says,

> I guess we were always taught to follow what you thought was the right path and treat people how you'd like to be treated and I think that was one of the major things that led me there to get involved [in the union]. You can see when people aren't being treated properly, especially if it's a certain group like women. Men won't just put up with it but women would at that time. I think there's more women now that would speak up and out but years before, they wouldn't bring their problems forward. That was the main thing.

Direct, thoughtful, and plain speaking, she chooses her words carefully and inspires trust. In the late 1960s, the sister Northern Electric plant in London was already organized, meaning the workers had already joined a union, the UAW. Around this time, Moses was part of the organizing drive at Northern Electric as a committee member. The organizing committee would plan and execute a strategy to speak with the workers about joining the union and getting them to sign a card signifying their desire for the union.

In the same year, once a majority of the workers had decided to join the union, Moses was elected to chair the bargaining committee. The committee would meet with the employer and negotiate the terms and conditions of their workplace contract. Moses chaired the bargaining committee for two rounds of negotiations in the early 1970s. In those days, she says, they had "men's jobs" and "women's jobs." When there was a layoff, this meant that if the company decided to eliminate women's jobs, men, in "men's job's" who had less seniority, or were newer to the company might keep their jobs while longer-serving women would be laid off. "It became clear how unfair those different classifications were, and they amalgamated them for a single seniority list," says Moses.

She found being chairperson of the bargaining committee exciting but also difficult. This meant she was the leader of the union in the workplace, not only negotiating the contracts, but also ensuring that management abided by them during the intervening years.

Most of the men in the plant were okay with Moses being chair, as she had worked with them. She was the shop clerk who did payroll and overtime, so they depended on her to ensure their paycheques were accurate. "I didn't have a problem with most of them."

Some supervisors challenged her, but as union leader, she learned how to deal with them.

Being chairperson of her huge plant, Moses attended the UAW Canadian council, which met every few months, as one of the very few women. "I remember Roxie [Baker] but thinking right now, I can't recall any other names that were there. There wouldn't have been many others. It was a different time. I guess maybe the women might have been more hesitant about taking the job on."

Bob Nickerson was their union national representative at Northern Electric and became her mentor. After Lorna Moses was elected for two terms, he approached her about a staff job.

"I was surprised," she says. "But I also gave it an awful lot of thought because I thought I will be going into a group where there's pretty well all men and I thought they might have chewed me up for breakfast and then chewed me out for lunch."

In 1975, the UN International Year of the Woman, Moses joined the UAW-Canada staff as the first woman organizer. Her job as a staff organizer would be to try and build workplace committees to encourage workers to join the union. The staff organizer needs to understand the law and workers rights to advocate for the union. Meeting workers before and after work and on weekends, meant long hours. But it is exciting work, helping workers to exercise their rights and improve their workplace. Moses would remain on the UAW/CAW staff until she retired in 2001.

UAW hiring was traditionally based on leadership experience in the workplace. With little or no additional training, new staff were thrown into the job and relied on other staff when they had questions or problems.

Like any workplace, Moses says, some would test you out. "But I was quite pleasantly surprised. In the organizing department there were not that many of us, but they were all men, and they were older men. They were always there for help if I needed it."

Moses led an important organizing drive at Fleck Manufacturing in Centralia, Ontario:

> Many women just wanted to go to work. They were there for one purpose: to make more money to complement their partners' or their husbands' wages, to make a better life for their family. And they were prepared to put up with whatever they had to put up with to do that. There were some women that were a little bit more progressive than that. But on average the people saw themselves as average housewives who were out there trying to make a better living for their family.

She says that some male co-workers at Fleck were on a power trip. They used bad language and ran roughshod over the women. It was mainly the women that led the organizing drive in the workplace.

Once a workplace is organized, the union brings in a national representative to help with collective bargaining. First agreements can be very difficult since the union is a new structure for both the workers and the employer. The first collective agreement at Fleck, achieved after a bitter strike, was instrumental in enshrining union security for all workers into Ontario law.

After organizing for about seven years, Moses asked to join the servicing staff. Servicing meant working with existing workplace bargaining committees to help them in contract negotiations and later helping them use their rights under the collective agreement. She was the national representative serving about twenty-five to thirty bargaining units, workplaces, from Peterborough to

Kitchener, including the Northern Chain, which now included a plant in New Brunswick. She explains,

> This is a job you do mostly on your own, working with local bargaining committees. Most of the people that you were meeting up with on a first-off basis, they didn't really know anything about you, and you didn't know anything about them. I think women just found it a relief that they were going to talk to another woman about some of the problems that they had. I'm not so sure that they would have come forward if it was a man that they would have to talk to. And some men, the way they present themselves, wouldn't be somebody I really want to talk to about the things I need to talk about.
>
> Most of the committees that I worked with were fine, but mind you, there were a few on some of the committees that you could not have worked with. Some men were traditional in that era and very difficult to work with.

She also found some managers very difficult.

> They were used to telling women what they were going to do rather than maybe putting it in a little softer way. I remember this one man, and we were having a problem with the safety posters that they needed to put up in the plant. It wasn't anything about the poster. It was about him. So anyway, I said, "You have to start placing the safety posters around where people can see them and they know what needs to be done." He said to me. "There will not be any safety posters in my plant." I said, "Well, I beg your pardon, but there will be safety posters in your plant."
>
> I mean a safety poster! Come on. You were just trying to get organized. It was the first agreement for a newly organized plant. He was the person that the company sent to the bargaining table, and I thought, we got bigger eggs to crack than this one, for heaven's sake.

"I got that one stopped very easily," Moses adds, and then goes on to talk about workplace harassment:

> In some of the plants it depended on how far management would let their folks that dealt with harassment go. Because in a couple of cases where there was harassment by management, it wasn't being dealt with. Of course, when some people see people harassing and nothing's happened to them, well, then, they start the bad behaviour, too. So what I did in those cases, I just went around them. And there was one plant in Peterborough that had a hotline where you could call the operations management in Philadelphia.
>
> One of the people on the committee got me the hotline number, because what was happening is there were women being harassed, and it wasn't being dealt with at all. So I called the hotline in Philadelphia, and I told him exactly what was going on in his plant, and I said, "Maybe I'm bringing you old news. I don't know. But I'm calling you, because the picture in that plant is not healthy at all."
>
> And he was very ready to hear what I had to say, and at the end of the conversation he said "Give me a couple of weeks, and I will get back to you on what I've been told." So, I said, "That's fine," and I thanked him for the conversation that we had.

The manager did get back to her at the end of the two weeks:

> He said, "I listened to your concerns, and I've taken your concerns up with the management in the plant. And he said, as of this conversation, the person that was causing the problem, they're no longer with the plant and he said that the management at the plant level has been told that they have to concern themselves with cleaning up the messes in the plant." And he said, "You were right." I got that one to stop very easily.

Also in her career in the union, Moses served as assistant to then-president of the Ontario Federation of Labour Gord Wilson, and she was seconded by the Canadian Labour Congress in the early 1980s to organize bank workers. Bank machines were just coming in, and many thought the workers would be ready to join a union. That was not the case.

"Most workers aspired to be managers," says Moses, "which was unrealistic, but it meant that most didn't want to join a union."

Over her long career, she was also caring for her mother who wasn't well. She hired homecare workers on two shifts each day to cover the time she would be working from early morning to late at night. When Bob White was president, he did give her some additional time off, but her family responsibilities were challenging.

Still, she loved her job. "I really enjoyed it. It gave you a broadening view of what different workplaces are like. I enjoyed it all except the bank workers."

She found it gratifying when people would come up to her and thank her. To this day, she meets retirees from Northern Electric who thank her for their negotiated pension plan that they won with a strike:

> One guy came up to me in the grocery store, and he said, "Do you remember me, Lorna?" And I said, "Yes, I remember you." And he said, "Well, I want to apologize, and I also want to say thank you." And I thought, "Oh, what! What's this all about?"
>
> "Well, I want to apologize, number one, for being so nasty about trying to negotiate a pension plan." And he said, "I'm here today to thank you for that pension plan because I have lived quite a nice retirement with that pension."[15]

Organized Working Women and the OFL Women's Committee

With more women joining the paid workforce in the 1970s, there was renewed interest by women to join unions and renewed interest from labour to recruit them. In 1975, the United Nations International Year of Women, a group of women from Toronto Labour Council used the opportunity of a labour council women's conference to form a feminist group called Organized Working Women (OWW) "to organize and empower unionized women." Working women in Saskatchewan formed a similar organization.

There were few women in union leadership positions, although there were growing numbers of women in the workforce, including in unionized workplaces. OWW was open to any woman from a unionized workplace. The official founding of OWW occurred in March 1976; over two hundred women attended.

Two key leaders in the creation and early years of OWW were its first president, Evelyn Armstrong from the United Electrical Workers (UE), and Dorothy MacKinnon from the Canadian Union of Public Employees (CUPE 79). Deirdre Gallagher who later worked for the United Steelworkers of America (USWA) was hired as the first executive secretary in 1977.

OWW was an activist organization. They organized conferences open to all union women, offered training often denied women in their own union, developed policy, and advocated for change. Most importantly, they practised solidarity with women's strikes and other actions. "As a young union activist, I found their events exhilarating" says Peggy Nash. "We were challenging powerful employers, governments, and unions, and fighting for change for women."

The activism of the OWW prompted union women to press the Ontario Federation of Labour (OFL) leadership to form an OFL women's committee, which the leadership agreed to do in 1978. The OFL committee had the advantage that the women on the committee were representing their unions, and they could put their union's muscle and money behind decisions. They supported the important women's struggles of the time, such as childcare, abortion rights, and affirmative action, and they advanced policy papers on these and other issues. They also provided influential support for strikes, especially those involving groups of women, such as those at Fleck, Radio Shack, and Eaton's.

Cuthbertson recalls,

> You just went around the [OFL women's committee] table and heard that war had given our mothers this expanded notion of women's role in the workforce and in the world and then they were all sent back to the kitchen against their will. My mother said to me once, it was like putting a chick back inside its shell, and she resented it enormously. She had been mobilized in the war, and I think a lot of these wartime women passed on those memories to their daughters.

Cuthbertson believes that almost all the women on the OFL committee knew their mothers' lives had changed or they were somehow affected by the war. It had given gave them a lived experience of women's abilities and potential, passed on to their daughters.

The impact of OWW and then the OFL women's committee cannot be underestimated. Under OWW's influence, a number of the women who were key activists in the early 1980s began to take on positions in their unions and then decided to put their energy into the newly created OFL women's committee.

"OWW was a wonderful organization," says Cuthbertson, who was briefly its president, "but it had a limited mandate because its members weren't officially representing their unions." She says the women on the OFL women's committee, because they were chosen to join the committee by their union, represented the power of their union:

> It gave the women on the OFL committee more clout and resources than could the OWW. We could bargain with men in the unions, and thus we could bargain indirectly with employers. We all had such demanding jobs within our own unions that it was difficult to be effective in both organizations [the OFL and the OWW].
>
> I think that it's important for women who come after to know that not everything comes easily. You have to fight for progress. But we had this great gift being part of a fighting organization [the UAW] and that allowed us to be able to do progressive things. Most unions wanted to be on the right side of history. With some notable exceptions, and I don't want to whitewash all of this, the core of the staff, and certainly the leadership got on board, and that's why the male allies are such an important story too.

Remarkably, when the OFL women's committee was first formed, it was co-chaired by two men. This was because there were no women on the OFL executive board. Each union would choose a leader from their union to be on the executive, and none were women. And none of the men would give up their place. This is why women began to advocate for affirmative action seats on the OFL executive. Each executive member of the OFL chaired a committee. Bob Nickerson from the UAW supported the formation of a women's committee and, knowing there were no women in the executive, went to the OFL President Cliff Pilkey and asked to chair it. He was joined by Moe Koeck from the USWA as the other co-chair.

Bob Nickerson, who hailed from Windsor, was a UAW service rep who was known for being a tough negotiator. In 1978 when he was posted in Toronto, the UAW asked him to represent them on the Ontario Federation of Labour executive as a vice president.

Nickerson says that early on, he had to take a course at the Canadian union's education camp on the shores of Lake Huron near Port Elgin, Ontario. He was sent there to take a seminar to be an instructor for the union. At that time there was a woman vice president of the UAW in the United States who spoke to the Canadian group. Nickerson says,

> I picked up a lot from her. As a woman she was running with all of the women's issues at that time. And the UAW women's department in Detroit was a real learning process for me. I then got the opportunity to go to Detroit. I learned "Watch what is going on. Don't shoot your mouth off, pay attention, learn what's going on until at least you got your head in it, and then you can start to get into it."

Barb Nickerson, Bob's wife, was also a strong influence on his feminist evolution.

"Shelley Acheson came to me and she was raising shit," says Bob Nickerson. Acheson had been a member of the OWW since 1976 and became its president in 1978. She was named the OFL human rights director in 1980 and was the person that was eventually appointed as the coordinator for the women's committee at the Federation of Labour.

Bob Nickerson said it was Acheson who raised the point that women's issues were always on the last day of the convention, which ended at noon. By then half the delegates would be gone. If there weren't enough delegates left for a meeting quorum, resolutions would get referred back to the OFL executive without any debate on the floor of the convention. This often happened to women's resolutions.

In response to the pressure from women in several unions, the executive moved the women's agenda from Friday to earlier in the week. Then the women went about organizing for their goals, with the help of some allies like Nickerson.

He said they strategized about ensuring that women lined up in front of each microphone on the convention floor to make sure that key women like Julie Davis would get a chance to speak. Davis was a leader from the Canadian Union of Public Employees (CUPE) who later served as executive vice president of the Ontario Federation of Labour. Her voice at the mic carried weight.

Once women had the chance to present their resolutions to the entire convention earlier in the proceedings, where they were able to showcase key women leaders from different unions who were advocating for better representation, they began to make significant changes.

In 1983, five years after the formation of the OFL women's committee, women won the first comprehensive labour affirmative action measure and added five women's seats to the OFL executive.

OFL women's committee and others, front row from the left, Peggy Nash, Edith Johnson, Bob Nickerson, Barb Nickerson, and Carol Phillips. Photo: OFL.

Chapter Two

Union Women Winning Victories, 1978-1985

A Solid Foundation

Early Congress of Industrial Organizations (CIO) organizing of production workers expanded during the Second World War when women's labour was in demand. Women activists during the war years pressed for equal pay and better representation of women in the union. Initially the UAW supported these demands to entice women to join the union but, by the war's end, the equality demands had merged into the fight against Nazism and for democracy and human rights. These principles were foundational in the post-war years.

After the war, workers and their unions continued to fight for a better world, and they struggled for progress through withdrawing their labour, when necessary. The Second World War generation benefited, albeit unevenly, from the promise that democracy and stable industrial jobs would lead to a better life. Discrimination held many workers back, and Canada's geography meant that some areas fared much better than others. However, as the economy expanded, union-negotiated collective agreements improved workers' standard of living, and many found they could, for the first time, afford to buy a home and even a car. Their taxes paid for public education and eventually public health care. Their children's lives would be better.

It was 1942 when Justice Rand ruled on the formula that all workers had to pay union dues. By 1978, what was known as the Rand formula, had been negotiated in many other collective agreements. But it was not the law.

That was about to be tested.

Expanding Demands

In the 1970s, Dr. Henry Morgentaler opened a clinic in Montreal to offer reproductive services to women. Abortion was illegal, and his clinics were highly controversial. He was jailed in Quebec for violating the abortion law. He went on to open twenty clinics across Canada and twice challenged the abortion law, a challenge he won the second time. He was awarded the Order of Canada for his work on women's reproductive health. His clinic in Toronto sparked fierce demonstrations and was firebombed. A woman's right to abortion was a very charged debate that united the women's movement, including the women of the UAW.

Canadian Labour Congress (CLC) women's representative Sue Genge recalls back in the early days of women organizing at the OFL, then-President Cliff Pilkey and feminist activist Judy Rebick talking with some key women at the beginning of the OFL Convention:

> I remember this very well, and they said to a bunch of us, "you feminists have to raise the pro-choice issue at this convention. We need the labour movement on side." And we're like, "Oh, my God, we can't even get them to support childcare. What are you talking about? You know we have no women on the executive. We don't have a women's committee." "No," they said "you have to do 'choice.' And this is why." And Rebick argued this for an hour or so. And finally, a bunch of us said, "Okay, I think this is right," and we were scared shitless. It's a difficult debate. But we got it partly because of Cliff. He was absolutely firm. That's the first time the OFL took the pro-choice position, and the rest of the country followed.

The committee members were strong feminists, and they were determined to make sure that the women's issues were moved front and centre. "Women's issues became hotter issues over time," says Nickerson. "Eventually, a guy like Bob White got up and they started speaking on women's issues."

Sue Genge recalls that not every union was similar:

> I've always worked with CAW women and feminists. There were women on the committee who weren't particularly feminist. I think sometimes unions that appointed women who were not feminists went around to the staff saying, "Please set up women's committees in locals where they're appropriate and make sure you don't have any feminists on them."

She continues: "There was a healthy competition among unions and the cross-fertilization of ideas." She recognizes that this process would be critical later in her time at the CLC:

> Through the Women's Committee, we would hear all these ideas from unions like CAW or CUPE or CUPW, and we'd take them back and say these guys are doing this, and we should be doing that. Cross-fertilization was really important. CAW would lead on a number of initiatives like childcare. So there were all kinds of different ideas that came out such as in CUPW.

More women were coming into the union movement, noted Nickerson, but there was no balance on the OFL committees. There were more women in the workforce but none of the male leaders were recognizing that women were working in the workforce and were also doing the work at home, which limited their ability to be active.

Eventually, Nickerson says,

> The men started understanding that if they didn't go along [with women's issues], they were gonna get themselves in a mess of trouble. So, they started lining up on that basis. And I'm sure [Bob White's wife] Marilyne White had a lot to do with making sure that Bob White came around, too.

Nickerson stayed on as co-chair of the OFL women's committee until 1992, by which time things had been moving very quickly and the affiliated unions started taking more action.

Fleck Strike, 1978

> "That first morning of the strike, every one of us was scared to death," says Mary Lou Richard, 30. "I climbed in the car and my legs were shaking. And when they brought out riot police against our picket line . . . hundreds of cops, a helicopter . . . they had these shiny black helmets and big riot sticks. Jeez, it was like the movies."
>
> —*Toronto Star*, 18 Oct 2011, "May 1978: Fleck women put fire back into feminism"

Getting a first collective agreement at a newly organized workplace is often difficult. Some employers just don't want to recognize the union. That was the case at Fleck Manufacturing in Centralia, Ontario, in 1978.

There, it took a mighty band of eighty women to stand up to their employer and the police. The women took part in a heroic 163-day strike that led to the Rand formula being enacted into law in Ontario in 1980 and in federal law in 1984. This protection was extended to other jurisdictions in Canada in the following years.

Fleck Manufacturing workers were paid just over minimum wage to produce wire harnesses in an old aircraft hanger. It was so cold in winter that the women often worked in snowmobile suits.

> In the beginning Fleck looked like a routine, first-contract bargaining situation. It was a small auto-parts plant with 140 employees, mostly women. Conditions in that place were simply terrible. It was infested with rats and mice. The safety precautions were negligible, the machinery was dangerous, and there were only four toilets. To make a bad situation worse, a good many of the women were being sexually harassed by men in senior levels of management.[1]

UAW-Canada Director Dennis McDermott assigned Al Seymour as the UAW servicing rep to bargain the first collective agreement at Fleck. Seymour and McDermott's assistant Bob White had come up in the union together. Seymour says they were familiar with gender discrimination as an issue because in their first negotiations in their own workplace they fought to eliminate pay inequities for women in the 1950s. (Seymour remembers attending his first UAW-Canada council meeting where White was to ask for strike support for their members in their woodworking plant. There were no women at the council, "just forty-five to fifty all old grey-haired men, so these would have been the pioneers of the union.")

He credits the Fleck strike with bringing women's issues to the forefront of the union. He recalls that the union was certified at Fleck without a vote since that was possible then with at least 65 per cent of the members signing union cards. National rep Lorna Moses had organized the plant (see chapter 1). The members elected three women to the bargaining committee to represent them: Sheila Charlton, Fran Piercey, and Mary Lou Richard.

After months of bargaining, the talks were hung up on the issue of union security and union dues paid through the Rand formula, which had become known as dues checkoff. The union would not back down.

Fleck had hired a company out of Toronto to do the bargaining and they made it clear that the employer would never agree to the Rand formula. With the strike due to start on a Monday morning before the 7 am shift start, the employer reps called a meeting with the union reps for 9 am the Friday before. It was puzzling since their position was unchanged. Their motive only became clear later. Also at nine that Friday morning, the OPP were meeting with all the members of the union at Fleck to advise them that if they wanted to cross the picket line that was perfectly legal. The police told the union members that anyone who attempted to stop those who were crossing the picket line would be severely punished by law.

Al Seymour remembers Charlton reporting to him:

> The women were scared about what they were hearing, and some of them, there was no question, she thought, would go into work, but she was quite confident with a number of people that she had talked to, that they still would have a number of people supporting the strike, who would participate and wouldn't cross any picket line to go to work.

For the Monday morning start of the strike, Seymour said he decided to bring "a couple of carloads of guys" just in case. But this is what he found at the picket line on Monday morning:

> The first thing I was amazed at before even getting there, was the number of women that were there with their picket signs and singing solidarity, and it was amazing to think that after what they had gone through with the provincial police talking to them about charges. They were very courageous.

Eighty women walked off the job. They were mostly young, on average twenty-one years old. Forty were too intimidated to join the fight. Once the picket line was up, things soon became violent.

Not long after Seymour and his guys arrived, a school bus came in loaded with some new people that the company had hired, supervisors and some of the women that were prepared to cross the picket line to go to work. They were scabbing the strike.

The OPP arrived, in what appeared to be riot gear, with "shiny black helmets and big riot sticks," as reported by thirty-three-year-old Fran Piercey:

> I couldn't believe all that black gear was coming straight at me. We had to pretend to be a lot braver than we were. You know, most of us are mothers, and we've been bringing up our kids to respect the police. And here we were, walking a picket line, getting shoved around, getting so scared and angry that we were shouting stuff you wouldn't believe.[2]

Al Seymour remembers how the OPP pushed the strikers out of the way to allow the scab buses into the plant:

> The women would join us to push back in front of the buses. The cops were grabbing them [the women], and of course it was in March, and we had a lot of snow up there at that time, and they were throwing the women into the snowbank.

The plant was owned by the Conservative MPP and Deputy

Minister of Industry and Tourism James Fleck. Many wondered if the massive police presence would have been as great were he not so powerful.

When the OPP wanted agreement from the union to let trucks through, Seymour and the chairperson from the union local at the nearby Northern Electric plant, Rene Montague, refused. They were thrown in the cruiser and sent to jail at the OPP headquarters in Exeter. After fingerprinting they were told that they were charged with obstruction and abusing police officers. They were told they had to sign a peace bond that would mean they were banned from the area.

Seymour told them he was part of the negotiating committee trying to settle the strike which he couldn't do if he was banned from the area. They told Seymour they didn't care and if they signed they would be released: "But if you don't sign, we will keep you locked up."

"I told Rene to sign because if he didn't show up for work, he could be fired," Seymour remembers. "I don't think I'm going to sign but I'm going to call the union's lawyer first."

The lawyer told him at first not to sign but later decided it was better to sign and appeal in court, which is what Seymour did.

It was not only the OPP that pressured the women. In a 1980 article, Constance Backhouse wrote,

> Jack Riddell, the Liberal MPP representing the riding in which the Fleck plant is located, visited the plant on March 20, 1978. After a half hour visit, he walked to the picket line and threatened the employees with possible closure of the plant unless they ended the strike. Riddell made statements to reporters accusing the union of using devious methods and threats to get the workers to join the union and go on strike.[3]

Backhouse further notes that there was also support for the strikers:

> Taking a somewhat different stance, after a face-to-face meeting with a number of the strikers in April, Dr. Bette Stephenson, then the Ontario Minister of Labour, in an almost unprecedented

> move, endorsed the position of the strikers in their battle for union security. Stating it was "inappropriate" in this day and age for an employer to resist union security, she came down firmly on the side of the strikers.[4]

"So these women were lionesses," says Wendy Cuthbertson, then on the UAW national staff:

> The lioness does all the hunting, the birthing, the training. I think they're pretty good at what they do. When people say they fought like a lion, I say, no, they fought like a lioness. First, it was this critical issue on the Rand formula, and also the fact that there was violence on the picket line. So I sat down with Bob [White] and I said why don't we fight this as a women's strike. And Bob said "Go," so we did.

Men in the union from other locals came out and reinforced the picket line. Support poured in from local unions in the area, including from the large Ford plant in Talbotville, near London. "The days they came out, the Fleck plant was closed down," says Seymour.

Wendy contacted other feminists in the union and in the broader women's movement. And she reached out to Organized Working Women, headed by Deirdre Gallagher at that time, as well as to the International Women's Day Committee. They produced a leaflet about the strike that was papered all over Toronto. The plan was to bus women from far and wide to the picket line to support the women strikers and keep the plant closed to scabs.

"And the deal was that we couldn't even get the buses paid for by the union." says Cuthbertson:

> We had to pay four bucks a person for the honour of getting up at 2:30 in the morning and going out to Fleck. No bathrooms in school buses, right? So there we were trying to time the buses to the last subway train. We were at Yonge and Bloor, I'm stress smoking, because I had no idea if anybody's actually going to show up at that hour. And then all of a sudden

> women came pouring out of the subway from the last train. We knew we had to get to the plant early because the plant starts at seven. We needed to meet at the subway because most women didn't have cars. I was with my 19-year-old sister who was also stress smoking.
>
> Women came streaming out of the subway stations, a murder of women. It was just overwhelming. The buses were so packed, my sister and I ended up on the step by the door because there were no seats left. And off we went to Fleck.
>
> Of course the Toronto cops were standing by the subway stations. They'd no doubt seen the leaflet too, and they probably called ahead and told the OPP, "We don't need violence on the picket line, there's 400 women coming your way." And so, we closed the plant. There was no scabbing that day. There were a couple of cops on the rooftop. It was a brilliant blue-sky day. Women came with their babies in strollers. It was an unforgettable event.

The strike came at a time of union strength and a growing women's movement of second wave feminism. It drew thousands of other union members, many other women supporters, and the support of the Ontario NDP.

Al Seymour says,

> I'll never forget that day. They closed the plant for the day. There were busloads coming in from Toronto and Hamilton with all the women who showed up.
>
> Afterwards we played a little game with them one time. We told them we're gonna have another demonstration of women show up. But we had no plan. We got somebody to phone the cops and said, Oh, they're planning on this big women's rally on us, whatever date it was. And so the only women that we had that were going to show up was just a car with Barb Seymour, Barb Nickerson, Georgina Anderson [who in 1992 becomes an instructor in the new women's leadership training, described in chapter 4], Sharon Kennedy, and Beulah Harrison. There were about six women and 400 cops, and they got the plant closed for a day.

Workers strike Fleck Manufacturing in 1978 for better wages and safer working conditions. Photo: LFP Collection; Western University Archives and Special Collections.

Victory

As a result of pressure from the women striking at Fleck and lengthy discussions with then Ontario Premier Bill Davis, the Ontario government changed the law to make the Rand formula compulsory for all collective agreements in Ontario. This meant that everyone in a unionized workplace had to pay dues and everyone in the union got the protection of the union. A group of courageous, determined women supported by the labour movement and united with the women's movement became stronger together. And won a huge victory for all workers.

"It was the highlight of my career," Seymour says, "to be involved in women's struggle for equality." He confirms that the strike helped put women's issues front and centre in UAW and many other unions—"Pay equity, childcare, affirmative action, all the issues you can think of that affected women. It led the way within our union and CLC and the Ontario Federation of Labour, and other federations of labour across Canada."

As a result of the Fleck strike more women got involved in the union and their voices were better listened to than before.

Women join Fleck Strikers in a show of sisterhood and solidarity. Photo: LFP Collection; Western University Archives and Special Collections

"The Fleck strike showed women, and it showed men, especially in our union, 'Look at what they did at Fleck,'" says Seymour:

> I mean, it was a women's strike. Let's face it. There were no men involved, and the only man that was involved in the committee, and that was myself, probably should have been a woman but our union was guilty, too, of not putting women on staff. Fortunately, now that's changed. . . . Going through the strike with those women, an all-women strike, it certainly made me a better person in relationship to working for and supporting women's issues, no question.

This five-and-a-half-month strike by a determined group of eighty women united with others eventually won the Rand formula in law for all Ontario workers.

Allies and Solidarity

A fight like the one at Fleck can teach a lot about allies and solidarity. When the Fleck women were invited to head up the

International Women's Day (IWD) march in 1979, Cuthbertson learned that the IWD committee had proposed a motion that had strong support, to exclude men from the march. That stopped her in her tracks. She argued strongly against the motion.

"I couldn't go along with it," she said. "A male-dominated union had organized the Fleck plant and men had closed the plant for twelve days. They were our allies. Women had closed it for one day." The motion was defeated, and men were allowed to join the march as they are to this day.

There was another concern. The Fleck women noticed there were lesbians in the IWD march. They were unwilling to march with the lesbians. Cuthbertson told them, "Those lesbians had been out to the Fleck picket line in solidarity and had helped close that plant."

She says Sheila Charlton was quick to respond: "That's enough for me," and she marched over and introduced herself to the IWD women, thanked them for their support, and the Fleck women joined the march.

Solidarity for the Fleck strikers took many forms. Theatre Passe Muraille actors from Toronto spent a couple of days on the picket line and created a play about the strike that ran for two nights with sold-out performances. Madeleine Parent, the famous union organizer from Montreal, spoke and then UAW-Canada Director Bob White. The Fleck strikers took in the play, and Cuthbertson says they were so moved by what they saw. All their challenges in the plant, their uncertainties, their struggles on the picket line, all their emotions were captured. And they finished the evening event by singing the labour anthem *Solidarity Forever* and "just blew the roof off the theatre."

Fleck Victory Changed Everything

The Fleck strike taught the women's movement that not only could they fight to change laws to improve women's rights but united they could also collectively bargain through the union to advance women's rights, and thereby improve the rights of all workers.

As Wendy Cuthbertson puts it, "unions were a long lever":

> The strike certainly radicalized the Fleck strikers. The Rand formula for women in semi-rural Ontario at that time would have been a very abstract thing, but by the time they were fighting for it, it became a very real thing. And the strike radicalized me. There was something about the fight, actual bargaining objectives that you could win with a fight, that you could change things with a fight. It changed me.
>
> You were part of this enormous organization; I think about the UAW and other unions. If you get unions involved in a fight like this you have real power. A long lever can move a heavy load. So, I became a different kind of feminist, focussing on what could be accomplished through union power, in the wider society as well as at the bargaining table.

The Fleck strike cemented once again women's place in the union and in the labour movement. It was this band of tough, determined women that had finally won this key to union security. At the same time, a generation of second wave feminists in Ontario was learning about unions and their role in achieving women's equality. It's been observed that the strongest bond in the world between the women's movement and the labour movement has been in Canada—and that is directly attributable to the Fleck strike. The relationships forged through this key struggle would go on to shape both movements for decades to come.

The role of the Fleck strike with its explosion of publicity and the leadership of women like Bev McCloskey, Roxie Baker, Edith Johnson, Lorna Moses, and Wendy Cuthbertson were all having an influence on the union. And as more local women's voices were heard in meetings and at microphones, women pressed for the right to have their voice included in the union's Canadian bargaining program. The Fleck strike had changed the union.

Women's Victory Yet to Come

In 1979 Roxie Baker and the UAW women's committee, with Edith Johnson and Wendy Cuthbertson, put together a bargaining agenda for women that was adopted and added to the union's program. "I had met Roxie Baker over the Fleck strike," says Cuthbertson:

The CAW national leadership during GM talks, while Wendy Cuthbertson looks on. Photo: Wendy Cuthbertson.

> Edith was the staff person for the union's women's committee; Roxie was a member. She was quiet but persuasive. There were just three or four of us. Childcare was a key demand although our program covered all the bases for women's issues. But we didn't get any of it in that round of bargaining, not one. The union negotiators meanwhile did get paid education leave (PEL) and legal services. We were at the Royal York Hotel, and the guys were congratulating themselves, "What's left to bargain—we got everything."
>
> "Well, no," I said, "we didn't get any of the women's program."

But that would change in just a few years.

Maureen Kirincic: I Was Not Going to Let These Guys Beat Me

In February 1973, just two weeks after she got married, Maureen Kirincic got hired in a small Windsor area plant with about twenty women and a couple of men. A few years later, while on maternity leave with her first son, she heard that Chrysler was hiring. So in

1977 she became one of the first fifty or so women hired there along with the 13,000 men working in Chrysler's three plants, and she became a member of UAW Local 444. A few women were hired on full-time, but most were hired as temporary, she says because the company claimed that so many of the women wouldn't stay even though they were experienced.

The company never asked them why they left, but it was obvious to the women. From the time they walked into the plant until they left, wherever they went there was a commotion. Men would jump around like monkeys and make monkey sounds "whoo whoo whoo." When the women went on break or to the washroom, there was an uproar from the men. Kirincic recalls,

> They'd fill condoms with petroleum jelly and put it wherever you're working. Or they'd shit in a pizza box and put it at the back of the van [on the assembly line]. Then they put so many pages of pornography all around your work area and in the van. I never gave them a reaction. There were only a few of us in all of chassis at that time, and one other woman would get so upset and cry, and the more she got upset the more they went after her. Some men told her directly that she and the other women were taking jobs from the men who had families to support.
>
> If any of the guys befriended her, somebody would say "She's a big slut."
>
> Like, we were all sluts in the plant, and we were all going there because we wanted a man. That was the common thing around the plant, depending on where you worked. Maybe because my husband worked there in another plant, and I had other family friends that worked there, I was kind of left alone. I'd get it, but not like some of the other women would. It was tough. But I was not going to let these guys beat me.

The rejection and harassment continued even at union meetings. "What the fuck is she doing here? What does she want? She must need a man." That was the reaction to her showing up to a Sunday morning union meeting, even though she wore a wedding band and everyone knew she was married.

A much older man named Jimmy who had been a member

of the union executive, overhearing some of the sexist comments, whispered to her "You know, you're the most important person at this meeting." She just stared at him in disbelief because she was thinking of not coming back.

"No, you have to come back; that's the only way there's gonna be changes. We've gotta open up our eyes. And you guys [the women] gotta make us."

"I never left my work area," she says, "because even if you went to the bathroom, you were heckled. So you brought your lunch. You went only when you had to, because you didn't want to walk down the aisle."

There was a layoff, and she managed to get hired in another plant in the area and became a member of a different UAW local.

There things were much worse. She discovered they had two seniority lists, a separate one for women. "So you're telling me," she says, "I'm laid off on the street, and this Johnny-come-lately, he's got this good job in the area, because it's a little bit heavier job? Well, the president of the local didn't like me after I complained about that."

A senior person in the union told her to leave it alone, that the local wants things that way. But Kirincic bid on a job at the bottom of the main seniority list, the men's list, and she got it. One or two other women bid on the male seniority list before she was laid off.

Men in the plant would routinely verbally harass the women. "One old guy kept talking about my ass, and I told him to stop."

Eventually she and a couple of other women went to the local president for help. He berated her for thinking that she could change things there just because she came from the Chrysler Local. He told her she was mistaken. "You think you're so hot and mighty cause you come from Local 444? You think you're gonna change things?"

> Eventually there was a meeting with the executive to raise a few of the issues the women had such as a guy exposing himself in the parking lot, and a woman found a rat on her car at work. One time I left my thermos at the plant in the lunchroom and came back and found I had a comb in it.

She took it further to the area staff rep, but he encouraged her to work it out in the local union. A different staff rep did advise Kirincic to protect herself in case the men tried to set her up for a charge of theft. She was very careful. The leadership of her former Local union (at Chrysler) offered to escort her in and out of the plant if she wanted protection.

Finally, she was recalled to Chrysler. But she had to bump to a different plant with even fewer women.

Shit-House Meetings

Maureen Kirincic remembers how the shit-house meetings came about:

> Only two women were bumped into plant 3, and at that time there were probably 8,000 men there. We both went in on the same day. They had me downstairs in the pit [under the vehicles], on the main floor of plant 3, and they put the other woman on up in the paint shop. She and I would talk, she said, yeah, the guys would just change their clothes in front of her. And one guy stripped right down, and she told him, "I'd be embarrassed. My nine-year-old son's got a bigger pecker than you."
>
> I know downstairs they would do their normal monkey stuff, but they weren't mean because by then the reality was, the women are there to stay.

Washrooms were the big issue. Women had to walk from one end of the plant to the other to get to the washroom.

> At that time, you had six- or seven-minute breaks to run to the washroom. Well, I couldn't even make it to the washroom in seven minutes. So, then they had the skilled trades guy bring his little golf cart. He'd come and get me and take me to the nurses' station, or to the canteen to go to the bathroom. But then, as more women came into the canteen, they didn't want us to use their washrooms. So, we use the nurses' washrooms, and then the nurses didn't want us to use their washrooms, so we were using the office washrooms. Again, for us to get back in time, we couldn't do it.

The company tried to place the women strategically on jobs closer to the washrooms. Kirincic began holding what local union leaders called "shit-house union meetings."

> Women would run to the washrooms. I went around and I'd say, don't rush back. There's one toilet. There's six of us. They're running, running, not getting a coffee, not getting anything, I said. Take your time. We gotta go to the washroom. Don't rush. So they were all on time. But I was always the only one that was late.
>
> We'd have no tampons. I remember going to the union "Why are there no pads or tampons in here?" They said the guys keep stealing them, and we can't keep them up. Bring your own from home, that was the attitude. "We're not paying for your tampons."

So then they built a washroom in the roof above her workstation, and they put in three stalls so she wouldn't be late. "They literally built it in the rafters above my workstation. But I was still late till the day I left the plant. And I still held shit-house union meetings."

1982: Hired on Staff

Lorna Moses who had been hired in 1975 as an organizer, was moving from organizing to servicing. Edith Johnson from Local 27 in London had also joined the staff in 1975 to head up women's programs and retired workers. In December 1982, UAW-Canada Director Bob White asked Kirincic to join the union's national staff. Kirincic told him,

> I've got grade 10 education and a hairdresser's licence, and just factory experience.
>
> But he says, "Nope, you're the one. You don't have to have a degree to know what workers want." He says, "you gotta have a heart and your heart will tell you what's going on, what you should do."
>
> And he was right.

After getting the call in December, she didn't start on staff until January. But she never went back to the plant after the holiday break. A lot of the union guys didn't think she was qualified because she hadn't been to the bargaining table, and that made it politically challenging for her to return. She says she never even cleaned out her locker. She just left: "Don't forget, being a big local, you had a master bargaining committee. Ninety per cent of the people that were [union] stewards that had never been to the bargaining table."

She loved organizing. And she was good at it. She has direct blue eyes, short blond hair, a solid frame, and a straight in-your-face manner that builds trust. You just know she's someone you can count on. And she's someone who takes no bullshit even though plenty got thrown at her.

After six months on staff, Kirincic discovered she was pregnant. Doctors had told her she was unlikely to ever conceive again, but being based in Toronto, only going home on weekends, seemed to work miracles. "Oh, God!" she thought. "What do I do?" She wrote by hand a short "private and confidential" note to Bob White, apologizing that the pregnancy was unexpected and promising to take the minimum amount of time off. She sealed it, and gave it to White's assistant. She got a handwritten note back congratulating her and telling her to take whatever time she needed, given the staff agreement had no maternity leave language but leave in general was 100 per cent pay for the first year, and the next six months at 50 per cent. He reassured her to take what she needed.

Kirincic remembers having more trouble with some of the older men on staff. She recalls a staff union meeting where one of the older guys complained that if she was getting paid leave (for pregnancy), then they should be able to get it too. Pat Clancy, an older staff rep firmly on the political left was conducting the meeting and told him that when he got pregnant, he'd get the same benefits. Kirincic didn't take one day more than employment standards allowed (four months at that time) because of the peer pressure from the old male union staff.

Years later there was a collection for a woman who the staff believed was the first pregnant staff woman. Kirincic had to remind them of her experience as the first pregnant staff woman many years before when there was no collection, no cards, just grief from some colleagues because she needed time off.

When a new person was named to the staff, they were often assigned to a different community to organize or service. Kirincic was from Windsor but was assigned to Toronto, working with an old-fashioned rep named Jack Possuns. She praises his effectiveness as an organizer, and she appreciates the training she received through him. He came up in the union with Bob White, and they had a similar organizing style.

She would drive home to Windsor whenever she could, often on weekends until her family was able to move to the Toronto area. "As soon as I came home, I did all the laundry, and I'd try to cook for the week. I mean it was tough. Fortunately, my husband was a good cook and supportive."

She says she'd drive home rather than stay overnight whenever possible, and she and her husband did their best to at least have one parent at home with the kids for a meal. "In hindsight, there's a lot of regrets. I'm sure every woman or every person has some. How much time we had to leave our children. I loved the job but I have regrets. I try to make it up now with my grandchildren."

Kirincic is also proud of her work as an organizer, such as organizing the huge casino in Windsor. She had trouble with a supervisor in the union, criticizing, second guessing her, sending her nasty notes. She documented all of it and took it higher to get him to back off. It worked. Her time defending herself in the plants served her well. She knew how to fight. She did not let the guys beat her.

1984: Split from UAW

As Maureen Kirincic recalls, the split from the UAW involved tough negotiating and felt risky:

> And then in 1984, we started talking about the breakup from the UAW, and I remember it was scary times when we were talking about leaving. It depended on how much the UAW was gonna give us in a separation. It was unanimous among the staff that if we had to, we'd go on half pay or whatever.

In Big Three auto bargaining, Bob White told her after they had bargained anti-harassment language "this is in there because of you, that he says we've got that because you brought it to our attention. He said it was me that made the changes in the women's language."

At the next national staff meeting, she says White was asking them all how the new language was working out. How was it in the plants?

> And oh Christ! You got all the men saying it's fine, there's no problem. I listened to about the fourth or fifth man talking about how great everything was in the plants for the women, and I was just boiling and boiling and boiling and I got up and I told Bob, I said, "I came to this fucking union for help and you guys did nothing. I'd pay somebody a thousand dollars to break somebody's leg before I'd ever come to this union for help for anybody. You put good language in, but you don't do fuck all."

And she left the room.

Lorna Moses, who had been sitting next to her at the meeting, came to her room after. Kirincic recalls,

> Bob [White] came to me after and he says "You should have stayed for the discussion," and I said, "Well, I'm sorry, I still feel that way. I would not come to this union, anybody in this union for anything. I'll pay them before I'll come to this union for anything." He said, "There's gonna be a lot more changes again because of you. The women in the union can thank you."

Canada's Charter Rights for Women, 1982

In January 1981, the UAW Canadian council, the union's parliament, formed a women's advisory committee. This would give women a greater voice in the decision-making body of the union. Roxie Baker was part of the committee, and both Edith Johnson and Wendy Cuthbertson joined as staff members. They met a few times during the year, and daycare was a top priority. Support for childcare was essential if women were to be full participants in the union and in society. The UAW-Canada's brief in support of

The 1980 UAW council women's advisory committee, Edith Johnson on the left, and Georgina Anderson fourth from left, beside UAW Director Bob White. Photo: UAW.

negotiating childcare in collective agreements was passed out to all council delegates.

In April that year, twenty-four first-time Canadian delegates attended the UAW women's conference in Michigan. At the Canadian women's conference held that September, childcare activist Pat Schultz was the keynote speaker, and the conference proudly displayed the banner: "A Woman's Place Is In Her Union."

With the passage of the Charter of Rights and Freedoms in Canada in 1982, after much pressure from feminist groups, equality rights were enshrined in the Charter, which became foundational for equality struggles in the legal domain. Stories of women's struggles for equality everywhere were uniting women from all sectors, and achieving results!

However, by the early 1980s, the US and Canadian sections of the union began to take different paths. Wendy Cuthbertson said that while the Canadians owed a debt of gratitude to the UAW parent union for spearheading so many progressive changes, the United States under President Reagan was not union-friendly.

With deregulation of key industries, like the airlines, and the undermining of labour security laws, unions were under pressure to limit demands for progress or in some cases to take concessions.

There were also other differences. Cuthbertson remembers how the US progressives were focused on equality and were uncomfortable bargaining provisions like maternity leave that would only apply to women.

In contrast, in Canada Justice Rosalie Abella, in 1984, delivered a groundbreaking report on Equality in Employment, where she emphasized equality of outcome, or equity. In her view, if women or another group needed special accommodation, such as maternity leave, to achieve equality of outcome, then this was the appropriate path. Abella's work shaped the approach to equity in employment for decades to come.

Childcare, 1983

The war years changed the perception of what could be bargained. For women to become the essential workforce it was during the war years, they needed nurseries for their kids. In the sixties and seventies when women came back into the workforce in large numbers, the issue of childcare once again jumped to the forefront.

The women's movement was seized with the issue, and organizations like OWW and the OFL that passed a daycare paper in 1980, adopted policies advocating for it. For union women, it was clear that they wanted to use the power of the union to bargain for childcare. It was also a key argument for why women needed unions, as Cuthbertson explains:

> So there was this kind of cross-fertilization. We in the UAW and the OFL women's committee did a paper on childcare and toured with the proposals to probably six or seven cities. I think it was just an incredible example of how important it was to have this alliance, born out of Fleck, between the women's movement and the labour movement, because they saw what labour could do, and we saw what issues the broader women's movement was raising that we could support, such as choice.

The UAW bargained childcare at Canadian Fabricated, which was Roxie Baker's plant in 1983. In that plant of mostly women, childcare was a pressing concern.

Bob White's assistant Buzz Hargrove bargained this breakthrough: two cents per-hour-worked to create childcare. The problem was that it wasn't enough money and, according to Cuthbertson, they didn't have a plan. What the union found out later was how expensive and complex childcare was.

There was a lot of membership pressure on Baker. Not all the women in Canadian Fabricated supported the childcare initiative because they would not benefit. Others wanted the benefit but there wasn't actually a new facility for them. Cuthbertson, from the national staff, was put in charge of implementing the fund, but they faced steep challenges due to the complexity and cost of the care. In the end, they were able to subsidize five spots in existing centres rather than creating new spots. It was an imperfect solution.

Years later, employment declined in the plant and the fund declined. In 2001 the plant, then owned by Johnson Controls, closed and the work went to Mexico. But Cuthbertson still calls it a breakthrough: "The plough had gone over the ground."

Roxie Baker's plant would pave the way for future successes and, in her entire career, that 1983 agreement with all the breakthroughs they negotiated makes her most proud.

Roxie Baker's Childcare Subsidy

Roxie Baker grew up on a farm in southwestern Ontario, married, had three kids, then moved with her husband to Stratford, Ontario, to search for work. She was sewing Arrow shirts for seventy-five cents an hour. As a member of the Amalgamated Clothing and Textile Workers Union, she began her involvement when the staff union representative asked her to attend a union conference. On her return she was recruited by her co-workers to take on the position of president of the local union when no one else would run. She stayed there for six years until the plant closed when the work was transferred offshore.

She then got a job at Canadian Fabricated in Stratford, a much bigger plant where employment fluctuated between 800 to 1,200 workers. Can Fab, as the workers called it, made trim, seat covers, and door panels for American Motors vehicles. Roxie got a job as a cutter, heavier work cutting through foot-thick layers of fabric, but this move meant a big pay boost to $2.10 cents an hour.

She had her eye on one of the two quality control positions that made better pay but required being able to read blueprints. The man who had held one of the two positions got his training on the job. Roxie wanted the same opportunity but was denied. This injustice angered her so much she took a night course for about four months. Then she got the job.

Starting out at Can Fab in 1974, she had vowed not to get involved in the union, but she was pulled back into activism. The full-time union staff rep asked her to join the UAW resolutions committee of the UAW Canadian council. She learned the union was trying to involve more women but she was the only woman on that committee and later became the chairperson.

"Attending council was much different then, with probably less than half dozen women delegates," she said. There would remain only one woman on the resolutions committee for many years to come.

Once again, in her plant of about 80 per cent women, the workers called on her to lead them as president, and she was elected to that position in 1974, the first woman to hold this top job. At that time, there were many inequities in the plant: a sweeper (man) made more than a sewer (woman); there were other wage inequities and two seniority lists, one for the men and a separate one for the women. She was determined to make change.

Her plant was the first in the union to negotiate leave for the union's paid education leave program whereby a negotiated fund would be used to offer union members training and leadership education.

The Stratford Labour Council started a daycare committee in November 1980, and the following year they put out a four-question survey about daycare services in the city. The need was high as Baker knew well from members in her own plant.

In 1983, Baker's bargaining committee set the goal of a child-care subsidy for the membership. "No one thought they could achieve it," she said. "Women would take time off when their kids got sick but then come to work when they got sick."

In that round of bargaining, they won two cents per-hour-worked to put in a fund for childcare. At the same time, they won parental leave for child adoption, language to eliminate sexual harassment, and a number of other gains.

Roxie Baker held many elected positions in the union and in her community including, to name some, first woman president of the Stratford Labour Council, member of the board of governors at Conestoga College, NDP campaign manager, Ontario Federation of Labour executive member, first woman elected to the UAW/CAW council executive, and later first woman elected to the national executive board. When the union's education centre established its own childcare centre in 1989, they named it the Roxie Baker Childcare Centre.

First UAW-GM Affirmative Action Language, 1984

Cuthbertson remembers that since GM and Ford were separate agreements, not tied to the American agreements, they could do things differently. The first step in moving the language forward was to present it to the union's master bargaining committee.

It was Cuthbertson who was asked to present equity language to GM for the Canadian side in 1982. None of it was achieved to her great disappointment. While they were unsuccessful in 1982, they were determined to succeed the next time:

> We were in bargaining and met with the UAW General Motors master bargaining committee, which was fine. No problem at all. So I was asked to come to the Ford bargaining committee and tell them about affirmative action and why it was important. I got beaten up [she says with a mixture of fury and astonishment]. They had gone out for lunch, got a little drunk, and when they came in, they said they weren't going to be "pussy-whipped" by some woman in the union. It was just awful.

No one spoke up in her favour or defended her. She was mortified.

When Bob White found out later that day, he was furious. Cuthbertson continues:

> The next morning, he read the riot act to the Ford master bargaining committee. He said "this policy has been passed by the collective bargaining conference. It's Canadian council policy. It's the union's policy, and we will bargain it." And he just laid it out. By this time, I think they were sober.

GM had kept women working throughout the war and they continued to hire some women. Whereas, after the Ford wildcat strike in 1942, Ford's solution to the equal pay issue was not to hire any women, and they didn't until 1976, which was around the time the UAW began hiring women on staff in Canada. "Ford was a sexist employer for thirty years," says Cuthbertson, "and I think that history matters. They never had to deal with women at union meetings or women running for election, even in the years when we were starting to do that kind of thing."

Eventually they had a breakthrough on affirmative action language. Cuthbertson says that in the early eighties it seemed that the union was always in major contract negotiations. She remembers one day when Bob Nickerson burst into her office and said "I think I can get affirmative action at GM. Write me some language."

So she and Carol Phillips, also by then on the staff of the union, put a paragraph together calling for the union to have affirmative action reps. Nickerson dashed off. And in 1984, he bargained one paragraph, the first UAW-GM affirmative action language.

The director of the Canadian arm of the UAW was Bob White. "The closest thing to a bona fide superstar Canadian labor has ever had," is how the *New York Times* described the UAW's charismatic Canadian leader in the spring of 1985.[5] This was after the Canadian leadership, at their Canadian council meeting in December of 1984 decided to separate their 123,000 members from their US parent union after fifty years, leaving the US union with only about one million members. The decision would be formalized later that year in September.

Bob White

Bob White dropped out of school and began at a woodworking plant near his home in southwestern Ontario. Before long he was the union leader of the plant taking them on strike. Al Seymour was a co-worker and lifelong friend. Bob soon came to the attention of the Canadian union leadership, and at age twenty-five he was a full-time union organizer on the union's staff. He later headed up the organizing department and enlisted 35,000 members to join the union. In 1978 Dennis McDermott left as Canadian UAW director to head up the Canadian Labour Congress and White was named as his successor.

White was recognized even by corporations as an astute negotiator, and the UAW continued to make groundbreaking gains at the bargaining table. He bristled at the demands for concessions by the auto companies, and in 1982 he led a five-week strike at Chrysler that was opposed by the UAW in the United States. The company had said the strike would bankrupt Chrysler and throw all the workers out of their jobs. However, the Canadians held firm, secured an additional $1.15 an hour and gained the US workers an additional seventy-five cents an hour.

The *New York Times* accurately described how White had irritated both the company and the US union with his decision to later strike General Motors for close to two weeks in defiance of the US section of the union.[6] This was wildly popular with Canadian members.

Marilyne White, Bob's second wife, was a leader in the flight attendant's union that later became part of the Canadian Union of Public Employees (CUPE). They had met in 1976 at a Canadian Labour Congress convention. "At that time the union was mostly male; the whole labour movement was mostly male," says Marilyne.

Bob was a naturally gifted speaker, even as a young man, and he read extensively. Inspired by the culture of the union, he also surrounded himself with strong women at work and was not threatened by them. Some men feel uncomfortable when they see a group of women. Bob would make a point of going over to them to crack a joke or poke fun, usually at himself.

Bob was a good listener. When feminist leader Judy Rebick asked him to speak at a pro-choice rally, to prepare he discussed the issues with Marilyne, wanting to know why abortion was an economic issue. Marilyne White says she explained it to him and, later, Rebick told her how great Bob was at the rally. He had listened and understood.

"It was the issues that taught him and other male leaders about women's rights," Marilyne says. "The OFL affirmative action policy made a huge difference. It meant that qualified women actually had a chance to advance. And campaigns like the childcare campaigns raised awareness."

Marilyne White continues,

> Bob understood that the culture of the union could be difficult for women but he couldn't 'un-appoint' anyone (on staff or in local leadership) or go around the politics of the union. He realized that the more women he put on staff, the better things would be . . . He saw the pushback of some of the male staff, but he just had to nudge them along and then wait till they retired. Bob continued his learning all his life, and some men just didn't.

Sue Genge, a retired women's department representative at the Canadian Labour Congress, recalls:

> I was working at the library when CAW was formed. I remember co-workers of mine saying, "Sue, can we join CAW? We have books about cars." Bob White was very popular in trade union movement and we loved him. Tons of people loved him, but I had to explain that it was not enough of a community of interest to have books about cars.

Neo-Liberalism and the End of the Post-War Era

The 1970s and 1980s saw forces of conservative political change buffet economies and challenge the progress made by working people and their unions. Neo-liberalism in the form of deregulation, privatization, and free trade ushered in an era when capital was able to shift investments globally to the sources of cheapest labour, lowest taxes, and greatest profit.[7]

The Bank of Canada's dramatic spike in interest rates in Canada in the early 1980s was a shock to the economy that sparked job losses and threw Canada into a recession. The manufacturing sector that had been a powerhouse fuelling the post-war economy was under pressure.

In 1980 one million Ontarians worked in manufacturing, a quarter of all Ontario jobs. The percentage was highest in the areas of southern Ontario along Hwy 401, in close proximity to the United States. In the early 1980s, 88 per cent of Ontario men had a full-time job in the sector. By the mid-1990s, the Canadian economy had shed hundreds of thousands of manufacturing jobs and by a decade later there would only be about half as many workers in manufacturing jobs in Ontario compared to 1980.

Free trade, automation, industry consolidation all played a part, but by now employers increasingly had the upper hand. Work life became more precarious for workers. Employers demanded contract concessions for lower wages and greater company flexibility.

The Canadian UAW members were proud of their union's history from its formation in Canada in the 1930s to the groundbreaking gains in the decades after the war. However, by the mid-1980s the strains between the US and Canadian sections of the union created serious conflict. As part of the US union, the Canadians were expected to negotiate in lockstep with the US leaders according to the collective bargaining program adopted by the union at its convention. When they came under increasing pressure to limit demands and give concessions, the US leadership buckled, and the Canadians began to chafe at the inability to bargain freely.

Canadian Workers Separate from US Counterparts, 1985

The Genie award-winning film *Final Offer* by Sturla Gunnarsson and Robert Collison in 1985 details the UAW-Canada negotiations with General Motors as the unity of the union came apart. The film documents the talks where the Canadians took a more militant stance with GM and refused to back down despite pressure from the international union.

The UAW Canadian council in December 1984 was an emotional meeting where long-time UAW-Canada leaders spoke of their history in the union but the need to chart a different course in Canada. The 350 delegates voted to begin talks to separate from the international union. It was not a unanimous decision and, even for those in favour of the separation, it was a step fraught with risks. Both sides had called the divorce amicable, but it was far from that. "It was not a friendly divorce, to say the least," says Wendy Cuthbertson. "It was quite bitter."

Feminist Influence on New CAW Constitution

The new Canadian union needed its own constitution, its own governing rules to operate. Bob White asked Wendy Cuthbertson to prepare the document based on the UAW constitution. She mirrored that document with Canadian adaptations.

Organizing women during the war years, and the fight for equal pay, led the UAW at its 1944 convention to mandate a national women's department in Detroit, women's councils in every region, and women's committees in every local. The union also held an annual women's conference in Detroit. Despite the retrenchment of the 1950s as many women were forced out of their jobs, these provisions remained in the constitution. The groundwork laid by decades of feminist activism in the UAW paved the way for the Canadians as they set out on their own.

Cuthbertson just included all the hard-fought equity language in the Canadian version, and when the leadership presented it to the council delegates, the language passed.

Hard-Fought Victories

In the early post-war period, women were pushed to leave the paid workforce and return to the domestic domain. But some women remained and continued to press their union for greater rights for women. The structures the union created toward the end of the war, such as women's departments, conferences, and committees, would also outlast the retrenchment of the 1950s and 1960s, when women were pushed out of many workplaces and back into the home. The memories of their potential from the war years could not be erased. Women understood their capacity to earn income and expand their rights.

These constitutional structures endured in the following decades until second wave feminists again took up the torch of equity and fairness. They did this with the power of the union to organize in their workplaces and fight for fair working conditions and wages. They would also eventually do this by expanding separate programs for women, 2SLGBTQ+ members, Black,

Indigenous, and workers of colour. But that would take time and the efforts of those who were following in their mother's footsteps seeking economic independence and fair treatment at work.

Second wave feminists built on the legacy of their mothers, creating structures like women's committees and affirmative action policies. They would demand childcare and equal pay for work of equal value. They would prove their toughness in the workplace and demand equal representation in the union.

Chapter Three

CAW Mergers Building a Sisterhood, 1985-1995

CAW Founding Convention, 1985

The founding convention of the UAW-Canada in September 1985 was a bold and exciting event. What delegates didn't know was that the details of the Canadian union's split from the international union had not been finalized. When the dust settled, for the union to get its share of the multimillion-dollar strike fund, it could not take the UAW name. It took a special convention the following June to proclaim the Canadian Auto Workers (CAW) as the new name of the union. The multimillion-dollar divorce settlement cheque from the UAW would help the Canadians get the new union up and running and rebuild its education centre in Port Elgin, Ontario.

Bob White, as the new president of the Canadian union, pushed to invest much of the money in revamping the old camp near Port Elgin to become a state-of-the-art union education facility. There the union would continue with its goal of fostering the inspiration of the union and training its new leaders. White would often say: "The head of the union was in Toronto, but the heart was in Port Elgin."

The Canadians were now on their own and could determine their own path in their own country. Part of White's vision was to play a bigger role in the political debates of the day from free trade discussions with the United States to deregulation to human rights. Part of that bigger role was to be a bigger union. Freed from the restrictions of the international union, White wanted to merge with other like-minded Canadian unions to build a bigger base and become a bigger force in Canada. He would also play a significant role on the international stage with other unions and with political leaders like Nelson Mandela.

Roxie Baker: First woman on the National Executive Board

After the Fleck strike, when women were joining the workforce in unprecedented numbers, after the affirmative action initiative at the Ontario Federation of Labour where women joined the executive board, after the union's support for reproductive rights and the struggle to defend the Morgentaler clinic, the time was finally right to add a woman to the new national executive board of the Canadian union.

With less than 10 per cent women members, with few women elected to local union executives, and very few women on the staff of the union, the leadership soon focused on Roxie Baker as the local leader who should be on the national executive. Baker seemed the natural choice. She was a long-time president of her local union, president of the Stratford Labour Council, active in

Roxie Baker (right) and Karen Malcho, in 1980, with a sign reading "A Women's Place is in the Home and she should go there directly after Work(ing)." Photo: UAW.

the NDP, a huge promoter of worker education, and recognized as a principled, determined leader. And it was her local in 1983 that had bargained the union's first childcare funds.

"Roxie was modest and would speak softly, but if she felt strongly, she wouldn't give in, there was steel there," says Cuthbertson. "People were impressed. Her accomplishments spoke for themselves, and people trusted her as honest and brave."

Baker would remain the sole woman on the national executive board for several years, but the push to expand the representation of women and racialized members would gain momentum in the next decade.

Carol Phillips: Strength of the Sisterhood

When Carol Phillips was in her early twenties in the mid-1970s, she was hired to work in the office in De Havilland Aircraft in Toronto. Her dad worked there, and employees were encouraged to recommend family members for jobs. "The De Havilland plant was pretty raucous," she says. "They struck every three years, whether they needed to or not, walk-outs happened regularly there. It was a wild place, the office unit benefited from that, but didn't really participate much. We even had a separate expiry date on our contract [that was] after [the plant]."

As a clerk in the engineering department where aircraft were designed, she found there wasn't a lot of interest in the union, so she ran unopposed and got elected to the bargaining committee. "I always remember this very British old guy who was a planner and did things like designed the Beaver and the Twin Otter and things like that. And he said, with very British pronunciation, 'Can you imagine, we are represented by a common clerk?'"

After one round of bargaining, she ran for the position of chairperson for the negotiations in 1981. Her goal was a common expiry date with the plant so that they could get the office issues addressed with the strength of the plant workers.

Phillips remembers the opening day of negotiations very well:

> Bargaining opening day came along, and opening day is pretty simple. You go in. You exchange (contract) proposals, you say

> Hello! How are you? Shake hands across table, that's it. I got up that morning and my water broke because I was pregnant. So, I thought, well, I went to those prenatal classes. It'll be a few hours. I'm not in labour. I haven't got any pains, so I call up my mother—though, big mistake—and say, "my water broke. So, it's probably today, but I have to go open bargaining, and it's no big deal. It's at a hotel." Next thing, I'm going to leave the house, my mother screeches up in the car.
>
> "No, you're not getting in that car by yourself." So she comes to bargaining. And my rep was Jim O'Neil, and Bob Nickerson, who was responsible for aerospace for the national director, was there too. My mother and I walk in. Nick looks up, and then says, "Who the fuck's this?"
>
> And I said, "This is my mother."
>
> And he said, "You can't bring your mother to bargaining."
>
> Anyway, I said, "Well, you know my water broke."
>
> O'Neil practically passes out. He just cannot believe it.
>
> And so I said, "Look, I have to get out of here pretty quickly. We'd better get started."
>
> So in comes the company, and Nickerson says something like, "Let's get on with this, because Carol's going into labour any minute. Her water broke, you know."
>
> Everybody knew my water broke. So we open bargaining, and I went to the hospital. I know exactly what day the bargaining started that year.
>
> I know also that that same old planner said, "This is what happens when you elect women."

"In those days we did things differently," continues Phillips, "and we grabbed on to opportunities differently. Two weeks later I was back at the table because bargaining was of course delayed for two weeks because we'd exchanged bargaining proposals."

> The next bargaining day was two weeks later and I turn up with (my son) Dylan. And there's a side room when we go back and forth, and you know, pass the baby around and we handled it that way, and then my mother watched him a lot of times, and we went on strike.

> That wouldn't happen today. It wouldn't be the expectation that you had to turn up. You had to be there, and you had to pretend that I didn't just have the baby. But I was also driven. I knew that if I did step back that was it. I was the first woman elected and the first chair, and that it was going to set things back. Those were the days that people would have said, "See? Told you." Exactly like that planner said, "It's what happens when you elect women."
>
> I was a little bit embarrassed. But I just kind of plowed ahead. But, on the other hand, I know why I did it, because you had to make those ridiculous choices. Also, I don't know about the history of this, but maternity leave was pretty short back in those days. I was through my maternity leave entitlement by the time bargaining was over.

Then Phillips heard that the union was considering hiring a woman on staff and that she was being considered. Ultimately Maureen Kirincic was hired, and Carol says she was irked because she had bargaining experience that Maureen did not. She was so irked that she applied for the job of women's director at the Canadian Labour Congress to replace Mary Eadie, a former deputy minister in the Manitoba government. To her astonishment, as a young woman in her twenties, she was hired.

"The audacity of it" she says. "I was young (twenty-eight years), Dylan was eighteen months old and I came straight out of the plant. My staff rep Bob Nickerson was 'pissed off.'"

"'You've pigeon-holed yourself now,' he said. 'You're going to be in women's stuff for the rest of your life.'"

Phillips had been to a UAW women's conference in the United States and to an OFL women's conference. But she still had limited experience. "I was as green as they come because I didn't know the sisterhood."

Her task at the CLC was daunting: to organize a national women's conference in three months at the Château Frontenac in Québec. She was terrified. She set about travelling the country to meet all the labour women she needed to know to get their advice. "I remember Nancy Riche from NUPGE [National Union of Provincial Government Employees] and Carole Gingras from the FTQ [Fédération du Travail du Quebec] being so helpful." She knew the success of the conference depended on the support of the labour women. Without their support she would not have been able to pull it off. And the conference was a huge success. Women's conferences at the CLC were a really big deal.

In her role at the CLC for eighteen months, she learned how supportive women could be. That hadn't necessarily been her experience up until then. "We were a tough, competitive union, and it was even worse for women activists. We hadn't learned the power of supporting each other. We were in such small numbers, often allowing ourselves to be played and pitted against each other for the crumbs that the guys were willing to share. So for the rest of my experience in the union, that was such an important radicalization that happened there."

Her big issue at the CLC was affirmative action. She shepherded this issue through, with the support of the president, Dennis McDermott. Despite the opposition of CUPE President and CLC Vice President Shirley Carr, it passed at the 1984 CLC Convention, and ten spots for women were added to the executive board.

Later that same year, 1984, Bob White invited her to join the staff of the UAW, as a service rep, with mainly auto parts units, mostly with women, many of whom would later be affected by the free trade agreement signed in 1989.

Phillips recalls,

> The CLC affirmative action measures made it to our bargaining tables in the Big Three [auto] negotiations. National staff representative Pat Clancy took this on with training sessions to organize around affirmative action spots. The goal was to hire more women, rather than just one here and there. To allow women to move into the trades and other jobs they were restricted from. They wanted to eliminate the Assembler 1 and Assembler 2 positions that kept women out of the better paying jobs. Affirmative action reps at each auto workplace did the audits, did regular reports, and learned leadership skills.
>
> I was quite disliked. I was expected to be a rep like all the others not a feminist rep. We really started getting involved in the broader feminist issues. I got on a bus to go to Radio

> Shack because it was a women's strike. The labour movement came but so did the broader women's movement. I benefited hugely from that.

Phillips would go on in 1988 to become an assistant to the president, the first woman to do so in the union. White told her that he wanted to send a message by appointing a feminist. She says he gave her "a long leash in terms of continuing to push affirmative action, harassment, and childcare."

Peggy Nash and Jane Armstrong: Airline Workers and the First Merger

As free trade and economic deregulation would impact the manufacturing sector, so airline deregulation would disrupt that sector. By the 1980s airlines came under intense competitive pressure that would ultimately see airline bankruptcies, mergers, and takeovers. For airline workers this began a period of insecurity and fightbacks to resist contract concessions.

The Canadian Air Line Employees Association (CALEA) had only about 5,000 members in 1985. With a large majority of women, most of their members worked as airline ticket and airport staff for large and small Canadian airlines. With US airline deregulation, the CALEA leadership could see the writing on the wall early on. CALEA President Tom Saunders knew his union needed to change to adapt to the more pro-business environment they faced. In multiple rounds of negotiations, employers were becoming more aggressive, and the tiny union had limited resources and no strike fund.

As CALEA headed into what promised to be challenging negotiations with Air Canada, they began exploring how the union could join or merge with a larger union to better serve their members. They knew the huge changes occurring in the airlines.

Saskatchewan-born Jane Armstrong was active in solidarity work with South Africans and the South African Congress of Trade Unions (SACTU). Getting hired in the early 1980s as a part-time librarian at CALEA gave her a chance to work with a Canadian union, albeit a tiny one, with about 80 per cent women members.

Peggy Nash had worked for Air Canada at both Pearson

airport and then in the ticketing office in Toronto and had been a health and safety rep, developing the union's first health and safety policy. She had been hired by Saunders as the union's education and communications director, joining a team of service reps, and a lawyer—all men—and Jane Armstrong the part-time librarian who later served as an organizer and researcher.

Armstrong and Nash were highly motivated to advance gender issues in the union.

Nash pushed for the union to hold a women's conference and got Saunders's approval, even with an impending dispute with Air Canada. He at first wondered why they needed a women's conference when they had a majority of women members, but Armstrong and Nash persuaded him that women were not as involved in the union as they needed to be. CALEA would need its members more than ever, especially if they ended up in a strike with Air Canada.

Nash and Armstrong partnered to organize the first women's conference in the airline union. It drew these women together for the first time to speak about issues like harassment, pensions, new technology, part-time work, and shift scheduling. The conference not only educated but also mobilized women in the union who would soon be out on strike. It was a tiny conference in February 1985 of only about fifty women. Future Ontario Cabinet minister and Canadian Senator Frances Lankin, then the women's rep for Ontario Public Service Employees Union (OPSEU), gave the opening address. Workshops followed on topics such as pensions and health and safety. At a workshop on sexual harassment, almost every woman indicated that they had observed or experienced harassment, not surprising in a public-facing job in the 1980s. What was surprising was that none of the male service reps had any inkling that this was an issue.

As expected, the conference unleashed greater momentum in the union when they needed it. Many of those conference participants did not hold an elected union position but became activists during the strike. Some later ran for leadership positions in the union.

When an Air Canada manager said that many of the women just worked for "pin money," the union pounced and the members were outraged. They united with the women's movement and

CALEA members on strike in 1985 against Air Canada. Photo: CALEA.

Haviva Hosek, the president of the National Action Committee on the Status of Women, publicly condemning Air Canada's sexist comments. MP Margaret Mitchell challenged the Conservative transport minister over the erosion of full-time jobs at Air Canada. CALEA declared their strike in 1985, a women's strike, and women responded. Women like Cheryl Kryzaniwsky (already active) and others who had never been active in the union took notice and were steadfast on the picket lines. And some, like Kryzaniwsky, went on to play big roles (see chapter 4).

The 1985 Air Canada strike was a first for the tiny union. UAW-Canada Director Bob White was by this time a well-known national figure because of the tough rounds of auto bargaining he had led. He met with CALEA's national bargaining committee and then, when CALEA President Saunders had a heart attack, White joined the negotiations to send a message to Air Canada. He said he had no magic wand to pressure Air Canada but he declared that Air Canada was not going to starve out the workers, since they were not getting strike pay. White's presence broke a logjam and shortly after the committee and the company got a tentative agreement that was ratified by the membership in 1985. It was to be a defining moment for the union.

The previous December, White had invited a few reps from CALEA to the UAW Canadian council to observe the debate on whether to split from the US union. The speeches were passionate and emotional. Nash says "We had the privilege of a front-row seat to this historic event and hearing the speeches about the importance of the union, and building a new progressive path for members, oh, I still remember the feeling, it just was so inspiring. That inspiration stayed with me for a lifetime. When working people decided to act together, to take charge of their own future, they are a power than can improve lives very directly."

The proposal to split from the international union passed overwhelmingly at that meeting, December 1984.

CALEA leaders knew it was time to merge with a larger union to be able to better represent their members. They had some key criteria for merger candidates. Armstrong was on the CALEA committee at that time looking for a merger. Having a women's department and education programs were a priority, and most importantly, having a strike fund. They were also looking for a Canadian union.

The CALEA merger committee met with the main unions they were considering and chose the UAW. One of the key reasons in favour of the auto workers union was the presentation to the CALEA committee by UAW-Canada director of communications Wendy Cuthbertson. She spoke of the union's women's director Edith Johnson, the annual women's conference, and local union women's committees, all structures that the union had created as a result of women organizing decades before.

CALEA had none of these structures. But what CALEA could offer the auto workers was a national membership from every part of Canada, a new and important economic sector, and an influx of women members. This meshed with White's vision of a truly national union, committed to women's and human rights, and a national platform for UAW's labour voice.

With the Canadian UAW's separation from the international union, leaving it free to make its own choices, the CALEA members voted to merge with the UAW-Canada in 1985. They were the first union of what would become many Canadian unions to make the same choice. This was a first step in Bob White's vision of a larger Canadian union movement.

September 1985, UAW-Canada was born. "We were so proud to be members of this organization that was making life better for Canadian workers," said Nash. "I was eight and a half months pregnant and wouldn't have missed the convention for anything. Delegates, me included, lined up to get White's autograph on their convention program. We knew this was history in the making."

"I think there were five women on staff out of about seventy when we merged with them," says Armstrong. She was assigned to the organizing department, joining Maureen Kirincic. A key issue with women workers was harassment. To show the workers that the union could get action, Armstrong says, they would send a letter to an employer threatening to take them to the Labour Board or the Human Rights Commission if they didn't stop all harassment. That usually got action and would give a boost to any organizing campaign.

The women from CALEA brought a different perspective to the now CAW. "They didn't work on the auto assembly lines, but they worked on another form of assembly line. Electronic monitoring was an issue, where the number of keystrokes you hit in a minute were calculated on computers and used to discipline workers."

Armstrong believes that the influx of airline women encouraged the existing women members in the CAW. "Being able to join with these other women at education sessions, there was this feeling that they could make progress on issues that may have been seen to be secondary."

CAW organizer Jane Armstrong celebrates with a group of workers who just settled a long strike with CIBC Visa in 1986. Photo: UAW.

After the merger, Nash was going to stay in the airline group that was now a local union on the UAW-Canada (soon to become CAW). Cheryl Kryzaniwsky was the local union president. As the union was taking its first steps of independence, Nash went into labour and off on maternity leave with what would be the third child in a recombined family—his son, her son, and their son.

While still on leave, she got a call from Wendy Cuthbertson and then from Bob White, inviting her to join the national staff in the communications department. The chance to work directly with Cuthbertson and White was thrilling, but she was torn. How could she leave her three-month-old baby?

Cuthbertson assured her that the union would accommodate him. Peggy and her partner Carl Kaufman talked it over. He was a leader in his own union at VIA Rail. He understood the opportunity that was being presented, and he made the unselfish offer to take a year of unpaid leave, to stay home with their sons. Like for most women, childbirth and parenthood is an emotional roller coaster and a financial penalty. Nash got the job of her dreams, but Carl lost a year's wages, and that precious time with her son was irreplaceable. Later they would pay for caregivers and daycare and live the stress that many working parents face.

Soon after, just before her first day on the job, Wendy Cuthbertson called again. "Welcome to the UAW staff. I'm afraid we need to send you to Calgary."

There was a strike at Pacific Western Airlines and it looked like they were close to an agreement, so they needed help to create a ratification brochure for the members.

"Calgary?! I can't do that. I'm breastfeeding. What about my baby?"

"Don't worry," she added encouragingly. "I booked a sky cot for the flight and I booked a childcare agency to be on call if you need support once you're there. And there are some new fathers on the bargaining committee; they will love having a baby there."

"So at age twelve weeks, our son Thomas flew with me to Calgary, where indeed some homesick fathers made a huge fuss over him. It was actually a good way to start on the job. I had been so anxious about leaving him and this way I didn't have to do that."

Back in Toronto, she rented a big and noisy milk-pumping machine. Anne Chetwynd, who worked with Nash, would guard the door. Nash would put the little bluish sacs of milk in the freezer on their floor of the national union.

"What the fuck is this?" asked one of the staff reps when he opened the freezer door, probably looking for some lunch to pilfer. Nash remembers his disgust when he found out that it was milk from her body. Men have such a strange relationship with women's breasts.

Union jobs mean long hours and unpredictable schedules. Nash felt terrible stress and guilt leaving her baby time after time. She had already suffered through this with her first son. As a local union activist, she had too many meetings and conferences. But she was determined that she was in a fight for workers rights and women's equality, and that meant doing the same jobs men did and it meant fighting for supports like childcare to be able to do it. It's just that getting there was hard.

Jane Armstrong was facing similar challenges, becoming a single parent. As much as she loved organizing, balancing organizing with a young family was tough. "I had a small son and it was difficult to leave a baby and head out to an organizing drive at 2 am in the morning, because somebody had got fired in the middle of an organizing drive." She eventually transferred to the union's communications department, later becoming the director.

Armstrong reflects on how much the women in leadership and on staff needed the support and help of other women. "It was a male-dominated union, and even though the top leadership were good, the kinds of work we did, and the commitment we had, it was pretty crazy."

"Even though the union provided childcare at major events, it closed at a certain time, but the meetings that the men were often chairing didn't end when childcare ended. So we would organize to have others pick up our kids, and sometimes they went back to various rooms to sleep, or we drove our kids back to the city."

She also recalls meetings where one of the only women would make a point and there would be a nod, and then on to the next speaker. Then three speakers down, some man would raise the exact same thing that the woman said, and suddenly there was like strong agreement with the suggestion. And the women would look at each other with a nod of recognition.

Jane Armstrong's activism and union work continued for almost two more decades. She held the role of communications director for ten years until 2004, where she was instrumental in the creation of the women's advocate program and the union campaign "Break the Silence" (see chapter 4).

Human Rights: First CAW Conference, 1986

One morning soon after Nash joined the staff, Bob Nickerson burst into her office with his usual gust of exuberance. "You're on the council human rights committee, ok?" Then without taking a breath, "You get with them at the next council meeting and see what they want to do."

On the list of getting the new union up and operating and while facing challenges from employers, a skeptical media, and nervous members, Nickerson probably saw this as an important but small item to take care of.

"But," she said hesitantly, "with Wendy on leave, and me doing her job and my job, and with a baby, I just don't want to overextend myself."

"It's the human rights committee. They just talk about human rights. It'll be fine."

At the first council human rights committee meeting in the new Canadian union, it was both a getting-to-know-you session and a call to action. The leadership on the committee, all men, were frustrated that human rights issues were falling under the radar. Employers were getting away with murder.

As an enthusiastic new member of the CAW, but not from the auto workers culture, or even an industrial worker, Nash was a bit apprehensive about the committee meeting. But they welcomed her as the representative of the union administration. Far from being just a discussion about human rights, the committee insisted that the union hold a human rights conference—as soon as possible.

She agreed unconditionally. They suggested guest speakers and they wanted key topics of racism and harassment. Her job was to make it happen.

The CAW human rights conference would be the first conference of the new Canadian union, held that same year November 1–2, 1986. No one in the administration knew how to run a conference, how to send a call letter, how the costs would be calculated, or the bills paid. This had all been handled in Detroit by the international union. This would be the test. And this new person to the union, this airline worker, who was feeling like a hyperventilating rabbit, would be the person who had to make it happen.

From the call letter to the billing, from the topics to the fees for guest speakers, everything was breaking new ground in the union. She was a frequent visitor to Nickerson's office to get him to approve spending. "The Canadians were very dependent on the UAW in the United States," he says. "In collective bargaining we would gather all the expenses, hotels, meals and so on, and just send it all to Detroit to be paid out of the strike fund. The Canadians did not have an independent financial structure."

Dr. Linda Murray: Racism and Sexism as Tools of Division

There were several conference plenary speakers, but the highlight was Dr. Linda Murray, a community health activist from Chicago. Murray punched out a hard-hitting speech to the ninety-three delegates about how management used racism and sexism to divide the working class and why fighting for the rights of all workers would strengthen solidarity and the power of the union. She appealed to workers to join together to fight racism, and to not let employers use racism and sexism as a tactic of division.

Her speech was persuasive and inspiring. After a prolonged standing ovation, they opened the floor for questions and comments. Auto workers are well schooled in speaking their mind with working-class eloquence. Speaker after speaker applauded Murray's remarks. There were also complaints about the companies and how they were using racism to divide workers, which Murray had explained well. They emphasized however that the union was not blameless.

Then came comments by Leroy Bell, a union executive member from Local 199, General Motors in St. Catharines. A large man with a booming voice he rose in the expansive assembly hall to make his point. He spoke quickly and emphatically. As a Black man, he expected management to use racism against him, just as they would use sexism, to try to divide workers, to pit them against each other. What he could not tolerate was the union leadership and members who bought into racism, who called him racist names or his union sisters sexist names. "I love the union," he said, his eyes glistening. "If you're gong to call me something, call me brother. And for the sisters, if you're going to call them something call them sister. Don't divide us. Don't weaken us." Bell's emotional appeal reinforced Murray's message.

His comments hit with force. Delegate after delegate pressed the union to commit it was not just going to talk about harassment but was going to take action. As a neophyte on the union staff, Nash resolved that the union would take action, and she made this commitment before all the delegates. She breathed their skepticism in deeply and vowed not to let them down.

After the staff meeting where Maureen Kirincic had issued her frank challenge (see chapter 2), after the opening of the floodgates of the human rights conference, anything besides effective action by the union was a betrayal. Nash reported as completely and forcefully as possible to the union's officers and locals what recommendations the conference had produced. Human rights committees were already constitutionally mandated by the union, yet another important institutional structure. They were called on to be more proactive in educating and enforcing human rights.

"While the delegates were pleased that the CAW was holding its first human rights conference, several expressed the view that expectations have now been raised and that concrete actions and activities should now follow," is how the report ended.

Nash was assigned to work with Carol Phillips, at that time the union's women's representative, to come up with a plan for dealing with harassment. They did.

Call me Sister, Call me Brother: Harassment Policy and Procedure

Phillips convened a group of women on staff and from local leaders to discuss harassment and possibilities for a procedure for dealing with harassment. Problems with management were somewhat easier to handle using the union's grievance procedure. But getting issues like pornographic pictures taken down or misogynistic graffiti removed remained entrenched problems. Co-worker harassment was much tougher to deal with.

Most of the women members worked in places like auto assembly, aerospace, and other large manufacturers that were overwhelmingly male dominated. What many of the women spoke of was the difficulty of raising issues with an all-male leadership in the workplace and the local union, a problem compounded if it was one of those male leaders involved in the harassment. They also raised the need for confidentiality to avoid a backlash against the person complaining, combined with the need for a quick resolution. Word travelled quickly in the plants, and women or racialized workers were easily labelled troublemakers or complainers.

They also heard about another related issue: if a union member made a complaint against another union member, and the company disciplined that person, the union would defend them but there was no one to defend the union member who had made the complaint. Co-worker harassment was a big issue. Taking this on would mean challenging the culture in the plants.

They began drafting a procedure along with a policy that aspired to build solidarity and ensure that all members claimed equal standing in the union. Leroy Bell's remarks inspired the name of the policy, "Call me Sister, Call me Brother."

The policy aimed to embrace Dr. Linda Murray's framing of harassment as a management responsibility and also a tactic to divide workers. It called on the union to aspire to respect everyone and to ensure workplaces that are safe and healthy.

> Harassment in the workplace is cruel, destructive behaviour that is not only damaging to the affected individuals but which in the case of co-worker harassment, can also eat away at the very foundation of our union. . . . By respecting our brothers and sisters and confronting harassment in the workplace, we can build a stronger and more effective union.[1]

The policy laid out a procedure to follow if a member faced harassment and it offered them the ability to report the harassment to anyone they felt comfortable with in the union. It also offered the union a chance to try and resolve the issue informally and quickly. Where that was not possible a complaint procedure was put in place to push for a quick investigation and resolve while trying to protect the confidentiality of the complainant.

This policy and procedure were an important step in trying to change the culture of workplaces. The pinups had to come down, the comments and catcalls had to stop, and the retaliation against complainants had to stop. That at least was the goal. Of course it would be imperfect, but the key was getting the policy out far and wide, educating the local leadership, and holding them accountable for upholding the policy. The union didn't want local leaders washing their hands of the issue and just hiring outside investigators. They knew that without the buy-in of the elected leaders, workplaces would not change.

The union's top leadership was supportive. The policy was debated at the national executive board and then brought to the council where local leaders gathered. It was presented as a requirement for a modern union to protect its members.

These normally opinionated and outspoken men sometimes went quiet and didn't speak against it. With the top leadership on side, no ambitious local union leader was going to risk saying the wrong thing. But their silence spoke volumes. It would be a long, bumpy process to change the culture of these industrial workplaces. Pinups could come down, but opinions could harden below the surface and bubble up in the coming years.

The union created a package of materials, including the harassment policy, the procedure, posters, videos, complaint forms, and a question-and-answer document about harassment. Some progressive local leaders would genuinely try to uphold the policy and support complainants who used it. Others just ignored it and tried to squash complaints from going beyond their local union.

The policy would evolve over time as the understanding of human rights evolved and the union gained more experience in handling complaints. The enactment was imperfect. Without a doubt harassment continued to happen and life was miserable for far too many CAW members, but the local leadership was held accountable for failing to treat harassment seriously according to the policy. Even national staff representatives, in rare cases, ran afoul of the policy and were taken to task.

There was no list of fixed consequences for different types of harassment. Each case was assessed individually. In some cases, verbal harassment might mean an apology was in order. In some serious cases, people faced serious discipline and the union recognized that it was merited.

Something else changed. The policy created the space for local activists who were elected as council delegates to get to the microphones and speak at the council meetings in a way that was new. They could speak about the topic of harassment and about human rights more generally. This would be a permanent change that would just grow over time.

Today with the backlash against "wokeism," some people bemoan that the left has gone down a blind alley, abandoning class politics for identity politics. "Do we really care if we have Black bank presidents or if leaders like Margaret Thatcher are elected?" they ask. Class is often overlooked in the focus on identity politics. Identity politics without class solidarity is simply striving as an individual. Yes, some will succeed but at the expense of the many.

However, there is no question that Dr. Linda Murray was correct when she argued that sexism and racism (and discrimination against all other identities) disproportionately hurt some workers but divide all workers. Solidarity is about making sure we can all succeed, that we can stay united and be stronger together. The new Canadian union adopted this harassment policy and became proud of its role as a trailblazer on this difficult issue.

Childcare, Why It Matters

Support for childcare has been a demand from working women for several decades. When women were essential during the war years, employers found a way to offer care for children. When men returned, it fell, again, to women to look after the home and family.

At Canadian Fabricated in Stratford, Ontario, Local 1325, President Roxie Baker along with then-assistant to the UAW-Canada Director Buzz Hargrove, bargained the first money in the union for childcare, the union got a tough lesson about the costs of childcare. Not only could the union not create a childcare centre, but it also couldn't even buy enough spaces in existing centres. Pressure grew on Baker and the union leadership to get the program up and running. Kids couldn't wait and their parents needed help. Finally, the union bit the bullet and offered a small subsidy for some members who had centre-based care for their kids. What was needed was more money, lots and lots more money.

Ken Gerard was the president of Local 444, the same local union as Hargrove, representing Chrysler Canada workers, and others. He was a towering figure in the union, very committed to advancing the union's bargaining goals, of which childcare was one. In the 1987 Chrysler bargaining, he negotiated half a cent per-hour-worked to go into a fund for childcare, the largest childcare fund ever negotiated in the private sector. This was another breakthrough, but still not enough for the need.

When Gerard died suddenly of a heart attack in 1990, Larry Bauer was the natural successor. He was very tough and provided strong leadership for the local. Nash remembers Larry in bargaining at a Toronto hotel, when they were trying to push for more childcare funding:

> He pulled me into a small meeting room, one-on-one: "Why is this a union issue? Why should I push for more money for childcare? Tell me why this should matter to my members."
>
> I should have been ready but this was unexpected. I realize now he was just preparing arguments for bargaining.
>
> "Well, so that they can get help looking after their kids while they're at work," I stumbled. "More women are coming into the plant and they need help with their kids, especially because they work shifts. Childcare centres aren't set up for shift work."
>
> "My mother always worked," he countered, his eyes unblinking, challenging me. His big hands looked like they could just as easily crush me as he could persuade me in an argument. "We would get ready, put our coats on when my mom left for work, me and my sister. We'd go to the end of our long drive. There were two chairs there and we'd wait there for the bus."
>
> I don't remember how long he said the wait was, but I remain with the impression that it was a long time. I thought of two small children, in all kinds of weather, waiting at the end of

> the drive for the bus, their mother long gone to work to put food on the table. She had no choice. I couldn't help it. Tears started to well up in my eyes. My fear melted, and I saw that little child who really should never have had to go through that.
>
> "That's so sad," I said. "No kid should have to do that. No parent should be forced to do that."
>
> He just turned and left. And he went in and hammered Chrysler for childcare funding for shift workers, his members, and bargained double the amount, one cent per-hour-worked for the thousands of Chrysler workers. He would go on to more than quadruple that in 1993. But in the meantime, his commitment to childcare was realized in the creation of a Windsor childcare centre for shift workers.

The union hired childcare experts Martha Friendly and Laurel Rothman to guide them through the process of setting up the centre. Something unique was created: a childcare centre set up to cover shifts, with cots for kids to come and leave at all hours. The union also created an in-home program where members could

CAW 1987 childcare poster, with Bob White at the opening of the CAW Childcare Centre in Windsor, Ontario. Photo: CAW.

take their kids to a provider's home, or a provider could come to their home, all subsidized by the childcare fund.

The services expanded to Oshawa where another centre was created. However, the funding, and the need, was always precarious and fluctuating because of layoffs. The workforce was reduced in numbers and it was the older members, who no longer had young kids, who remained. It became tough to argue for the funding and the services declined.

What became a permanent change though was the provision of childcare for union functions. All CAW conventions and council meetings would offer childcare and, at the CAW Education Centre, a state-of-the-art Roxie Baker Childcare Centre was established. When union members came to learn, they could take their kids to the centre of care.

Annie Labaj: Affirmative Action in Action

"It never got real until you walked into that factory and you realized why they gave you a column number and letter for your job location, because the factory is so large, it's so you don't get lost," says Annie Labaj, one of the early hires of women in the assembly plant. There were only about 10 women and over 1,200 men on her shift in the plant. She had benefitted from the struggle led by the women in UAW Local 222 that three years earlier had changed the Ontario Human Rights to prohibit discrimination on the basis of sex. Now there was just one seniority list, not a separate one for the women.

GM was aggressively hiring at the time Labaj applied, so men were not losing jobs because of the change to seniority rights. However, she says,

> At that time, many of the men didn't want to work with women. They felt women couldn't do the job. But it wasn't just about taking the job. They didn't want to work with you. Some men saw the workplace as a man's cave, a place to spend time with the guys, and all of a sudden they felt like now that's gone.

At that time, women were able to punch out five minutes earlier than the men. A hangover from WWII when the employer let

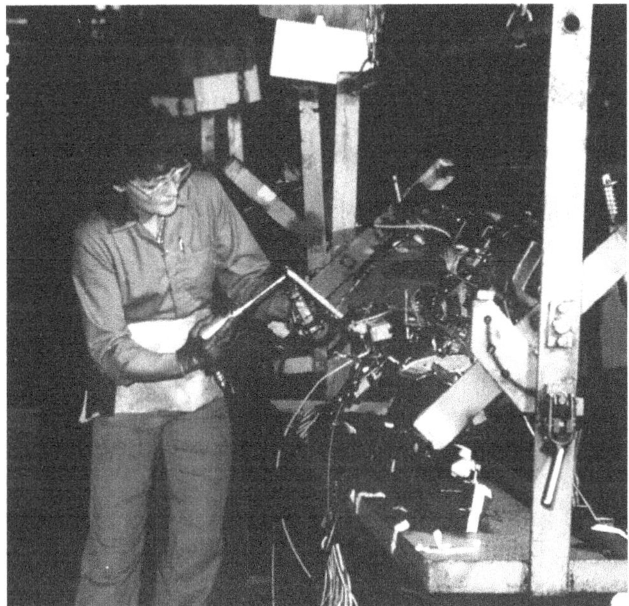

Annie Labaj on the job at GM in Oshawa. Photo: UAW.

women go five minutes before midnight to avoid being responsible for giving them a ride home. The women got to walk through the clock line-up. "You can just imagine how much fun that was," says Labaj.

The truck plant was greasy and dirty, and the lowest seniority workers got the worst jobs. The few women there were continuously asked why they wanted to work there and why their husbands couldn't support them. "I made it through to Christmas, got through my probation period, then just after Christmas shutdown, they laid me off."

Labaj was one of six children of Ukrainian immigrants who came to Canada in 1950. She married at seventeen to a man who worked at Chrysler and gave birth to a daughter. In 1973, she applied at GM thinking that if she needed to work and be away from her family, she wanted to get well paid. They called her for an interview the following week, and she started work three days later.

Shift work in the plant made life difficult. With no childcare, she and her husband worked different shifts.

I think that's why it was so easy to get involved with the

> campaigns around childcare. It wasn't daycare; it was childcare, for workers that had to work shift work.
>
> It was challenging. You really didn't see your partner except on weekends. You end up having separate friends and separate social circles. That could have been one of the downfalls of the marriage. It never lasted, so I think shift work had a lot to do with it.

After the layoff, she was called back to the wire and harness department, which was a different world. Cleaner and friendlier, better hours, and it was mostly women, many who had worked there for a long time. She got to meet some of the women that had changed the Ontario Human Rights Code that had impacted the collective agreement and eliminated separate seniority lists.

The women in the north plant were much more involved in the union and attended union meetings. "You walk in there [to union meetings], and you hear the debates," she says. "The women made these great speeches and the men listened." Then she was invited by one of the guys to join the local union women's committee. She figured it was a safe way to get introduced to the union, not knowing that there were two rival caucuses.

One of the committee members, Bev McCloskey, made a motion that instead of having an election, they should expand the women's committee since there was so much interest. The eight of them were acclaimed. To her surprise they wanted her to serve as the chair to take the committee in a fresh direction with more action than just writing letters. They wanted to deal with pinups in the plants. They wanted more opportunities for advancement in the workplace such as doing relief work instead of being overlooked. And they wanted the health and safety issues women had at work addressed.

The trailblazing Local 222 women were there to guide and help whenever needed. Labaj remembers Helen MacInally, who she knew as a cool local mom who drove a big Cadillac. Seeing the power of her and other women's voices in the local was inspiring. "The thing that really stuck in our minds was that it could happen, we could make changes."

That was already proven, as they had eliminated separate

seniority lists. They told Labaj that when they first started the campaign, it was more out of self-interest. They did not want to quit or move with the jobs to Windsor; they wanted to keep their jobs in Oshawa. But in reality, it helped all women when their struggle was successful. These women were inspiring role models, as were women like Vi Pilkey who was an active member of the Local 222 women's auxiliary (later the family auxiliary). They were politically active and involved in various campaigns.

They wanted women to get involved. Encouraging women to learn Robert's Rules of Order would allow women to participate with confidence in local union meetings and not worry about getting ruled out of order. They wanted women, not just on the women's committee, but on all the local union committees. And women needed to have their voices heard whether it was for political action or recreation or education.

Labaj understood that union education was important and attended the union's family education program the first summer after being elected. As a committee, they attended the UAW-Canada women's conference. The one thing that was most noticeable was that the handful of women at the front were vastly outnumbered by the men. The speakers were all men. "Of course, we all sat there looking at these men who were telling us we could be leadership women all the while knowing that they truly did not understand the challenges that women faced in the workplace." Still, the local union women went every year to the women's conference because it was a great way to connect, find out what was happening in the union, and learn what other women were doing in their workplaces.

Two major concerns for women were childcare and harassment in the workplace. For the pinups, they got creative. They cut out paper-doll-like clothes to put over the pinups on the walls saying "all these poor women don't have any clothes, so maybe we should clothe them." Others decided that they would get male pinups. The guys got really offended, she recalls. Different women had different strategies, and they didn't reject any of them. They tried different things to see what would work. They were just trying to figure out how to survive and make changes in a male-dominated workplace.

In 1985, Labaj and co-worker Mary Ann Green got appointed

to a joint affirmative action committee that was tasked with identifying barriers to employment. A census was needed to develop a plan for the workplace, but they faced a huge backlash and had trouble even getting people to fill out the form, never mind developing a guide for the employer for future hiring. So, they focused on skilled trades where few women were employed. Labaj says,

> One of the best kept secrets was around apprenticeships for the skilled trades. The guys would all tell each other when you could go and apply for the apprenticeship, but never shared that knowledge with the women. We didn't even know what the qualifications were. So we met with skilled trades to find out.

They then met with Durham College, to help develop a course to increase women's skills so they would be able to qualify for the apprenticeship programs. When an information session was held in an attempt to engage the 20 women from the plant required to run the course, to their surprise, 120 women showed up.

The program's success was honoured with the Employment Equity Award from the Ontario Women's Directorate. For the twenty women attending the program, childcare costs were covered as well as eight hours of time off work for job shadowing. The program opened the door into the trades for women, not only course graduates, by the late 1980s.

By this time, the Canadian region of the UAW had broken away from the United States and formed the CAW. Bob White, the first president of the CAW, saw an opportunity to advance affirmative action in the union by hiring more women as national representatives. One of the first openings was in the education department. Labaj, with previous experience as a local discussion leader, was the successful candidate for that position in 1987.

By 1988 the union was just developing a harassment policy. "It was great that there was something clear and concrete, a package that we could give people in education classes, collective bargaining, and at union functions."

Labaj remembers the union's first human rights conference:

> I thought it was one of the best conferences that I had attended because people were starting to understand that change was needed. Members were open to the idea of change and wanted things to change. That conference made me feel that we were moving in the right direction. We were actually going to make changes that were not possible while we were a region of the UAW. As the CAW, we could focus on issues important to our Canadian members. Not only were we Canadian, we were progressive.

In the education department Labaj worked with many departments helping them to develop workshops and courses, always including a gender perspective. She coordinated the CAW women's conferences.

> We tried to discourage men from attending, but some locals would always try to send the guys saying "we wanna learn about these issues."
>
> Great, we'll have a workshop for men where they can discuss with each other on about how are you going to support the women at the local.

After the 1991 CAW convention in Halifax, a paid education program specifically for women was created. Labaj worked on the development of the women activists course and later, while working in the international department, began inviting trade union women from Mexico, Brazil, South Africa, and Mozambique to attend the course. They would take that course, adapt it to their culture, laws, and reality to make it work in their respective countries. That cross-fertilization continued for many years. "You often wondered, like with each country having their own laws, each country having their own challenges, how do you relate to them? But there's something about women, that we can relate to each other, regardless of the culture, regardless of the language."

Labaj felt the impact of the women activists course at the annual Women's March in the year 2000. "In every city we hit, we saw a wave of CAW posters. It just showed that the number of women had changed in our union." It was less than ten years since the start of that program. It was a rapid transformation, and she knew these programs really helped.

She has some disappointments. Childcare is still such a struggle, one that her daughter now faces. The CAW-negotiated childcare program closed due to layoffs, so now much of that work needs to be done again. "It is just going to be another battle. I can see that, as I think of all the young people still struggling to get childcare. We didn't quite get there."

She was also sorry that Carol Phillips abandoned her bid to run for secretary treasurer of the union. "I felt it was time for the face of the union to change. I don't know if we would have done well or beat the machine, but I mean it would have been great to try. In the end it was her choice."

What is she most proud of? "I think it is the progress women have made as a group. The work needs to continue as a lot of fights remain for women. It cannot be done by one individual. All women, must push in one direction, from many different areas."

Merger with FFAW (Fishermen Food and Allied Workers)

Mergers and building a bigger presence were part of White's vision for the new Canadian union. In 1988, Richard Cashin, a former member of parliament and then-president of the Fishermen Food and Allied Workers Union met with Bob White. Cashin was frustrated with his union's membership in the United Food and Commercial Workers Union (UFCW), based in Washington, DC. It was a proud and storied organization, but Cashin and his members felt they were not getting the representation they needed, and they were determined to leave this union and join a Canadian organization, the CAW.

White agreed to try to win the support of the FFAW members, and this set off a furious campaign between the CAW and the UFCW that split the labour movement for many years to come. "We went around Newfoundland to help develop materials for the campaign, visiting small fishing villages and outports to hear Cashin and inspired local speakers," says Nash. "Fishermen who prided their independence in their dangerous industry, spoke about self-determination." The CAW won the campaign in 1987, and the Fish, Food and Allied Workers Union (FFAW-CAW) was born.

There were already storm clouds gathering as to the sustainability of the cod fishery. Five hundred years after the arrival of Europeans on the Newfoundland shores, where the water had been so thick with cod that it seemed inexhaustible, the fishers themselves could tell that the cod stocks were declining. The federal government scientists and fishery officials had ignored them. Overfishing mainly by giant factory freezer trawlers, many of them from other countries, were scraping the bottom of the seabed, destroying spawning grounds, and were depleting what had been a plentiful resource for centuries.

By 1989, federal fishery scientists knew cod was overfished to the point of collapse. It was an environmental disaster. They drastically cut their estimates of the cod stocks, declared a moratorium on the cod fishery and threw the industry into turmoil. It was the equivalent of the collapse of the entire auto sector in central Canada. Except for Newfoundlanders, alternative work was rarely an option. Fishing was not only what they did but also who they were.

When the lack of cod shut down the cod fishery, the Fishermen's Union sprang into action. To help with their fightback campaign, they hired a young reporter named Lana Payne. Payne didn't know a lot about the fishing industry, but she supported the union and had a public profile in Newfoundland based on her work as a journalist. She had written stories including about the rancorous decision to move the union from the UFCW to the CAW. It was Bob White, then-president of the CAW, who had agreed to provide the funding to create the position she was being hired for. There at the FFAW, Payne built her labour activism, forged in the union fightback to deal with the crisis of the collapse of the Newfoundland cod fishery.

Lana Payne: Learning through Crisis

Growing up in a working-class family in Newfoundland, Lana Payne learned early on the value of union. Her dad had a disability and without the insistence of his union to have fair access to jobs in his trade, he probably wouldn't have had much of a chance. She went to work as a journalist and put her union background to good use, winning the first grievance ever filed in her workplace. She soon left journalism for a job with the Fishermen's Union, headed by Richard Cashin.

She joined the union in November 1991. I learned a lot from [Cashin], even though he stayed until only June of 1993 so I didn't get a lot of one-on-one working time with him. But every moment was valuable." Cashin was legendary, a great orator and a great writer. Young Payne was impressed that he would take the time with her; she was always asking questions. "I learned as a journalist there is no stupid question. In fact, the stupid thing to do is not to ask the question and make a mistake."

By 1991, many fishers were already unemployed, and fish plants were closing. By 1992, with a collapse of the cod fishery, the government imposed a ten-year moratorium. The industry was in full crisis. The union's job was to protect the workers and the communities. This would take a major campaign to mobilize communities and push governments to act. It was then that Cashin hired Payne on a six-month contract to do research and communications. She would remain there for seventeen years.

Her years with the FFAW were challenging as she was the only woman working with an all-male staff. She was the first woman hired on the staff of the union, in addition to the support or secretarial staff, and while there she remained the only woman. At first, she was paid less than the men, but she eventually took care of that.

It was a small staff at the FFAW, and everybody had to help with the union's work, whether bargaining, organizing, or political campaigns. This feisty upstart union always seemed to be in a fight whether in bargaining or taking on the government. Payne says,

> We were in a fight every year with somebody. For God's sake we shut down shipping lanes and oil company lanes. This was the nature of the fight. We always were confronting power in that union. I had seventeen years of confronting power. How could I not know how to do it after that? We had to understand how to do that smartly and strategically, and sometimes just with brute force, because that sometimes is what's left, and then you negotiate afterwards.

> I learned so much about how to lead through a crisis. Twenty thousand people thrown out of work July 1992. There was a profound sense of loss. How does a union survive if the members aren't working? You felt it every day. And the only way the union could survive was to build hope that we could get to a different place.

Fish harvesters were fearful of losing their vessels if they couldn't make loan payments. The union fought for compensation and retraining. They had a vision of what the future should look like and who would own the fish. Corporations fought with local fish harvesters trying to earn a living in small communities. Their struggle was also about families, communities, and about the future of the province. The union had to fight for compensation, for survival, and it needed to build hope for a better future.

FFAW Women Find Their Voice

The union became what is called a social union, because their struggle was for jobs, but not just about jobs. Women were especially concerned about the impact on their communities.

It was a crisis and, at Payne's insistence, the union needed to find a way to make sure that women and the issues they highlighted were heard through the crisis, and were front and centre. "So we organized, we got grant money, and the union put in money," says Payne. "We organized the provincial women's committee. We had women go around talking to women."

"And through that struggle," says Payne, "women found a bigger voice in the union. We were organizing around issues that nobody else was talking about. So, it was like, 'take your space sisters, work.' This is where we got to show that we belonged at these decision-making tables."

Union leaders began to say, "What do you mean we have decision-making tables in the union that have no women on them? How is this possible right now?"

The union produced a report about the cod moratorium's impact on women. "You didn't ask for permission on these things," says Payne. "You just started a project and made sure women got involved."

"Even though Bob White wanted us to be a social union way back in the day," says Payne, "it was really the women that turned us from a progressive, industrial union to a progressive industrial, social union." Payne learned from other women in the union such as Julie White and Peggy Nash who both had headed up the women's programs. Payne remembers Nash telling her you need to know when to have your elbows out and when to keep them in. In other words when to take on the fight, when to take up space, and when to keep your powder dry, a judgement call. One of the fights she did take on was changing the name of the union from the Fishermen's Union to the gender-neutral Fish, Food and Allied Workers Union.

Ultimately, she understood that there was no place for her to go in the organization. "I mean, you know, I wasn't going to be president of that local. I wasn't even going to be secretary treasurer so I was standing still for a long period of time."

As a woman, there's a wall. You know when you've hit it. Cashin never fished, and neither did his successor, Earl McCurdy. But the members trusted their leadership. Payne had thrown her guts into the union, and she loved it with every fibre of her being. But gender was a deal breaker, as it was to be for so many women in the auto union. And while Payne was helping members with employment insurance appeals and workers compensation, she didn't have the direct bargaining experience that a union service rep would get. She was doing the research to prepare for bargaining but never got to the bargaining table.

She left the FFAW to lead the Newfoundland and Labrador Federation of Labour where she could again unleash her organizing and activism skills. She remained there until Unifor was created and she came back to the union to run for the position of area director. And eventually, president.

Mildred Skinner: Affirmative Action in FFAW

The FFAW national executive board in the 1990s included just one woman, Mildred Skinner. Mildred had got into fishing with her husband out of economic necessity in 1989. "I got into the fishery when I married a fisherman," she says.

Her involvement in the union increased after the cod moratorium:

> When the moratorium happened, it was one of the worst times in the Newfoundland and Labrador fishery. And what I discovered was that there was a lot of us [women] on the fishing boats, but we weren't recorded anywhere. The men were all recorded as union members but the women as crew members weren't. There was no data on us. So, when it came time for compensation from the federal government because our industry was shut down, we found ourselves without compensation or in that program.

Skinner raised this with a union staff rep who fought with them to get compensation and eventually the women became full union members. So Skinner became interested in the union.

Mildred Skinner, Hermitage Bay, south coast of Newfoundland, lobster data collection. Photo: Jeff Roberts.

In 1996, the FFAW council member in her region representing the inshore fishers was retiring, and at Payne's suggestion, he asked if Skinner would consider running for the inshore council seat. She would be the first woman on the inshore council of FFAW. "When I arrived, I was green as grass, so I talked with people and I listened a lot," she says. She became close with Payne as the only other woman in a room full of men. Now the union has affirmative action seats.

Payne insists that, while affirmative action seats can be made token, "It's important to get women in the room, and that you have to start somewhere if you want to make change. If you get your foot through the door, you can build from there."

Mildred Skinner was re-elected and held on to that seat until she retired in 2015. She later became a field tech for fishery science with the FFAW, collecting data for Fisheries and Oceans Canada (DFO), so that they know what species are in the ocean. This is key for the future as the collapse of the fishery was based on the lack of accurate data at the DFO.

Tina Pretty: Fighting Sexual Harassment

As a young woman Tina Pretty was hired to do office work for the FFAW in St. John's. After several years she became the assistant to the president of the FFAW, Earl McCurdy, the successor to Richard Cashin.

The fishing union had a board and in the early years, as a young woman, she found it difficult to deal with them. She recalls a board member who often came into the office:

> Oh gosh! The things that man would say to me as a young woman was just disgusting. It was sexist. It was harassing. It was unacceptable. And you know, you just didn't have anybody to go to. You just figured somehow you must be bringing it on yourself. You start thinking, well, I shouldn't have worn this top today, you start questioning. He would just comment on the way you looked in your clothes, or he would tell me what he would like to do with me sexually in the office in very coarse language. It was horrible.

> When you get that women's advocate training, and maybe it comes with age as well, you start to speak up. You may not always speak up for yourself, although I certainly would now, but you can speak up for another woman.

Pretty tells about a time when a young woman co-worker was getting harassed by a tall imposing guy who came into the office from time to time. She says he was one of those people who invaded women's personal space and made them uncomfortable. He also said some terrible things. The woman came to Pretty for help.

Pretty found that the union was reluctant to take on the man since he was a high-profile leader in the FFAW. So she took him on. She pulled him aside and asked him to confirm what he had said to her co-worker, and he admitted it. So she said,

> You know something? I don't like it. And I really don't want to hear it anymore. But this is a young woman who comes every day to work, and this is not what she's coming to work for. She's coming here to work, and she doesn't need to have unacceptable behaviour directed toward her.

He was really taken back. And his behaviour changed. If he continued as before, Pretty didn't hear of it.

> Nowadays, young women will put those comments on social media, so hopefully men keep their comments to themselves. You'd like to think that our education programs empower women, and that they also change male attitudes so that these things don't happen. It's not just changing behaviour but it's changing minds.

However, Pretty says, to this day, that sexual harassment is under-reported.

> But it's little increments, just like everything, just like closing the wage gap and childcare. It's just hammering away, being persistent. And over time things change. Younger people are not

> going to tolerate things the same way. Younger women aren't going to be the same. I think they're stronger, and with social media, they just do not seem like they are going to put up with the same nonsense that we did.

Two Steps Forward

The new Canadian union was established and spreading its wings. CAW members were confident in their union's leadership and felt a sense of momentum. The union's rebuilt centre in Port Elgin became a state-of-the-art education facility. It remains a tremendous source of pride for all workers who attend education programs there. For workers to get the chance to engage with other workers, to learn about the bigger world and engage their intelligence and creativity, it is an inspirational achievement.

But there were storm clouds. The pro-business initiatives of free trade, deregulation, and privatization would impact Canada, and Canadian jobs, for years to come. Soon the Canadian economy would soften, and the CAW, like other unions, would face workplace closures, outsourcing, and demands for contract concessions. This would put downward pressure on workers' contract gains and job security. This was happening just as women, human rights activists, and other progressives were pushing for governments to do more of the work of creating an equitable society. The push for affirmative action in male-dominated workplaces would run headlong into massive layoffs and plant closures.

"It's not the right time" would be the refrain from companies, and sometimes from the union, for affirmative action or human rights initiatives. Eventually though, both the composition and the culture of the workplaces would change.

The CAW joined with the rest of the labour movement and with progressive groups across the country to mount a spirited and effective opposition campaign to free trade. Bob White and Council of Canadians Chair Maude Barlow would be invited to two televised debates with Alberta Premier Peter Lougheed and business spokesperson Tom D'Aquino, moderated by the highly respected host of the flagship CBC current affairs program *The Journal*. In this 1988 election, with its focus on free trade, the anti–free trade side battled convincingly. Nevertheless, free trade championed by Progressive Conservative leader Brian Mulroney eventually won the election. Canada would have free trade with the United States in 1989 and the Liberal government under Jean Chretien would campaign against expanding the free trade agreement with Mexico, only to sign the deal when in government in 1994.

The overall impact, as we see now decades later, is an increase in inequality. Union members lost jobs through international competition; the downward pressure on social programs with tax cuts to compete with the United States and a pro-business culture left behind far too many Canadians.

In the subsequent chapters, we will examine events that sparked calls for more progress on equality rights, but also events that created more downward pressure on jobs and against equity measures.

Chapter Four

Tragedy and Transformation, 1990-1995

Tragedy, Struggle, and Hope

In 1989, the year of the birth of the world wide web, a momentous change captured the world's attention. After decades of the Cold War between the West and the Soviet Union and its satellites, mounting protests led to the destruction and the fall of the Berlin Wall. Francis Fukuyama called it the end of history, and there was hope that instead of investing in the military, there would be greater investment in shared prosperity.[1]

On another cold, dark evening less than a month after the fall of the Berlin Wall, on December 6, 1989, news began to trickle out in early evening about a terrible event in Montreal, Canada. On the evening news that night, the stark horror was clear: a heavily armed young man had entered a school, the École Polytechnique de Montréal (now Polytechnique Montréal), where he went into engineering classes. He separated the women from the men and proceeded to shoot them. The toll was fourteen killed, many more injured. A massacre in a country that saw itself as open, progressive, and peaceful.

The debate began almost immediately. Was this a random madman? Surely, he was crazy, some said. However, the gunman had left a statement blaming feminist women for his failures. Instead of a random exception, it was quickly seen as a symptom of the misogyny and violence that all too many Canadian women, and women around the world, faced daily. It was symptomatic of an epidemic.

Three days later journalist Stevie Cameron wrote a moving opinion piece published in the *Globe and Mail* entitled "Our

Daughters, Ourselves": "Fourteen of our bright and shining daughters won places in engineering schools, doing things we, their mothers, only dreamed of. That we lost them has broken our hearts; what is worse, is that we are not surprised."

Cameron captured the fury and grief that so many felt about this attack on these promising young women. She also understood that harassment, violence, and other barriers were still the reality for women around the world. What the hell was going on and what could we do about it?

Women who had been struggling against gender-based violence with few resources or recognition were called on to share their expertise. As people were grappling for answers, like many organizations, the CAW put out an initial statement about that terrible event. The Montreal Massacre, as it became called, sparked calls for gun control, especially from the families of the victims. In addition to the many women's voices advocating for urgent change, there were initiatives like the White Ribbon Campaign, an effort by men protesting the acts of violence and offering positive role models. It later sparked the CAW postcard campaign "Six things men can do to end violence against women."

Nationally the tragedy is officially remembered and commemorated every December 6. The event would also reverberate in the union for decades to come.

The Era of Growing Self Employment

In the early 1990s, there was a severe downturn in the economy. This was a period of job losses and declining productivity, followed by stagnating employment, insecurity, and lowered expectations. Self employment grew rapidly. Working people fell behind, and many never recovered. While many women lost jobs, this era was especially hard on men. The traditional expectation that men would provide for their family was upended with a growing public sector that employed many women.[2]

In September 1990, the politics of the province of Ontario swung dramatically. In a snap election, the NDP led by Bob Rae won a surprise majority government, defeating David Peterson's Liberals. This was the first win for the NDP east of Manitoba, thrilling NDP supporters and shocking business groups.

Rae tried to use the opportunity of government to make major changes with laws such as those banning scabs or strikebreakers and establishing employment equity, and much more. However, he also made the mistake of trying to override collective agreements to reduce the provincial deficit. This undermined the NDP and split the labour movement for years to come.

Nonetheless, the opportunity presented by an NDP government in Ontario became a key focus of the labour movement. Some trade unionists were hired by the new government, including Carol Phillips, Bob White's assistant, who was named director of public appointments.

With Phillips's departure, Bob White named Peggy Nash as his assistant and director of women's programs.

A New Era of CAW Women's Programs, 1990s

The gender equity measures established in the union decades before were a significant foundation to build on. When Nash began in the position of director of women's programs, she didn't understand how unique these women's programs were. The union's constitution included the requirement for a women's department, for the CAW council to have a women's committee, and for each local union to have a women's committee. The union was also required to hold an annual women's conference, which Nash was then tasked with organizing, working with the council women's committee.

At the next meeting of the CAW council, the women's committee members also met. They were all local leaders who had worked their way up through the tough politics of their local unions. Shocked like most Canadians by the Montreal Massacre, they wanted the next women's conference later that year to focus on the issue of violence against women.

This was not a traditional bread-and-butter issue for the union, but given the statistics that pointed to widespread incidence of gender-based violence and abuse, CAW members would likely be representative of those numbers. Also, the union had a history of engaging on broader social concerns, which meant they didn't stop at the workplace. They engaged with their members broader lives on health care, housing, and community services. Gender-based violence was an important issue that the union had not up to that point adequately addressed.

StatsCan Study on Sexual Violence

CAW members probably faced the same issues as the general population. In 1993, StatsCan published the results of a study on sexual violence as experienced by women in Canada:

> The report estimated that 51% of Canadian women experienced at least one incident of sexual or physical assault since the age of sixteen. This figure masks important details showing that women experience multiple acts of male violence: 39% reported sexual assault, 29% physical and sexual violence by a marital partner, 16% by a dating partner, 23% by a friend or acquaintance, and 23% by a stranger. One-quarter of women who were physically assaulted by a spouse were also sexually assaulted. Eighty-seven percent of women had been sexually harassed and 80% of women aged sixteen to twenty-four were sexually harassed in one year.[3]

Gender-Based Violence: CAW Breaks the Silence

The union partnered with feminist community leaders who were the experts, inviting them as conference speakers and workshop leaders. As expected, the conference that year in 1990 was intense and emotional. The widespread abuse, harassment, and violence in Canada was indeed reflected in the union's membership. Delegates shared their personal stories and quickly learned the scope and root causes of the problem, and the urgent need for change. All who attended were deeply affected.

While the women's conferences were designed for women, at that time they were open to men as well. Some male leaders came as a joke and spent their time goofing off or hitting on women. Worse, they took up spaces badly needed by women in the union. There were also a few male leaders who genuinely wanted to support women members and who wanted to learn more about their issues. National executive board member and president of Local 200 Frank McAnally was one of these. He was shocked by what he heard.

The conference goal was not to encourage women to disclose their situation even though they had councillors standing by to offer support. They did encourage the delegates to understand harassment and violence as a societal as well as a personal issue. While they offered individual help, they encouraged the delegates to think about societal challenges. The pain some of the women felt was intense. For many this was the first time they had opened up about what they had faced. Women spoke about being attacked in the military, by family members, intimate partners, co-workers, random strangers; it was overwhelming. Issues that had not been discussed in the union before, now were on the agenda.

The women's committee decided that the conference was just the beginning of a conversation on the issue of gender-based violence and that the following year's conference should focus on solutions. Some women objected to men attending the conference the year before, especially given the sensitive nature of the discussions.

At the next conference there were some women-only workshops. Just banning men from attending would have created a backlash, so they took a quieter approach. Annie Labaj from the education staff would contact men who registered, not to prevent them from coming, but to strongly encourage them to instead send a full delegation of women from their local union. The conference was clearly for women. Men soon got the message.

Those at the second conference on gender-based violence in 1991 produced a long agenda for action. They recommended changes to legislation, policing, government policies, community organizations, housing—specially second stage housing—funding for women's organizations and shelters, and it also set out an agenda for the union. They wanted to beef up the access and training for the union's harassment policy and procedure. They wanted women in the workplace to have another woman with whom they would discuss issues of harassment and violence, especially in male-dominated workplaces. They wanted to get more women hired, to have effective employment equity, they wanted women facing violence to not face penalties from their employer if they were absent. They wanted more women leaders in the union.

The 1991 conference was a watershed moment. The women

delegates called for many substantive changes both within the union and in broader society. The women's recommendations would set out goals for the union for the next several years. The issue of gender-based violence would be revisited as a topic for every women's conference after, for decades to come.

Solidarity in Diversity Constitutional Convention, 1991

There was a sense of urgency coming out of the CAW's second women's conference. Women knew that calls for judicial reform, gun control, police training, or money for housing were longer-term goals. But they were counting on their union to address the pressing issue of violence.

Frank McAnally understood the urgency and advised the committee on how to navigate the procedures and more importantly the politics of the union's national executive board. They prepared a document for approval by the national executive board in time for the union's constitutional convention later that year in Halifax. Unlike a bargaining convention, this convention, held every three years, would focus on the internal policies and programs of the union. It would be an opportunity to advance the key conference recommendations that pertained to the union itself. Time was short.

Following the women's conference, Nash crafted a policy on violence against women and an affirmative action policy and got Bob White on side. He understood the importance of these efforts and fully supported the work. Ultimately with the approval of the union's officers, the national executive board adopted the proposals and they went to the 1991 convention in Halifax. White agreed to the proposal of the convention slogan of "Solidarity in Diversity" to emphasize class values that grounded the changing makeup of the workforce.

The statement says in part:

> SOLIDARITY IN DIVERSITY
>
> Recognizing the diversity of our union and working to ensure fairness in all our structures and activities, means building a stronger union. It means creating a union where all members can become active knowing that their rights will be respected;

> where all workers see themselves reflected in their leadership and in the activities of the union; where all members committed to the union can aspire to leadership; and where, when we call each other sister and brother, and when we claim solidarity, we know that this is truly so.

To reinforce that this policy had the full support of the top leadership of the union, it included a statement from White as a key endorsement introducing the paper:

> Solidarity in diversity—the theme of our 3rd constitutional convention—challenges our union to give new meaning to the words that the "union makes us strong." We have built a dynamic union from coast to coast. Our strength can only be maintained by acknowledging our differences, by embracing what is unique about all segments of our union as well as our shared values.
>
> Now, with women and visible minorities making up a significant proportion of our membership we have to expose the sexism and racism that poisons workplaces and destroys solidarity. We have to build for the future a union whose leadership at all levels reflects the membership.
>
> To that end, the affirmative action policy commits the CAW to recognizing and removing barriers to participation from women and visible minorities, such as combatting discrimination and harassment, developing special education programs and building our leadership to be representative of the membership.
>
> Our union has a strong history of fighting for progressive social change. To call each other sister and brother and truly mean it, we must build solidarity through diversity.
>
> *In solidarity*
> *Robert White, President, CAW Canada*

The paper contained thirty-five commitments adopted by the union, such as expanding affirmative action seats on the national executive board to a minimum of two women, a minimum of one worker of colour and one woman on the Quebec executive, and for local unions to make their executives and committees similarly representative. The policy called for extensive education initiatives including development (by the union) of leadership courses specifically for women and workers of colour. In collective bargaining, the policy called for negotiating training courses paid by the employer for employment equity and anti-harassment measures, pay equity, and childcare.

The many recommendations passed unanimously.

There was also a strong resolution committing to take action on violence against women. When they presented at the convention the room was unusually silent. "We held our breath" says Nash. "When a local president went to speak at the mic, we squirmed nervously. Would he challenge the statement and speak against it? Instead, he told an emotional story about sexual violence committed against him as a child. This kicked off several speakers sharing experiences and a real appreciation of the importance of the union acting on the issue. This opened the floodgates and affirmed that the union had an important role to play in to ending violence."

This convention represented a turning point in the union. Of course, not everyone was on board, but the leadership understood the importance of working-class inclusivity. There can be no solidarity if everyone is not part of the union.

Cheryl Kryzaniwsky: President of CAW Council, 1995

Cheryl Kryzaniwsky called her union staff representative, Greg Spencer, who had become a good friend. "I've got to meet with you right away. I've got a huge problem. And I need your help."

Kryzaniwsky's story begins in 1983, in the same union with Jane Armstrong and Peggy Nash and at about the same time, the Canadian Air Line Employees Association (CALEA), just before its merger with the UAW. As the elected chairperson of a group of three hundred workers at Air Canada reservations in Toronto, Kryzaniwsky had been encouraged by the union president, Tom Saunders, to run for a position on the union's Air Canada bargaining committee. If elected she would be the first woman to hold that position, representing a group of about 75 per cent women. She was thrilled and felt that her work to that date had really prepared her for the position. The CALEA had only about five thousand members, and they were in for a difficult round of bargaining at Air Canada.

For her, it was not to be. After trying for many years to conceive a child with her husband Chris, she finally got pregnant. This was not compatible with months of collective bargaining. So she had called Greg.

"Greg is one of those just nice guys," she says. "I sat down in a booth across from him in this bar."

"So, what's up?" he asks.

"I'm pregnant."

There was this pause, and then he looked at her and he said, "Well, it isn't mine!"

"Of course it isn't yours!"

"Well, you kind of made it sound like I should come to this meeting because I had a personal stake."

She said, "Well, you do, because I have to tell Saunders that I can't be on the bargaining committee, and I don't know how to do it."

"Saunders is a family man," he replied. "He'll be so happy for you. Just forget it and move on."

She was relieved but a bit sad to miss out on this opportunity.

Because of Kryzaniwsky's maternity leave, the union reached out to union activist Diane Hollingshead in Alberta, who was the first and only woman on that bargaining team. As described in chapter 3, it was the first strike by the union at Air Canada. It was tough for Hollingshead as the only elected woman on the committee, with four men and three male staff reps. She would go on to play an important role in the union (see chapter 5).

After her maternity leave of about sixteen weeks, Kryzaniwsky returned to work with the union already on strike at Air Canada. They weren't quite sure what they were supposed to do, so they decided to open up a childcare centre in a nearby church for members doing picket duty. Kryzaniwsky remembers pushing her infant son Michael in a stroller on the picket line.

Air Canada tried to keep the reservation centres operating. "Supervisors would come along to do our jobs, and we knew them all, so we'd say, 'Oh, Hi, Bert, Hi, Jackie, good to see you,' and in they'd go."

By this time CALEA was in merger talks with the UAW, and Bob White had become involved when Saunders had had a heart attack. When White heard about the supervisors, he put a stop to it. "A bus came and dropped off guys from Local 707 [the UAW local at a large Ford operation in Oakville]. They were big guys, and they were intimidating," says Kryzaniwsky.

"They asked the strikers what are [the supervisors] doing in there? "And we said, Oh, they're doing our jobs."

"Well, they're not gonna do that anymore," said the guys. "We have to put pressure on Air Canada. We're going to close ranks with you. When a supervisor comes along, we're gonna tell them they can't go in."

The women were mortified. "We knew someday we're gonna go back in there and we're gonna have to work with them. We just didn't understand enough about trade unionism at that time. We didn't know that we were really supposed to hurt them. We just thought we could bring them to their knees with maybe, 'please, and thank you.' I'm not sure what the hell we thought."

With the determination of the membership and the support of the UAW, the union was able to resist the concessions that Air Canada was trying to force on them.

Shortly after, CALEA President Tom Saunders told Kryzaniwsky that he would be joining the national union, the UAW, as part of the merger agreement, and asked her to consider running for president of what would become a large UAW local union. As Kryzaniwsky remembers it,

> The election campaign was an incredibly hard battle. I think it was because I was the first woman, and even a lot of women thought that it was still a male role.
>
> I remember coming home to the farm from work one day. We had a long driveway up to the house off Highway 9. And there was a brown paper bag with my name on it like a lunch bag, between my front two doors. And it was cash. It was probably two or three hundred dollars cash. Jane Armstrong had dropped it off. She was going from the national union to Port Elgin, and she came along Highway 9. She had asked people to help me out financially.

It was difficult to campaign from coast to coast with no social media and no budget. But in 1985, Kryzaniwsky eked out a slim win.

Merging with the CAW, many of the staff from CALEA transitioned to the national union. The new president was left with a skeleton team in the local.

She had three years to prove herself until the next election. "And so, I worked my ass off. But I had a new baby, too, right? I was struggling to learn what I needed to learn. I needed to find childcare, and I needed to find it quickly."

Her husband was a flight attendant, so he also had non-standard hours of work. She finally found a local caregiver who was a lifesaver. She cared for Michael in her home but would stay overnight if needed.

"I remember my mother tearing a strip off of me like saying 'How on earth, after you've waited all these years for this baby? You're thirty-five years old. How can you put an ad in a paper to find someone you don't even know.'"

"And I remember thinking I just don't know what else to do." She fortunately found an exceptional caregiver who made her union life possible. Her doctor told her that at age thirty-five this was likely the only pregnancy she would have. And then she got pregnant with their second son, Steven, when she was forty. Then a live-in caregiver was the only answer. This was hard financially but the only way they could manage.

In 1989, Bob White called and invited Kryzaniwsky to join the executive board of the national union. She was hesitant given the balancing job she already had to be a president, wife, and mother. He told her she would be joining the sole woman on the national executive board, Roxie Baker, and it would give her and the airline sector much greater profile without much extra work.

She had to do some research to understand what the national executive board role would mean, but she decided to accept. After her bruising campaign to run for the presidency of her local, she wondered how to campaign for this position. White told her she didn't need to campaign. "No campaign necessary," she was told." We've got this. You are our choice, and that's all you have to be."

That's how the caucus system worked at that time. The leadership choice got support.

"I didn't understand that at all at the time," said Kryzaniwsky. "In the local union it was a knockdown battle with travel across the country."

"Don't put out a leaflet. Don't put out anything," she was told. "You are the caucus choice and that's all you need to be."

She knew there was another candidate running, Ken Maheux, president of Local 195, a big amalgamated Windsor local. The election was in Port Elgin at the union's education centre. It would be decided by a standing vote, not secret ballot. When Kryzaniwsky got there, her opponent had leaflets and buttons and she had nothing. "His team is standing at those big doors, handing out leaflets, and there were a few buttons in the crowd."

The candidates were asked to leave the room. Waiting outside the meeting room, the two candidates got to know each other, and it was very friendly. He told her,

> Cheryl, I think a little bit more democracy in our union wouldn't hurt, and that's why I put my name in. But I can congratulate you now, because that's how things work, and I think you'll make a great member of the national executive board, and I hope that we will continue to be colleagues and workmates.

Sure enough, when they went back in, her position on the national executive board was announced. As Cheryl and other women would find out, the caucus system could help you or hurt you depending on the leadership's decision.

She worked hard to build relationships at the national executive board. Baker, as the only other woman, became a friend. Like many women of that era, she carried a lot alone, the sense that she wasn't good enough, that she couldn't be both a mom and a leader, that she was taking on too much:

> Like most women, I internalized the failures. They're mine. They're not the system. It wasn't because board meetings were at 5 pm. It was because I needed to figure out how to get to a board meeting at 5 pm. I was just too afraid to say anything about why the schedule didn't work for me.

One time there was a national executive board meeting in Port Elgin, a three-hour drive from her home or office. The national executive board meeting was before a council meeting, so it meant being away from home for nearly a week. Another time there was a board meeting on Mother's Day weekend:

> I remember thinking, "Oh, my God, my kids, my husband." You know everybody's gonna be so upset. But I didn't say anything. I do remember going to the art gallery in Southampton and buying myself a very useless, very expensive piece of art because I was just trying to make myself feel better about the fact that I was in Port Elgin over Mother's Day, and not at home with my family.

The first time she did say something, she was already the president of CAW council, a very senior position in the union. The president of council was also a member of the national executive board. Childcare finished at 5 pm but the national executive board would go on later:

> I would get a call from the childcare centre, asking, "Do you want us to take your kids to dinner?" I would say, "Yes, please. I'm going to be here another forty-five minutes." I remember my son Steven saying to me "Mommy, how come you always choose meetings over us?"
>
> And I remember being broken, absolutely broken, thinking, this is what my kids believe. "I don't always choose meetings over you. Sometimes I have to, but it's not always." And he said, "Well, you know the other kids, they don't get taken by childcare workers to dinner."
>
> So mine were the only kids ever that were left. And I remember saying to Hargrove, you need to set the time of the national executive board (NEB), and then you need to live by it, because I'm struggling with childcare. The next NEB meeting, I remember him looking at his watch and childcare was till 5, and it was 5 to 5, and he said, We're just gonna do one more item. He looked at me. "I promise you, Cheryl," he points me out, "that we'll be out of here, you know, 5:15 at the latest."

> And I remember at 5 to 5 I got up and I said, "I'm terribly sorry, but childcare closes at 5, and I'm going to pick up my kids." And I remember feeling shame, that I was the only one that wouldn't stay for that item on the agenda.

She had become the president of CAW council in 1995 when then-President Frank McAnally from the Ford Windsor local union was appointed to the national staff. The person who was earmarked to replace him, Jim Ashton, had died unexpectedly, and Kryzaniwsky was tapped to run for president, the first and only woman to do so.

She served one term, enjoyed the position and never heard any criticism. But she had supported her former local president, Tom Saunders, for the position of national secretary treasurer against the caucus choice of Jim O'Neil. She did so out of loyalty, but he dropped out when he was not selected by the caucus.

Then they wanted her out. Cheryl agreed to meet with Carol Phillips and Sam Gindin from the national staff:

> I was learning [as council president], and I think I was doing a really good job. I never heard anything to the contrary. But they decided that they wanted to profile [Ken] Lewenza, and they wanted me out, and so they sent Carol and Sam who met me at a Holiday Inn on the 401.
>
> "Look, this is what's going to happen," they said. "You will not serve another term as president of CAW council, and we think that you should use this to your advantage." They were very clear that it might be time that I came on staff, and that if I came on staff now, I could call the shots about what position I wanted.
>
> I remember Sam saying, "I think you'd be a great director of education. It's a high-profile position. I think you would love it. But you know we want you to think about it because you can. You can stand for election a second term. But you know how the system works, and they don't want you. And so you're not gonna win."
>
> I felt awful. I wanted to do another term. I felt like I was just kind of learning it, and that I was doing a good job at it, and that I had more that I could do. Some of it was bureaucratic technical

> stuff. Council never had an agenda, and I wanted an agenda, and I wanted an opening time and a closing time, and I wanted things to run in order. They hated it, and they pushed back. But delegates liked it.
>
> I wasn't changing the world but I really loved it.

She had won her third round as local union president without opposition and was well liked in the local. She loved the work in the local and loved being council president, and they wanted her to step down:

> I regret not running and losing and staying in the local, because when I was in the local as a local union president, I had respect. They asked me questions, didn't point a finger and tell me what I had to do. But that's what happened when I went on staff and I never liked it. I didn't like being told what to do, not really having an opinion.

She came on to the union's national staff in 1998 and stayed as a

Cheryl Kryzaniwsky, first woman president of CAW council. Photo: CAW.

staff director for seven years, but left early, at age fifty-five. She retired and never regretted it. "But they wanted Ken Lewenza, to profile him as a future president, and at that time there was no way they were ready for a woman president and no way they were ready for a president not out of the Big Three."

More Women in Leadership

> Tell me, and I'll forget. Show me, and I may not remember. Involve me, and I'll understand.
>
> —From the introduction to the women activists course, 1992

A key recommendation of the 1991 women's conference was to create more union leadership opportunities for women and racialized workers, especially in male-dominated workplaces. It was difficult for women to rise in the union because their numbers were small, but even where there were more women, it was usually the men who rose to leadership positions. The union needed to train more women leaders, to help them develop more confidence, and to help good union women to see themselves as feminists.

Some men in the education department were hostile to the concept of women-only education. They saw this work as not only undermining their expertise but, as they called it, "dividing the working class." It seemed odd that the lack of women in leadership or in education programs never seemed divisive to them. They grumbled, and women needed to find a way to get the job done.

The union needed a specialized program, one centred on women's experiences, where they would have the space and security to really say what was on their minds. The kind of program they envisioned was the opposite of the lecture-based, abstract presentations that often passed for education in those days.

Leadership Training: Women Activists Course

A new approach would cost money to develop, to hire someone who had the special skills and experience to write it. The union led by Buzz Hargrove in the early nineties faced huge economic hurdles with plant closures and layoffs. The immediate defence of workers' jobs and income was by necessity the priority. There was little ability or appetite to spend the union's resources to hire someone from outside to design a new education program for women.

With the NDP in government in Ontario, there was a funding program for outreach to women and other underrepresented groups. The union got a small grant to develop a course. Lynn Brophy, a CAW member from the airline local was tasked with the job. She had a degree in adult education and, possibly more importantly, she was a feminist with a deep understanding of learner-centred education. Working women's experiences would be central to the course.

Brophy worked with others in the field of adult ed and feminism as well as women leaders and staff in the union. The course came together quickly and piloted in 1992 at the union's education centre. Brophy and Georgina Anderson (who took part in the 1978 Fleck strike, described in chapter 2), a leader from Local 27, co-instructed.[4] The concrete reality of women's experiences in their plant or workplace were central to the program. It built on their discussions and ideas to encourage them to find social solutions, feminist solutions, to common problems. It helped them develop confidence and the motivation to want to get elected in their local union. It encouraged them to see themselves as leaders and to see other women, not as competitors, but as allies, so that if one got elected, she would push to open spaces for others. Guest speakers, elected women, and staff were role models and they encouraged the women to take their full place.

The union was an even more difficult place for Black and racialized women, and few were in leadership. Black women Ena Morris, Josephine Ebanks, and Georgina Anderson were part of the first group of twelve, but much more work was needed to support emerging Black and racialized women. Brophy was skilled at helping groups break the ice. As exercises encouraged participants to share more and more about their experiences, they also began to open up about their strengths and weakness as individuals, their challenges, and their goals. The course sparked emotional responses on occasions, where women spoke of harassment, lack of childcare, and the sexism they faced. As well, many faced tough economic challenges and insecurity in their workplace.

As the women shared their experiences, they began to gain confidence and build solidarity. They also talked through solutions that they began to see, such as the need for social programs like childcare, the need for better enforcement of the harassment policy and procedure, and changes in the union to open up more positions for women.

The course was far from perfect but was still a huge success. It helped women become feminist union leaders. They took participant feedback seriously and made improvements. They committed to improve it with each class they ran.

In 2001, Julie White, the newly appointed director of the women's department, conducted a comprehensive review of the two-week women activists program. White began tracking the attendance of participants, and the review revealed that the majority of women attending were from the auto and manufacturing sectors, while women from sectors with insufficient funding in their workplace paid education leave program (PEL), such as health care, retail, and fishing sectors, were underrepresented. Under White's leadership the two-week program was restructured into two one-week courses: women activists and women in leadership. The new programs were a tremendous success, providing access and opportunity to all women in the union.

The makeup of the union's membership, which was growing and diversifying, needed to be reflected in participants attending the women's programs. Their restructuring provided participants with a better understanding of the complexities of women's work in all sectors of the union and built strong sisterhood bonds that still exist today.

White also oversaw the expansion of several new forty-hour programs, including the women's advocate program, women in collective bargaining, and women power and political action.

Helping more women become leaders in the union had been one of the many important recommendations from the women's conferences on gender-based violence, as well as from the first human rights conference. Women needed to see role models to know what was possible. They needed mentors who could encourage them and give them guidance. The women activists course was all that and more. It drew women into the union and helped them become leaders, advocating for traditional trade union goals but also for the goals identified by working women decades before. It would be transformational and would inspire courses for Indigenous, Black, workers of colour, and 2SLGBTQ+ members. The union was learning to reach out to members in a new and exciting way.

Lynn Brophy: Learner-Centred Educator

It was intense workplace monitoring and measurement at the Air Canada reservations office in Toronto that got Lynn Brophy involved in the union. When they merged with the UAW, which became the CAW, and Cheryl Kryzaniwsky won the union presidency, Brophy went to work for her in the local union. She says that "the union felt it could do anything in those early days; a lot of that feeling stayed for a very long time with me. These were the great days of the Big Three auto sector. There was lots of confidence. There was lots of energy."

She later left the local union on a leave of absence to go back to school and, because of her training in adult education, was invited to join the CAW auto parts training council, where she stayed for four years and became an expert in adult education through a working-class lens.

She describes two models of education:

> At universities, professors and lecturers are the stars of the show and the centres of learning. Students learn by reading and writing at a high scholarly level, as well as by listening to professors' lectures. Mostly, students must understand and explain various theories in their areas of study. This learning model has a tradition of students as passive learners who do not bring their own experiences into a classroom. Their job is to absorb what they are being told. It is a top-down model of education that works for the few rather than the many.
>
> In learner-centred, adult education, things work the other way around. Learners are at the centre and are asked to describe and contribute their own life experiences and observations. Learning starts from a place of lived experience of adults who build theory with the encouragement and guidance

> of discussion leaders, facilitators and other learners. It is a ground-up approach rather than bottom-down model of education. Adults are understood as people whose experiences in the world count as much as 'expert' theories.

Brophy says the lecture-based model of education leaves many learners feeling insecure and excluded. It starts with abstractions rather than being grounded in workers' lives. Women, who are already feeling insecure and excluded, are especially vulnerable. Also, she says university-style education excludes a lot of people who learn differently.

The lecture model was terrible for women because the last thing the union wanted was to alienate women. The goal was to bring women together and give them a safe place to talk and strategize. So the CAW women activists course was developed using a worker-centred model.

The director of education challenged the goal of the women's program. "It was easy to go after the women's program," says Brophy. "People would talk about 'dumbing down education.' I was always perplexed by that."

We had an activist program that was just for women, and we were criticized for 'dividing the union and the working class.' Meanwhile women in the union were well aware that what was actually dividing the union and working class were harassment, sexism, racism and homophobia. These criticisms about dividing the union were complete nonsense."

She says it got wrapped up in a discussion about identity politics and that it can be divisive:

> But really strong links can be made between identity, politics, solidarity, and working-class politics. It can be done in a way that isn't divisive. If it's done properly, it will strengthen the union. That was always our belief. I think any education program needs to be solidly rooted within the union.

She says there is a lack of understanding about what good participant-centred education does and can do. Some of it, she says, makes her cringe. Some of the exercises are juvenile and embarrassing for adults to have to do. The strength of what Brophy did was to build on workers day-to-day experiences. She brought them together to help them, not just to understand, but to strategize, about how to make change. It was transformative.

Brophy says she thinks the fear among people who didn't understand the concept of learner-centred education, was that they would lose control:

> [Those who described starting with learners' experiences as] "touchy-feely" always makes me want to say, "You have got to be kidding. You try being the butt of harassment in a majority male workplace, then talk to me about having a problem with touchy-feely where women are comfortable enough to share those experiences with other women in a safe learning environment." It's a fundamental misunderstanding of worker-centred education. And it's an odd position for people to take who are tasked with empowering workers.

Brophy says delivering the women activists program was tough because the participants said things that were hard to hear. There was a counsellor from a local shelter standing by during the program, which was something learned during the women's conferences on violence. When women speak about the barriers to their involvement in the union, invariably harassment and violence come up. These are very difficult topics. Sometimes women are speaking about their experiences for the first time. But it was powerful because they wanted to take action.

One of the topics she wishes was discussed more in the course was how to bring the information back to the local union. "We need to make sure that the leadership of the local unions understands what it is we're trying to do here. When you explain education in terms of strengthening solidarity it makes it easier to build support. And that support makes everything easier."

She recalls general union courses, especially for the auto assembly membership, where there might only be a few women in the class. They wouldn't speak up, and certainly wouldn't raise a topic like sexism or harassment. She believes there were, and still are, good reasons for doing separate classes for women: "That stuff about dividing the union and the working class by having this separate program, separate classes for women, was just flat-out wrong."

Brophy emphasizes how the women activists course was situated in the many feminist programs and events in the union. From annual women's conferences to commemorations each December 6, to anti-harassment training and enforcement of the policy, to pay equity, the content of the course was reinforced frequently in the union. "The course didn't just stand by itself on a little island."

The women activists course was transformational in helping trade union women become feminists. Brophy was later tapped to work with Carol Phillips when she had a team rewriting the paid education leave (PEL) program, and she led the training of local union discussion leaders:

> Women and LGBT issues were woven throughout the new PEL program. And twenty-five years ago, we were talking very specifically about a continuum of gender. I do not remember pushback on any of that. What I do remember pushback on, and what I remember discussion leaders telling me, was that sexism was always the hardest part of the program to facilitate.

Brophy's theory was,

> When you talk about sexism, women's attitudes, ideas, and about feminism, the women in heterosexual relationships go back home and speak to their partners and local unions about these things. Lots of changes were then expected of men around sharing household labour and childcare. It also affected local unions in terms of childcare and paying attention to the ways in which two women in a room with thirty men could and did limit women's participation.
>
> Women were asking for real change. It hit closer to home and had to do with the whole concept of sexism and the whole notion of feminism. The challenge with looking at the world through a different lens is that it's hard if not impossible to go back to the way you saw things before. That's why I was wondering if we could have made that re-entry back home a little smoother.

Participants in the women activists program at the CAW Education Centre, 1992. Photo: CAW.

First National LGBT Conference, 2000

The first national conference for the LGBT members was in 2000, after a national LGBT policy was passed in 1997. There was a lot of nervousness about people being outed. Delegates were invited by word of mouth. Then it was held every year after and there were other supports for 2SLGBTQ+ members.

The CAW began to participate in pride parades across the country, which provided more visibility and support for members. Then the CAW championed Marc Hall, an Oshawa high school student who wanted to take his same gender partner to the school prom. The Catholic school refused, and the issue blew up in the media. Lynn Brophy became involved as did Mike Shields, the CAW president of the large Local 222, in Oshawa. Provincial Cabinet Minister George Smitherman also extended support to Marc. Finally, the school relented, and another barrier was broken.

"I am told that in all the years that Buzz was the president of the union he never got more disgusting emails, letters, and communications than when the union was taking a stand around our call of support for Marc Hall," says Brophy.

Maybe, until he took a stand on gun control.

Employment Equity: Wins Lost, 1995

In 1983, the federal government had asked Judge Rosalie Abella to head up a royal commission on Equality in Employment. As the sole commissioner she was asked to examine the employment practices of federal crown corporations to determine ways of promoting employment opportunities and eliminating systemic discrimination with particular focus on women, Indigenous people, disabled people, and visible minorities (the term used).

The Abella Commission report published in 1984 advanced the idea that discriminatory actions should be understood by their impact rather than their intent. It proposed that to achieve an outcome of equality sometimes meant treating people differently. It recommended the creation by government of mandatory employment equity programs for government workplaces and crown corporations where systemic discrimination could exist.

Subsequently a group of four women from Quebec took a case to the Human Rights Commission charging that Canadian National Railway (CN) prevented women from getting hired due to their policies. An employment equity program was imposed on CN in 1987 that would result in the increased hiring of women.

In 1995 GM announced it was accepting applications for a third shift in Oshawa. About 15,000 people braved sub-zero temperatures in a line that snaked around the building and made for striking aerial photos that sent shivers down the spines of the existing workforce. With almost 10 per cent unemployment, the message to workers was they were lucky to have a job. Not one person was hired at that time. There was speculation that GM was playing hardball and getting ready for the next round of bargaining by creating job insecurity. Some GM workers said, "The only thing worse than working at GM was not working at GM." People needed those jobs. By the early 1990s, the optimism of the early 1980s had given way to a recession and great insecurity, and in 1993 the new federal Liberal government of Jean Chretien signed on to the North American Free Trade Agreement. Plant closures and jobs losses accelerated.

Bob Rae's NDP government in Ontario took up the employment equity challenge, which had been a campaign pledge. In 1993 they passed an employment equity law to advance employment opportunities for four designated groups, women, people of colour, people with disabilities, and Indigenous people, in keeping with the Abella Commission report and the federal employment equity act. The timing of this initiative was difficult given the economic climate with plant closures, layoffs, and cutbacks. The economic downturn in the early nineties had already put the Rae government on shaky ground. "The timing isn't good now" was the repeated refrain of why the hiring numbers of the designated groups could not increase. Thousands of existing workers were losing their jobs. Conservative opposition strengthened, and employment equity policies were a key political target of conservative organizers and public figures, arguing that white men would not get hired.

At that time, you often heard that if you're a firefighter or a police officer, your son will never be able to get hired for that job. These jobs were overwhelmingly male-dominated and not at all diverse, but the message was effective at raising opposition to employment equity. The union tried to use the opportunity with its mostly male members to argue that opening up some spaces for others did not mean that white men wouldn't get hired. With so much job insecurity, it was a difficult climate.

Tough legislation with effective enforcement should have been enough. Even though the auto and aerospace companies were federal contractors and subject to federal employment equity law, change was glacial.

By 1993, the likelihood of losing the Ontario employment equity law seemed real, so the union's goal was to bargain language similar to the Ontario employment equity act into the auto collective agreements that year as part of a suite of important equity measures. There were few women, Black, racialized, or Indigenous workers in the assembly plants and they continued to say that harassment was prevalent and finding support much more difficult.

In December 1995, in one of the first decisions by the newly elected Progressive Conservative government of Mike Harris, they repealed the employment equity law.

Auto Bargaining New Equity Issues, 1993

Many recommendations from the women's conferences were for union collective bargaining goals. This is the wonderful thing about belonging to a union. You don't have to wait until the right government comes along to make progress. Yes, it can help, but the union, through the power of the collective membership in bargaining can negotiate pay increases, better working conditions, benefits, and work rules that non-union workers can only dream of. It is a tremendous credit to workers and their bargaining committees that union workers make more money, are more likely to have a pension, and have made gains like paid maternity leave, childcare, sick pay, and health benefits that governments offered to other workers long after.

By law, employers were responsible to maintain a workplace free of harassment, and the union wanted to ensure they lived up to the requirement by adding extensive anti-harassment language to the collective agreements, including the right to refuse work because of harassment or violence. Employers were responsible for hiring, and they had discriminated against women and other groups. The union intended to bargain employment equity provisions. They wanted the company to recognize the issues of violence against women and to train their employees on equity and harassment. They also wanted women to be able to go to other women in their workplace with their harassment complaints or concerns about violence. Women needed better workplace representation. Nash outlines some of the challenges from this time:

> We had to first get these goals adopted at the union's collective bargaining convention. There are many competing demands for the union, but the CAW prided itself on being a trailblazer so our initiatives for human rights and women found support.
>
> Next we had to get the union bargaining committees to agree to make these goals a priority, and then we had to persuade the companies to adopt them. Because we had had important discussions around harassment and violence at our council meetings and conventions, and the bargaining committees, if they had disagreements, they didn't voice them. Also many of these leaders had been around the union for some time, and they understood that leadership meant stepping up on issues that might be challenging with some of their members, but that their job was to defend these positions adopted by the union.

These committees were almost all men, and they knew that ratification votes depended on improvements in wages, benefits, and working conditions for the majority. While they may have supported the union's stand on equity and gender issues, they tended to give the floor to Nash to make the arguments for equity issues with the companies.

Women's Advocate Program, 1993

Nash remembers one discussion before 1993 auto bargaining with a colleague, Bob Chernecki, who was also an assistant to CAW President Buzz Hargrove, really his right-hand man:

> I always found Chernecki good to work with. He had a real bark to his voice. But he was a good listener, supportive, and gave solid practical advice. I wanted women's representation in the plants, leaders that women could go to with harassment or other gender-based concerns, almost like a health and safety rep. As a former health and safety rep myself, I knew about this special system of representation and how effective it was at problem-solving.
>
> "Forget it, Peg, you're not going to get a whole new system of representation in the plants. Not gonna happen," he said. "No way the companies are going to pay for that."
>
> I pushed back describing how women's concerns were not being addressed. "How was a woman supposed to go to a guy to disclose she was harassed or is beaten up at home or was assaulted?"
>
> He gave me that look, like I was giving him a problem he didn't need. Then he offered: "What about time as needed? No guaranteed time, if there's an issue, they can get off the job."
>
> Yes, that was it. If there were no problems, the reps would not need any time. But when women or others were harassed, when they had issues of violence at work or a home, there would be someone they could talk with. The pitch to the companies was that these specially trained reps would be problem solvers and save the companies money. It would be an innovative breakthrough that could defuse problems for the worker and the company. Win, win.

> I charged out of Chernecki's office on a mission.
>
> "You still have to get that past our committee and the company," he called after me.

Nash was fired up. In that round of bargaining, they presented a whole suite of new equity initiatives to the auto companies, first at Chrysler, then at Ford and GM Canada. They bargained significant funding for childcare, up to $8.5 million over the three-year agreements. They also bargained language on violence against women specifically, including the provision for a woman facing violence who needed to remain at a women's shelter or recover from an assault to face no discipline and retain her wages. They had bargained the union's harassment language in 1987 negotiations, but this time they included the right to refuse work if a harassment complaint, essentially a health and safety issue, is not resolved. This initiative paved the way for the CAW to argue successfully for its inclusion in law in occupational health and safety law beginning in Ontario in 2010.

And importantly, they succeeded in negotiating the women's advocate program. This was a groundbreaking plan to identify women representatives in all the auto plants who would receive special training in harassment, violence, and community resources available to members.

This achievement by women was perceived in the media world as a soft story, meaning getting coverage would be difficult. Jane Armstrong, CAW communications director, had worked with Nash in the CALEA during the time of its merger with the CAW in 1985, once again working with Nash, remembers:

> This story was not going to interrupt the economy of Canada the way a strike might in an auto plant. So Peggy Nash came up with the lead paragraph, and the lead line being that we had achieved the women's advocate program and that notices and information about this program would be posted as soon as possible in the women's washrooms. The idea was to get the media to sort of squint their eyes and say, "Am I reading this correctly? What's this about?"
>
> The title of the materials and the awareness campaign was

> "Sometimes only another woman can understand." We had the press conference at the hotel where we were bargaining. [Ironically, it was male labour and corporate leaders who spoke at the news conference.] We got a great turnout, and that was the question the media wanted answered, "Why the women's washrooms?" We said, because the chances are if we put this up in the main male-dominated plants, it's going to get torn down. There would be a backlash. It was an enormously successful program that we were able to take to many other companies over time.

They had designed special pamphlet cases for the women's washrooms with pamphlets explaining how to contact the women's advocate. The advocates would research what resources were available in each community and produce materials for each location.

Michele Landsberg, then a columnist at the *Toronto Star*, wrote an article entitled "Auto union makes big gains for women," where she detailed the progress in the 1993 bargaining and said "These woman-friendly policies (childcare, anti-violence measures, co-op housing support, childcare funding) set a remarkable and influential example."

Under Julie White's leadership as CAW director of women's programs, the union would go on to negotiate advocates in many other workplaces, more than three hundred of them, even where women were the majority of the workers, because violence and abuse can occur everywhere. Today there are more than six hundred Unifor women's advocates. And in 2020 negotiations, following the women's advocate model, Unifor broke ground and negotiated with the Detroit Three auto makers a racial justice advocate position to support CAW members.

Breaking the Silence

Another union-led campaign Armstrong recalls was called "Break the Silence."

As the CAW communications director, Jane Armstrong hired artist Marie Laville to produce artwork symbolizing the women's movement. Laville created a striking collage with images of the women's movement over many years. The artwork was reproduced on placards that stood out in marches and rallies:

> Having to come up with the materials and the strategies was a real privilege and uniting with new women's movements was a thrill. We deliberately worked to find a young woman of colour artist to come up with the artwork for the campaign's poster—the concept was it had to represent all women and it did. It was fantastic. We turned it into flags. I remember the support that we got from the top leadership when we wanted to produce—I think they were eight feet by three feet wide—posters, and we sent them off to women's shelters. And a number of places like that. The Toronto Women's Bookstore on Harbord Street had it on the side of a building for years and years and years. It was very prominent.

The artwork was shared widely and it gave CAW women a sense of pride to know this was part of their contribution to the movement.

Armstrong held the position of communications director for ten years until 2004. "There's no question," she says, "that the top leadership in the union was willing to put the resources and the commitment behind doing the work on harassment and gender-based violence, and bringing it forward at the bargaining table."

But Armstrong also found there was a contradiction between the verbal and the actual, as in the activist support of childcare campaigns, affirmative action, and employment equity, and how the union operated. Staff positions were very privileged, but she felt there were gender inequities or racialized inequities in terms of treatment of staff. "I loved the work, and I was committed to the union. The men who are in top leadership positions, elected or on staff, they seemed to have their own support for grocery shopping, laundry, picking up kids."

There were some on staff who thought the women shouldn't be on staff, that women were taking the jobs away from some very deserving men. She says some men on the left believed that you had to win the class struggle first, before gender equity. "I remember in those education sessions thinking, oh, my! Unlike that advertisement 'You've come a long way, baby,' you felt more like— 'It was a long way to go, baby.'" She felt however that she was able to do some important work.

Still there were women in CAW workplaces and even on

Jane Armstrong hired Marie Laville to produce the Women Unite! poster for the CAW, symbolizing the women's movement. Photo: CAW.

the staff of the union who experienced harassment. She knew of another woman who appeared in a union harassment video and faced so much harassment and backlash in her workplace that she needed to move from her plant.

"It was a vibrant time and it was exhilarating. There were tough fights," she says, "But we felt like we were making progress." She is proud that, to her knowledge, the CAW was the first union in North America to have had a website. They also had a videography crew so they could send out videos without having to pay the mainstream media for footage. The work just expanded, and she was exhausted.

Armstrong took early retirement in 2004 for several reasons:

> Whether it was the crush of neo-liberalism pulling the union's focus into more bread-and-butter issues. There seemed to be this kind of closing in, and there were some very tough debates about the union's stand on "weapons of mass destruction" regarding Afghanistan, and Iraq. By 2004 I was finding it extremely difficult.

The pressure on unions was increasing, and union density kept decreasing. It was difficult, especially in the private sector. The union had expanded, with many mergers. "That meant a crisis in some sectors of the economy almost every day," says Armstrong. "Without childcare, and being on the road often, it became too much." She was paying up to $30,000 a year for childcare, borrowing and rolling it into her mortgage. "It wasn't sustainable."

Bread and Roses

As the economic downturn dragged on in the early 1990s, the federal Liberal government was elected in 1993 on its Red Book of progressive action, including a national childcare program, pay and employment equity, jobs, and affordable housing. Instead, faced with a severe economic downturn, it enacted some of the biggest social spending cuts ever in Canada.

In 1995 the World Women Conference in Beijing inspired women in the Fédération des femmes du Québec (FFQ) to propose a global plan to fight poverty and violence against women. This initiative was based on a Bread and Roses march that same year in Quebec calling for jobs and justice.

The following year, the labour movement and the women's movement joined forces on the Bread and Roses (Jobs and Justice) theme. Women across Canada organized community events, and then thousands converged in Ottawa.

Chapter Five

Women on the March, 1995-2000

The 1996 women's Bread and Roses (Jobs and Justice) march on Ottawa rallied women, especially labour women, from all over the country. It was an opportunity for women from different locals and different unions to unite with women's organizations in a common cause. It was a key moment in flexing our muscles. CAW women came out in force.

However, as much as the pressure stung the federal Liberals, with their empty promises of progressive action from their Red Book, little tangible change happened.

Then, initiated by the Fédération des Femmes de Quebec (FFQ) and the Quebec labour movement, there was a call for a global women's march. It would culminate on International Women's Day, March 8, 2000. World March of Women in the Year 2000 was launched, demonstrating women's ongoing determination to change the world.

This was a global effort to build awareness and push for change on the themes of poverty, violence, and gender equality. Nash was chair of the Canadian Labour Congress's women's committee. Women in the labour movement worked together in a way they wished their male counterparts could do. They produced postcards to illustrate and inform about the march's goals.

While participating was exciting and it drew many women into a kind of activism they had not joined in previously, the movement's goals still seemed far off. The Quebec women who had initiated the global effort, felt let down by the inaction of the Quebec government of the time.

CAW women joined the 1996 Women's March Against Poverty, leaving Vancouver as it made its way to Ottawa, under the slogan "For Bread and Roses, For Jobs and Justice." Photo: CAW.

Irene Friend: Change Didn't Happen Over Night!

Irene Friend was one of the first local equity reps at the Big Three auto companies and the first full-time employment equity coordinator for the CAW at Chrysler Canada. Friend got hired in a small UAW Windsor plant in 1969, and she was elected as union steward and plant chairperson. When, early in 1976, Chrysler was going to put a second shift on in their van plant, they were also hiring women. Friend was part of the first group of women to go into assembly line work at Chrysler in Windsor:

> It was a scary adventure at first to walk into a plant full of men. There were 25 of us out of about 2,500 men. They didn't want us there. They didn't like us there. It was a bit intimidating, and the place is huge. When they hired us, they said, "Okay, you can go to the plant now, and you have to report to such and such a place."

The World March of Women for jobs and justice, culminating on Parliament Hill in Ottawa, on International Women's Day, March 8, 2000. Photo: CLC.

> "What is that?"
>
> "Those are the pillars. You have to look up, find your spot, and go and report to that part of the line."

Friend continues,

> The fellows I worked with in my area were okay but it was interesting. The guy that worked beside me was really and truly a criminal. He got arrested on the line. Cops came out of nowhere, and every one of us is standing there with our mouths open, literally, when they arrested him. They didn't even shut the line down. They just scooped him up, and out he went.

There was only one other woman near her and they faced opposition from the men. Irene says "We went through a lot of crap the first three months that I was there." She and her husband Bob worked opposite shifts so that one parent was with their kids. "When I was on afternoons, one of the guys from the plant would call my house and if Bob answered the phone, there'd be all this garbage about 'Oh, I'm going out with Irene, and we're having this affair.'"

The callers eventually got tired of it. "I think they realized that this isn't gonna work, and that I was not leaving." She adds, "I didn't put up with anything on that line ever. So, if you treated me with respect, then that's what you got back, and if not, like, I could be just as vulgar as you."

During the 1980 recession, Irene was laid off for about eighteen months. When she was called back it was to a different location, plant 3:

> That was even scarier, because there were no women there, except for the women in the office and in the canteens. We'd heard all these horror stories about plant three. Almost all of us that got laid off ended up going to plant three, but you went back by seniority. As one of the first to be called back, it was the same thing, only on a way bigger scale."

Friend was later assigned to the paint shop, which she says was a good thing because it didn't matter that she was a woman:

> There was no BS going on, and I worked in a spot in the plant where you had to wear coveralls, so you all look the same. But where they kept the coveralls was in the men's washroom. So I made a decision right from the get go, I'm not gonna be embarrassed if they can't figure out to put those coveralls somewhere where I can get them. I go in there, and it wasn't very long before there'd be somebody out there with a handful of coveralls for me and that resolved that issue.
>
> Those guys were mostly great to work with. There were some crude comments from time to time, but that's probably the same, even in any industry. I had just made my mind up that this is a great job. I'm gonna end up with a pension at the end of the day and I'm making good wages, and I can do this.

She says the union was changing and bargaining was changing. The union first bargained a basic affirmative action clause in 1987 that required two part-time affirmative action reps, one for each of the two plants. Friend was one of the two, but when the other rep stepped down, she agreed to take on both roles. She worked with a management counterpart since equity was to be a joint program, similar to health and safety. This was the space that she could occupy in the union. She says "it would have been futile at that point to run for any union positions." There was no way to get elected. It took a few more years before that happened.

She jumped at the chance to do the equity work, which meant twenty-four hours, three shifts, off the line, working in an office that she shared with the skilled trades rep. They got on well. In 1990 bargaining, the local affirmative action rep was made full-time. A key part of her job was to conduct a survey for the federal contractor's legislation to which Chrysler needed to comply.

They conducted a corporate-wide survey with such a large response rate that government representatives visited to find out how the union did it. Irene Friend explains:

> I had made a point of going to every member in the Chrysler Windsor assembly plant, telling them how important it was to fill out that form. The local leadership reinforced that and they gave some legitimacy to the importance of it. We would say to them, "Listen, the government wants us to do this. So if we don't get a good response, you're not gonna have a job because we won't get a contract." Well, hello! You know you don't say those things to auto workers. "What do you mean? I won't have a job?" There's nothing like hitting them in their pocketbook.

Times were changing, and the plants were changing. She recalls that you always knew when there was a tour going through the plant. People wanted to visit an assembly plant in operation to see how a vehicle was made. "When a tour had women in it, the place would go berserk with whooping and hollering and cat calls. I said to the union reps, 'We gotta do something about all these cat calls and the only way is we've got to get management on board to hire more women.'"

The problem was the company wasn't hiring full-time at the point, only temporary part-time workers, or TPTs. They often hired young people to fill in for holidays and vacations, usually the son or the daughter of a member. "Well, when all those young women came into that plant on weekends to work, and you know what, Daddy doesn't want his daughter subjected to that. They're the ones that changed their behaviour. That was really a huge thing."

Then in 1993, the CAW bargained extensive equity language, including the women's advocate program, and language that protected women who faced violence at home or harassment at work:

> That really became a big, a big change in terms of having an employment equity plan and having a say in terms of who they hired, because that's never been our forte to be able to do. That's always been a management right and responsibility to hire. That was really the selling point especially to the union reps.

Friend recognizes the tremendous progress made over the years, but she did feel that even with supportive leadership, she often had to really push to make change. The leadership said she was like a dripping tap, there was always more. She would say the only way to turn off the tap was to get things fixed.

She says especially after they hired the third shift in 1993, they hired a lot of women for assembly line work. Young women have children, but they managed at Windsor assembly to be able to accommodate women, especially in the latter part of their pregnancy.

The union and Chrysler won a provincial award for setting a benchmark in pregnancy accommodation. Irene Friend remembers the effort it took:

> I went to the banks, the insurance companies, and different industries and nobody had any firm commitment in terms of a program of accommodation of women in their late stages of pregnancy, and we got to do that at Chrysler. Also, on the whole issue of harassment on the shop floor. We did that by bargaining joint training for both union and the company, and they had to sit together in the class and take the training, and that really started to change the atmosphere, as well.
>
> From the very get go when I walked into that first plant at plant 6 back in 1976, there was never gonna be a day when

> any one of those guys was ever gonna make me cry, no way. Because that was always there, "Oh, yeah, she can't do that. She'll be bawling her eyes out." Oh, yeah, not this one, man that was never gonna happen. And when I did get mad, they all knew I was mad because I was pretty vocal about it. I would put my jacket on, walk out the door and I'd slam every door I came to and I'm sure that they were all afraid that I would go to Turner Road [the local union office].

Change didn't happen overnight. It took a while.

Terry Weymouth: Electrician

In 1988 Terry Weymouth made the difficult decision to leave her job at the GM trim plant, where she worked as a power sewer to apply for an apprenticeship. This meant an initial pay cut, but her wages would rise over time, eventually matching—or even exceeding—her previous income. More importantly, it offered something new: a licence that would provide long-term job security and flexibility in the event of layoffs.

Over six years in construction, where she never met another woman in the trades, she earned her electrical 309A construction and maintenance licence while working on residential and commercial projects. Then 1993, when Chrysler added a third shift at the Windsor minivan plant, she was drawn back to the union rights she had once enjoyed.

From robotics and controllers to assembly lines and operational systems, the learning curve was steep and specific to the plant environment. Though there were two other tradeswomen, they rarely worked together. Even the basics—boots, coveralls, change rooms, and washrooms—weren't designed with women in mind.

When the CAW launched the women in skilled trades and technology awareness (WSTTA) program, to promote apprenticeships for women by using tradeswomen as discussion leaders, one of the women was Weymouth. A few years later, Terry Weymouth was appointed national skilled trades education coordinator, taking over the program's leadership.

Though the numbers are still not where she'd like them to be, she reflects proudly on the union's progress:

> I think we've done a really good job of making it socially acceptable for women to be in trades. When I started, it was unheard of. Now, it's a coveted job—by anybody. Those opportunities have to be available to all of us, and we have to keep pushing those boundaries. That's a huge success.

Weymouth also worked with a local non-profit through women's enterprise skills training, using the union's forty-hour women in skilled trades program to recruit women in Windsor and Essex County into the trades.

"There are still problems," she says. "There's still a lot of sexism, but you're only going to change that by getting more women in."

Mergers Bring Women Leaders, 1990s

The last decade of the twentieth century saw the CAW under President Buzz Hargrove continue its efforts to grow its membership by merging with other Canadian unions. At a time when the traditional membership base of the union was getting hammered by demands for concessions, layoffs, and workplace closures, according to the union, their expansion into new sectors of the economy added about a hundred thousand new members through mergers.

While some of these unions were very traditional, some brought in many women members and women who were or who would become leaders. Those women blazed a trail in showing what women could do in collective bargaining, challenging the stereotype that only men could take on bargaining.

A few of these unions had belonged to the Confederation of Canadian Unions, a labour central outside the Canadian Labour Congress, which had a history of militancy and Canadian independence. For example, the Canadian Association of Industrial Mechanical and Allied Workers Union (CAIMAW), a fiercely independent Canadian breakaway union from a US-based union, joined the CAW with approximately ten thousand members in 1992. CAIMAW members worked in industry, trucking, hospitality, and other service jobs. They brought into the CAW unique master collective agreements for workers at Kentucky Fried

Chicken outlets and White Spot restaurants that raised the standard of living for those workers who were typically without union representation.

Denise Kellahan: Gains for Service-Sector Workers

Denise had forged her leadership at White Spot, beginning as a young mom who was asked to run for elected office because she helped co-workers with problems. She seemed to be a natural for an official position and she ran unopposed, eventually becoming president of her local union, a large group of mostly hospitality workers. Kellahan encouraged her members to join the CAW in a merger and was elected to the national executive board of the CAW in 1994. She later joined the national staff as a service representative in 1999. Modestly, Kellahan explains:

> I was really just in the right place at the right time, when the union decided to increase the national executive board from one woman to two women. At the time it was a very male-dominated board. I look back and think, how did all this happen to me? I just feel sometimes like so privileged. I got to do all these things. It was an enormously challenging time servicing service-sector workers.

Her local union merged with a hotel workers union to become Local 3000 and focused on service-sector organizing and representation. Her efforts in the union aimed to help service-sector workers, especially shift workers, to have some stability and predictability in their lives. Her goal was to allow workers to maximize their hours of work to create the maximum number of stable full-time jobs, and to allow workers to bid on those jobs by seniority.

Service-sector workers were usually not highly paid, and it was challenging to convince the leadership of the union, for whom the auto sector was the priority, that it was a positive to organize in the service sector. Denise made this a priority during her time at the national executive board. “I had made the case that service-sector workers were undervalued, and there were myths out there that it was stop gap work. In all our hotels that were organized, many people work their entire careers there and they were unionized, so they had benefits."

She also tried to make the case for jobs that were very skilled. "Being a good server takes a tremendous amount of organization and people skills. A bartender should be a skilled trade; it is high pressure, tough work."

Kellahan says without a union, turnover in those jobs would be about 65 per cent, but with a union, that dropped to about 35 per cent. Some of our greatest achievements in that area made a qualitative difference in people's lives, and given that most in the service sector are women and workers of colour, it makes a huge difference."

Staff rep Roger Crowther led a ten-and-a-half-week strike in 1988, with nineteen picket lines on Vancouver Island and the lower mainland in British Columbia, that led to the first White Spot master agreement that so changed the lives of the workers there. The majority of the workers were women, and they could have a career at White Spot because of those agreements.

John Bowman, a national rep originally from Kellahan's local union, organized Starbucks at several Vancouver locations in 1996.[1] When they went on strike at Starbucks, Peggy Nash, joining the staff rep Roger Crowther, was tasked with helping them get a first collective agreement that provided wage increases, some benefits, and greater control over scheduling. Unfortunately, the turnover was great and the union did not expand the organizing. Eventually the group decertified in 2007.

Another staff rep from this group, Sylvia Simpson, bargained mainly in the hotel sector. She negotiated gains that allowed seasonal workers to maintain their benefits even when their hours dipped below the normal requirement by averaging the hours over a longer period. She established that English as a second language classes for the many South Asian workers, mainly women, were offered on company time so that the women didn't have to stay after their shift. This afforded many workers the chance to improve their skills and get better jobs.

Kellahan says that the union's affirmative action provisions helped these members:

> I firmly believe that if you didn't have some of the affirmative action spots women would have continued in the years that I was involved to have a problem getting elected to some of those positions. It was a culture shock for me when we moved into the CAW, because I did not experience that at CAIMAW. CAIMAW had equal number of women national reps in both British Columbia and Manitoba.
>
> When I would hear things about the struggle for women to be in top leadership positions, I would kind of shake my head and go "Wow!" Because, let's face it, people talk the talk about women's equality and all the rest of it, but did they practice it? I think we all know the answer to that.
>
> Looking back, I wouldn't trade it for the world. There were tough years, but I treasure every one of them.

Cathy Walker: Challenging Capitalism

Cathy Walker was raised in Burnaby, a suburb of Vancouver, with two progressive parents. Her mother was a peace activist who opposed the proliferation of nuclear weapons and the US invasion of Vietnam. Her father was a mechanic active in the Machinists Union. Walker joined the New Democratic Youth while in high school. She got active in student politics and the women's movement while at Simon Fraser University (SFU).

"After joining the Abortion Caravan in 1970, I left SFU and worked in an electronics assembly plant near Vancouver." The plant of about 110 workers was 90 per cent women and so she advocated for women's rights. The union was CAIMAW (Canadian Association of Industrial Mechanical and Allied Workers), an independent, progressive Canadian union. "When I discovered everyone at my lunch table 'had' to get married, I was amazed," she says. Birth control had only been made legal the year before, though it had been possible to get condoms from pharmacists who kept them out of sight behind the counter.

"I brought in fifty copies of the *McGill Birth Control Handbook* and put them by the timeclock," she says. "They were snatched up immediately by women on their way to the lunchroom. I brought in another fifty copies that also went quickly."

Because she had no children at the time, unlike most of the other women, she was the only woman from the plant who showed up at local union meetings, which at that time included another, larger plant in which the majority of workers were men. The men wanted representation from her plant, so she was quickly elected trustee of the local, then a couple of years later, vice president. When the elected president didn't show up at meetings, she became president three months later. "Throughout my involvement as a local union leader, I never let anyone know I could type, otherwise, as a woman, I would have been relegated to the secretary role forever, typing meeting minutes."

She got laid off at the electronics assembly plant and got a job at a telephone cable manufacturing plant in the local. Walker recalls,

> Back then, there were women's jobs that were boring and paid less than the men's jobs. Our work was uncomfortable, standing all day on concrete floors. We fought for and won chairs for our workstations. I also learned about the right to refuse unsafe work by refusing to work with a damaged hoist, and ensured that the hoist was repaired.

There had been a 1945 BC law "protecting" women from lifting anything more than thirty-five pounds. This got women out of the shipyards and out of the sawmills at the end of the Second World War to ensure men could return to "their" jobs (preventing the equivalent of another Winnipeg General Strike). Walker applied for a job as tester-inspector for which she was the only qualified applicant, given her science background at SFU. The company denied the posting. She grieved the denial but lost.

Then the NDP was elected in BC in 1972. One of the first things they did was to call public hearings into women's rights. Walker, along with other women unionists, "argued that the law was discriminatory against women, and our presentations were heard favourably by NDP MLAs Rosemary Brown and Colin Gabelmann. The next day the law was rescinded."

Although the tester-inspector job had already been awarded to a man, the next time there was a layoff, the women were kept on, rather than being replaced by men with less seniority. She moved into a man's job and found that not only was it easier than the women's job she had been doing, but it paid fifty cents an hour more, which was significant back then.

With the surge in Canadian nationalism in the 1970s, leading to many workplaces wanting to break away from American unions and many non-union workplaces wanting union representation, Walker's local rapidly grew to forty plants. She then became the full-time president. She was later to became a national staff representative.

Walker began bargaining collective agreements, handling grievances and arbitrations, and then, given she had won a couple of workers' compensation appeals for members, took on the additional responsibilities for occupational health and safety and the Workers' Compensation Board (WCB). There were many opportunities to make a contribution to improving workers' health and safety on the job by holding courses and seminars, visiting workplaces, and giving support to activists. The union was very public in criticisms of the lack of effective regulations and enforcement and were able to improve both.

In 1992, CAIMAW joined the CAW. CAIMAW leaders had been impressed with the courage of the CAW in breaking away from the UAW and felt they had much in common.

Walker was appointed head of the CAW health and safety department, and she moved from Vancouver to Toronto. Apart from the women's department and communications, she was the first woman to head a department in the CAW.

In her new position, she was able to make significant gains for workers in occupational health and safety. With her help, workers bargained better language in their collective agreements. They fought to ban asbestos, fight speed-up, promote ergonomics, and prevent cancer. These produced significant improvements in workplaces, collective agreements, with provisions for ergonomics and better standards for toxic substances. She also advocated for the union and made improvements in workplace regulations provincially and federally.

"We sent the *CAW Health, Safety and Environment Newsletter* to activists, using stories of their activism at the workplace to encourage others to fight back against the employers' agenda of production and profits over health, safety, and a clean environment," she says proudly. On behalf of the union, she published manuals and fact sheets and fought to improve legislative standards.

In the mid-1990s, the right-wing Ontario Harris government attacked workers' health and safety protections. Workers fought back, including with general strikes in the Days of Action.

Walker believes that women can make a major contribution to their fellow workers by getting involved in health and safety:

> Occupational health and safety is at the heart of confronting capitalism. Workers give up their lives, their limbs, and their health while employers only risk profit. Health and safety committee members must argue for and achieve more power to refuse unsafe work, to shut down unsafe equipment, and to make decisions about the workplace, including "management's rights" issues such as the speed of work. Workers' control over the workplace is needed, including what is done, produced, and how.

Clearly, Cathy Walker has lost none of her passion.

Laurell Ritchie: Commitment vs Personal Gain

The Canadian Textile and Chemical Union (CTCU) formed in 1952 under the leadership of Madeleine Parent and Kent Rowley. They led some very high-profile strikes such as McGregor Hosiery and Puretex Knitting, but their members were vulnerable to closures with the advent of free trade. Only seven hundred members remained when the CTCU joined the CAW in 1992.

Laurell Ritchie was an organizer who joined the staff of the CTCU in 1972, where she worked for twenty years. Her union was affiliated with the Confederation of Canadian Unions (CCU), a small association of independent Canadian unions. Ritchie became an elected officer of the CCU.

She was also an activist in the women's movement and her organizing focused mainly on immigrant women.

Ritchie was part of the CCU delegation that met with Bob White at the Westbury Hotel in Toronto to discuss a possible merger. The CTCU joined CAW in 1992. Madeleine Parent gave the merger her blessing. Their union became Local 40, based in Toronto, where they created an action centre that could offer space to progressives and help with organizing.

When the union joined with the CAW, Laurell initially continued as a Local 40 officer. A few years later in 1994, Ritchie was hired into the work organization and training department of the CAW and later was also posted to the pension and benefits department. She was one of the many women on staff who worked with what they called the "woman department," since it was one of the few departments with no staff.

Ritchie had learned early on from Parent and Rowley to value "a different kind of leadership," which might be quiet and soft spoken but commanded the respect of co-workers. "Early on I learned to take the measure of people by what they did out of commitment versus what they did for personal gain." She also took to heart the song "Bread and Roses" when it said "the rising of the women is the rising of us all." In organizing, men assumed because they were men and perhaps spoke better English in some workplaces that they should be the automatic union leaders, whereas, she saw quiet strength in some of the women who were taking ESL classes but had the respect of their co-workers.

Dignity issues were prominent in some of her early work. For example, at McGregor Hosiery in Toronto, management would refer to workers by their employee number rather than their name. A bargaining demand was that the employer refer to workers by their name rather than their number.

Ritchie found the hierarchy of the CAW challenging. She also struggled with the CAW practice of removing the organizer of a new bargaining unit, and replacing them with a service rep who had no previous connection with the bargaining unit. The staff organizer who worked with a committee and after months of work helped them successfully join the union, had to turn the bargaining unit over to the staff service rep who would help the workers negotiate their first collective agreement. Ritchie would have preferred the organizer stay involved.

She focused on economic issues such as the need for workplace adjustment programs tailored to women during the economic downturn in the early 2000s and the 2008 economic crisis.

Adjustment programs are designed to help workers when their workplace is reducing staff or closing. Helping them with employment insurance benefits, training, and new job opportunities lessened the negative impact of job losses. Ritchie knew that a larger share of women's jobs in auto parts, fish plants, and other industries were lost compared to men, but governments tended to focus on male auto assembly workers only.

The positives far outweighed any negatives for her in joining the CAW. Ritchie and many of the former CCU members were part of the union's hospitality council and the women's conference. Ritchie focused most on economic issues for women. For example, she joined the campaign to extend women's employment insurance parental benefits to one year, which was achieved in 2000. Then the campaign switched to provincial governments to ensure they brought their employments standards laws into line to guarantee women the right to return to their jobs after that longer paid-leave period. Improving employment insurance, reduced by the Liberals in the 1990s, is still a significant challenge.

Canadian Brotherhood of Railway Transport and General Workers Union (CBRT&GW) and Brotherhood of Railway Carmen (BRC)

In 1994, the CAW merged with the more than thirty thousand members of the Canadian Brotherhood of Railway Transport and General Workers Union (CBRT&GW). They added non-craft rail workers to the eight thousand skilled trades members, overwhelmingly men, of the Brotherhood of Railway Carmen (BRC) who had merged with the CAW in 1990. But in addition to rail workers, the CBRT included hotels, hospitality, health care, manufacturing, and fisheries workers. The numbers of women members were growing but the staff they brought were mostly men.

Marilynne Lesperance: At First, the Men Didn't Want Me to Succeed

While many of the CBRT members were women, there were few women in leadership or staff positions. Marilynne Lesperance was one of the women who joined the staff of the CAW after the merger and went on to play an important role as a service rep but also as a part-time staff member for women's programs. Lesperance is one of those people who seems up for anything, and her career in the union demonstrates that. At first glance she appears kindly, like a friendly aunt or perhaps a grandmother, but her smiling eyes hid a steel and determination that many underestimated during her career. She also has a wicked sense of humour.

She began working in 1979 as a school bus driver in Markham, Ontario, near Toronto. It was a job that allowed her to take her kids with her, but soon she was approached to help build a union there "because they said I had a big mouth."

So they formed a union and the bus company management was furious. "They were just wild that not only was there gonna be a union that we managed to organize, but it would be led by a woman, since I was president of the local."

She later became the business agent, which was a staff representative assisting with negotiating and enforcing the collective agreement, paid by the local union but working out of a regional office in Toronto. She had to be very hands on, attending school bus driver meetings and taking the questions and complaints of the drivers to the employer, because the workers were afraid.

When a job for a service rep came open, Lesperance applied for it. The then regional vice president of the CBRT&GW told her, "Marilynne, I'm sorry. I know you have the qualifications, but we're not ready for a woman."

"Okay," she said. "Well, human rights is coming in at 10 o'clock, and you can talk to them. Okay?"

After thinking about it, he told her "I will be stepping down in a year and by then maybe the people will be ready for a woman, and I can give you hospitality and nursing homes. If you wait for a year, you can have the national rep's job. Okay?"

She knew he was an honest man so she agreed, and in a year she got the national rep's job. But instead of hospitals and hospitality, the new regional vice president gave her all rail workers to service. "They gave me rail because they didn't want me to succeed."

They knew she had two school-age kids at home, and they gave her units in Moose Factory and Sudbury:

> And they had an agreement that I had never seen, where there

> was an article in there about you can't be let go or laid off. So, I said, "What does this mean?" And the vice president said "If you don't know, you shouldn't have this goddamn job. Get out of my office."
>
> They didn't think the rail guys would accept me but they learned to accept me. They learned that I worked really hard, I was always there for their questions. I took everything they said seriously, and I learned very quickly about the collective agreements of all the rail bargaining units.

She was not the first woman hired on the staff of the CBRT. A woman had been hired in BC but had only lasted four months. Lesperance was not going to quit.

She was in an on-again-off-again relationship with her husband, and he was not reliable. When she had to travel, sometimes she had a friend stay at her house, or she got a babysitter, and sometimes her husband was there. Like many working mothers she patched together a network of childcare. "I remember one time my son ran out to the car as I was leaving to go north, and he said, 'Who's gonna help me with my arithmetic?' And I said, 'That's your dad's job,' and then cried all the way north."

Merging with the CAW, she was assigned to the servicing department, which she says was a little bit daunting, "But it was really wonderful 'cause there was a lot of women compared to what I was used to, and if you had issues you could go to somebody for help."

She recalls getting sent to eastern Ontario to cover for a staff rep who broke his leg, at an auto dealership that was about to go on strike. The owner was in Florida and the son was running the show. He told Lesperance: "No woman's gonna tell me what to do."

She went to Buzz Hargrove and suggested he get a male staff rep in there to avoid having the workers out on strike unnecessarily. "If I have to sit beside you, you are going to negotiate that goddamn agreement," said Hargrove. "Nobody's gonna tell us that a woman can't do the job."

So she bought a bottle of Crown Royal to take to the local radio station and spoke to an announcer who conveyed her message on air. She said she was surprised given how many women bought cars that the dealership was refusing to deal with a woman union negotiator. "The old man got a plane back from Florida, and we got a deal."

PC World in Toronto was a company that hired almost all immigrants, mainly Black workers:

> They had great disdain for me at the bargaining table because I was a woman, and they locked us out, [meaning that the employer locked the workplace rather than the workers going on strike]. In twenty-seven years of being a staff rep, I only had two work stoppages, and both of them were lockouts.
>
> I went to Buzz [Hargrove] and said, it seems like we got a problem, we're gonna take over the plant. He said. "Okay." I don't think he really thought we were gonna take over.

They did, led by Lesperance. They locked the doors to make sure no one could get in. "A lot of CAW people showed up in solidarity, and we surrounded that building with over two hundred people for the whole time. They brought the police in, many on horseback, which was very intimidating for those outside."

This was during the Mike Harris government, and the lockout and occupation generated a lot of bad publicity for the company and the government. Eventually they got a deal. Lesperance was taken in by the police but was not charged. "We got increases. And the guys went back to work, and they were really happy. But it took a long time."

Lesperance was also assigned to work with CAW members at Union Station in Toronto, the country's largest train station. She recalls taking on Union Station management to get equal pay for women doing maintenance there. They were paid a dollar less because of a classification differential that supposed they weren't strong enough to use the floor polisher that was no longer used. Management laughed her off until she lined up a reporter to break the story in the *Toronto Star*, and they quickly agreed to equal pay. "At the next local union meeting all the women came in with bread and roses, saying they were so happy to get that money."

Lesperance was assigned to work part-time with women's programs when Nash was taking on more collective bargaining.

Lesperance remembers going to Newfoundland to assist women who were getting asthma from their work in the fish plants—but their real challenge was spousal abuse. The issue only came out because of a class she was leading, where women spoke of the abuse they faced in the dinghies. She understood how big an issue it was.

She loved the women activists program at Port Elgin. "It was wonderful, because people came out and spoke about their issues and about how to stand up for themselves. I saw a lot more women become active in the union, and not being afraid to stand up at union meetings and say this is wrong."

After those women's programs she got a lot of follow up from women who wanted the program in their local or wanted help to solve issues related to women. It made a tremendous difference.

When the union moved Lesperance's assignment out of rail, the members protested and wanted her back. She knew then that they appreciated her and that she had done a good job.

Marilynne Lesperance also served as the CAW staff union president negotiating with the top leadership of the union for the staff. "I must have been pretty naive but it worked out okay."

As the CAW merged with more unions, more women became members. There were miners, marine workers, and manufacturing groups that were mainly men. But there were now also thousands of retail workers at supermarkets, more airline workers, and health care workers, large bargaining units of mostly women, some of which were headed by women as workplace and local union leaders.

Diane Hollingshead: This Bargaining Session Is Getting Disrespectful

Diane Hollingshead joined Air Canada in Edmonton in 1979. Before long she was elected to the position of district chairperson, the union rep responsible for her workplace. Then out of the blue in 1984, she got a call asking her to join the Air Canada bargaining committee. Even though the membership was about 80 per cent women, she would be the first and only woman on the committee.

All the vice presidents and the board of directors, the presidents, and the servicing staff reps were men.

There was already a man from the same region Hollingshead represented on the bargaining committee, "So I looked like the token woman. Someone suggested we better put a woman on the bargaining committee." But she was happy to learn more about the union and to get out of the reservation office, answering phones all day was tedious, so she accepted.

That bargaining session beginning in 1984 was probably one of the most difficult the union had with Air Canada. It took eighteen months of bargaining and a three-week strike in May 1985. CALEA was also beginning a merger with CAW, and Bob White helped get the agreement. It was a successful first strike, and "I guess that's probably one of my strengths and one of my proudest moments is that we ended up opposing all the company's concessions." Hollingshead gained acceptance from the other bargaining committee members. And her local president, Cheryl Kryzaniwsky, was so supportive as an ally that she could run ideas past her. (See chapter 3 for the Air Canada and CALEA story and chapter 4 for more about Cheryl Kryzaniwsky.)

Diane Hollingshead speaking at CAW council. Photo: CAW.

> After that, I was hooked. I was not gonna go back and answer a telephone in a reservation office, because it was too boring. It really opened my eyes, being the only female on the bargaining committee with Air Canada, all the difficulties we were having with the business reps and the male board. That's what I guess really got me involved to be on the bargaining committee.

After the merger, with a new union structure, Hollingshead ran for the position of vice president of the pacific region for her local, which spanned across Canada. She held that position from 1985 until 1998. She attended the union's paid education leave program in 1988 and loved it. Then she took on the position of chair of the CAW council women's committee and was also very involved in women's programs in the union. She says the union's women's programs were fundamental. "That was the light at the end of the tunnel where you were able to really get together as women."

Then one day she got a call from Buzz Hargrove who told her that the only national staff rep in the region was transferring to BC.

"So he said, 'I want you to take the staff job.'"

Hollingshead said "No."

He seemed to not understand.

Finally, she said, "I need time to think about it. It's not something I was even looking at. It's probably something I'm not qualified for." Then she started thinking, well, if that previous rep could do it "Give me some time to think about it." She hung up.

The call came again thirty seconds later.

Hargrove said, "Diane, the fax is gone. You're now the staff rep."

"That was it. No discussion, no meeting, nothing. Within five minutes you were the staff rep. He probably couldn't imagine anybody would turn him down, and I don't know if anyone ever had. A couple of guys were upset that she was hired instead of them. But she says they would not have been qualified."

Diane Hollingshead was appointed to staff on April 12,1998. The guy she replaced had flown off to BC. She walked into the tiny office in the Alberta Federation of Labour building and saw "Mess, paper everywhere. Nothing found, no binders, no books, nothing." The CAW was in a dispute with the central labour bodies so she was instructed to leave that office, find another place, and in the meantime to work from home:

> I spent months with boxes and boxes and boxes of paper. I didn't even know the bargaining committees. I would cover the whole living room floor every day, every night. If I found a piece of paper for Loomis or DHL, it went in this pile. If this was a piece of paper for Porter Trucking, it went in this pile. And so I went through all the airlines and trucking. I went to couriers. I went to Engine Rebuilders. I went to the laundry. I went to hospitality, Coca Cola, Molson's. I did all this quickly, trying to understand. I basically started from scratch. None of them had clear collective agreements. It was a nightmare and that's what I spent probably my first four or five months doing. I hired an outdoor storage locker in Alberta, minus forty degrees, right, and I had things put in, my husband put in some shelves, and I finally got boxes, and I would label them, and then binders for the bargaining session, and that was my office. I would go there and pick up these plastic binders and you open them. They creak and they break. I mean, it's plastic. It's minus forty! That was where I had to store everything and then just work out of home until we got an office, and I got a part-time secretary, and then it was lovely.

My goal at that point, as a rep, was that I have to get out and meet the leadership. I put a letter out to all the leadership as well and even trying to find contacts of the different leadership. I phoned, and I met with every single local as soon as I could introduce myself. I tried to meet their executive. I got backlash from some bargaining committees in the first round of bargaining. But I worked hard to make progress for the members.

"I felt very alone as a woman," she says. "The majority of these groups were male. They were owner-operators or in manufacturing, or trucking."

She worked alone in her office with a part-time support staff person, another woman. Every so often something would happen that made them feel unsafe, and isolated. She reached out to some women in the BC office for support from time to time. "I had to get through this because I was going crazy."

> I just put my head down, and I rewrote every single collective agreement. I cleaned up those agreements. I'm really proud that when I left, people had a bound copy of a collective agreement. The membership actually had a book, and it was easy to read, and there was an index, and they could find working conditions and harassment language. I pushed like crazy to get same-sex language in there and toward the end, joint harassment policies. We got that into a couple of collective agreements. And that was the only thing, I mean, Alberta is Alberta. There was always this promise, so we'll get you another rep. We'll get you another rep right. But that that never happened. And even if it had, who would it have been?

Hollingshead really appreciated regional programs so that women didn't have to fly to Toronto to get to Port Elgin, Ontario:

> It was the best thing we ever did when they did some regional educational so that you could get some women just to fly to Vancouver for an educational, whereas their local union would not want to pay the greater cost to send them to a Canadian Labour Congress or a CAW course in Ontario. You develop really good close ties, and those women felt strong when they left, they felt powerful, and then it was really good to go back and work with them and push them and talk to the leadership, saying, "You know what, it's time you put this person on the committee." There wasn't enough of them by any means. There wasn't enough of them being accessible for women.

The union introduced courses on collective bargaining for women and public speaking for women so that she could encourage locals to send women to learn:

> One of the most important things in keeping my spirit up was having those connections, just meeting new people, other women, and some were from other unions. You could pick up a phone later on and have those conversations. So, I don't think there was enough women. They seemed to dwindle a bit.

Eventually she was able to get more women involved in those local unions and some even made it on to bargaining committees.

"Some of the biggest sexism was from company people. 'It's okay, honey. You don't need to worry about this, dear.'" One time Hollingshead was bargaining with a hotel and while she was prepared to let small things go, she finally called a break and they adjourned for the day.

> "I think we just need to adjourn right now."
>
> "What do you mean?" said the company person.
>
> I said. "No, this bargaining session is getting a bit disrespectful, and I think everybody needs to take a break. I'll give you a call."
>
> And then I had a private call with the individual. I wasn't gonna take him on in front of my committee. I had that private phone call with them, and I said, "You know, this isn't how I'm going to be treated, and none of my bargaining committee members are going to be treated like this. You're treating such and such just because she's a woman. So we can either take a really long break, or we can agree to get back tomorrow." And he changed.

But toward the end there was respect she says:

> Some of them would call me way later, looking for my help, wanting to know what to do with this harassment. Could I come in, and could we work together on this sort of thing, and they would call and ask for assistance. On what does this language really mean to you? That sort of thing? So it was good.

The key, says Diane Hollingshead, was to develop respect right from the beginning.

Anne Davidson: Negotiating from Naive to Experience

Anne Davidson joined CP Air in the 1970s, moving from a non-union job to a job in reservations that had union representation. She got elected as a union representative but later transferred temporarily to the airport. Back in reservations she again became a union rep and then moved up in the local union.

She was elected to a bargaining committee of seven men and was a regional representative at the Brotherhood of Railway and Airline Clerks. At that time, most of the workers in the reservations office where she worked were women and the airport workers were mostly men. She remembers having tough fights to get the union to provide childcare for union meetings.

She found union work stimulating and interesting. She quickly learned how the union dealt with management and felt that she could do that work. During the airline deregulation turmoil in the 1980s and after, their company became Canadian Airlines. Their union, the Transportation and Communications Union (TCU-Canada), merged their 3,500 members with the CAW in 1990. For company mergers they pressed for equality during mergers so that no workers at a carrier were disadvantaged.

"When you have women involved you encourage other women to get involved. We took advantage of the Canadian Labour Congress education courses in BC and we learned a lot about union principles."

Cutthroat airline competition had destroyed several airlines. Canadian Airlines, the second-largest commercial carrier in Canada, was in financial trouble. They invited Buzz Hargrove, Davidson, and a couple of the staff, including Peggy Nash, to a dinner meeting at the Sutton Place hotel in Toronto. In a private dining room, the then-CEO Kevin Benson, laid out his restructuring plan. He said that he needed a 10 per cent pay cut from the workers along with some other changes or the company was not going to survive.

Buzz laid into him: That was "never going to fucking happen," Davidson says, remembering with a smile, that she thought "Oh no, we're not even going to get dinner!"

When they finished their meeting, it was clear the company was determined to extract concessions. Davidson says,

> We came out of there, and I remember Peggy and Buzz, and Buzz putting his arm around me, saying "it's gonna be okay, don't worry."

> And I was naive enough to think it would be okay. But what I saw there was the strength of our union. When you're in that kind of crisis, it's like everybody in the national gets involved and is there behind you.

They quickly scheduled meetings, and Hargrove, Davidson, Jim Stanford, and Nash made presentations about how it made no sense to give concessions to the company who would then just use that money to cut fares to compete with Air Canada in a bid to drive down their market share. The union took that presentation to membership meetings across the country. Members were terrified that they were going to lose their jobs. There were no guarantees, but the leadership believed that the company was using that fear as a bargaining tactic to extract concessions.

> There was a meeting in Vancouver with the machinists' union (IAM) at the Richmond Inn. Our bargaining committee walked into the room with the IAM bargaining committee, headed by Dave Ritchie, the Canadian director of the union, and joined by

Anne Davidson at the centre of a media scrum during Canadian Airlines negotiations. Photo: CAW.

> Bob Rae. It was clear that Rae [who had recently been defeated as NDP premier in Ontario] was there to help the union negotiate their concessions.

Davidson also recalls Ritchie saying "Well, if you're not gonna make a decision, get the fuck out of here."

So much of this struggle was being fought in the media, and the union leaders knew they had to get their side out there as widely as possible. They would go out to brief the media frequently. Davidson had just been elected president and she says,

> I knew I could handle the employer, and the union reps, but the only thing that worried me was dealing with media. It was the one thing I was worried about. And then we're in a crisis. I would stand behind Peggy or behind Buzz, and listen to what they were saying, it was really a good education for me. Then you get the speaking points. I ended up forced to do media interviews.

The pictures of Davidson surrounded by media in a scrum about the Canadian Airlines crisis sent a message to a lot of women who were nervous about doing media. They weren't used to doing media and it was encouraging.

What was also striking about this struggle was Davidson was local president, Sue Schevinska the service rep, Nash was assistant to the president, and a couple of other bargaining committee members were all women. The members stood up to the company, the media that was pressing for a deal, the other unions who had all capitulated, and the federal government. The union held their ground and eventually got the federal government to kick in some money to Canadian Airlines so that, in the end, the CAW members had to give a little, but far less than any of the other union members.

Davidson was exhausted but gave a barnburner of a speech at the CAW council that December: "And then I spoke at the council, and I remember Peggy saying 'Don't cry, don't cry,' but you know you become so involved in it. You're living it, you know, it's just you. Really. You were exhausted, too. You were. I mean, it was so much pressure."

Afterward, a journalist told her that he remembered her being shy and quiet at the beginning, "but you're not so shy anymore."

> We did end up having to negotiate something, 'cause we decided we're better to go and negotiate and put that out to our members rather than have the board or the government force us, and we negotiated a better deal than any of the unions. Our members gave a little bit, but for a short time, and it bounced back. The others weren't so lucky. So people were happy with that in the end.

Despite threats to ground the aircraft and shutdown the airline, they kept operating and competing with Air Canada until, a few years later, they merged with Air Canada to form an even larger national carrier.

Davidson recalls that period as stressful and exhausting, but the most difficult time was the Canadian Airlines merger with Air Canada and the struggle of seniority. Would the workers at the smaller carrier (Canadian) go to the bottom of the seniority list, or would they blend seniority? "It was the most unpleasant, because we were fighting within our own union," she says. "It got nasty."

In the end, the only fair solution was to give everyone their full seniority, but it was a struggle to get there. Davidson and many other members had been through so many mergers—Pacific Western, Transair, Nordair, EPA, and so on. They knew the only fair way was to recognize the full seniority of each worker and not penalize them for companies driving each other out of business. "So I've had a lot of experience with groups that are divided as the new combined local bargaining committee was." But over time they learned to work together.

Davidson was then elected president of the new larger airline local union, now called Local 2002, the year of the merger. Leslie Dias from the Air Canada group was elected secretary treasurer.

Davidson served on the national executive board, preceded by Roxie Baker, Cheryl Kryzaniwsky, Denise Kellahan, and Julie White:

> When I did go on the board, it was quite intimidating at first, but it was good to have people that I knew like Julie and that I could talk to and ask questions, and 'cause you're quite isolated out in BC. I don't know everything that's going on in Ontario. I didn't know the structure of it at all. I kept quiet on some things because being from BC, I just didn't know all the background.

She says the auto guys dominated but she also got issues on the agenda. Davidson adds: "Well, I think the women's programs were excellent. I did attend those. I loved the women's conference; that was a real highlight. We tried as much as possible in our local to send people to that to really let people have opportunities." Women that they sent to courses from local or from BC, got involved. "I think the equity programs are really important. If people don't push for it, change doesn't happen."

Carla Bryden: Moving Up and Staying Rooted

Carla Bryden worked at the Credit Union in Antigonish, Nova Scotia. The sister of one of the women that she was working with worked at the Bank of Commerce that had a union. Her name was Marion MacDonald and they became good friends. MacDonald was a strong feminist, and while Bryden hadn't really thought about feminism, she learned a lot from her friend about sexism and feminism. "It was because of her strength that I was able to mobilize my co-workers to join the union," says Bryden.

They became what is called a direct charter to the Canadian Labour Congress. They were certified as a bargaining unit, but did not have a home union. The CLC assisted them with bargaining and servicing their members.[2]

In spite of her interest in feminism, when they first unionized, they right away elected a man to chair their bargaining unit of forty-five workers, 90 per cent of whom were women. "We relinquished our power and sent it off to a male to represent us. When I look back on that," she says, "I think it was part of my own insecurity and my own thinking. He, of course, would be able to do the job better than us."

That representation didn't work out well. Then with the encouragement of her friend MacDonald and the CLC rep who worked with their group, she began assisting co-workers with their problems and eventually was elected to represent them. She got a lot of push back from management. She thought about quitting but stuck it out.

Bryden wanted her small group of workers to succeed, and when she began looking for a larger union to affiliate with, she felt the CAW was the best fit. She and her members started showing up at CAW events to try and get themselves recognized. But they were such a small group in a difficult sector that they weren't taken seriously. Bryden remembers Bob White telling her that he would like to take the bank workers, but he wanted all of them across the country, in order to be able to make some gains, because one thing the banks had was lots of money to fight unionization.

In 1993, when they were still with CLC, Bryden led a strike at the Credit Union. The bank was creating more part-time jobs without benefits. It was the erosion of full-time jobs and benefits that provoked the strike that lasted more than six weeks. They got thirty dollars a week in strike pay from the CLC, but survived because before the strike they took out loans from the Credit Union that hadn't anticipated the job action:

> Yeah, in a small little town, you can imagine the community. But what happened was we got a tremendous amount of support from the provincial federation of labour, and from different unions across the province. We did get lots of donations from other unions like Nova Scotia Government Employees Union. I remember they gave us a lot of money to help us through the strike. And the mine workers in Cape Breton. Different unions came out on the picket line.

Halfway through the strike, management called them back to the bargaining table. The lawyer for the Credit Union, Bryden says, has since been discredited:

> He was always making sexual remarks to me, and I despised him with everything that was in me, because not only was he sexist, but he also would take the last dollar out of a worker's pocket. It didn't matter to him. He was there to support the employer

> and the employer only. They just offered the same bullshit. And they didn't think that a bunch of women were gonna go back out on strike.

The membership voted their offer down.

The Credit Union wanted that strike settled because the community was turning on them. The union held a big public meeting, so they could present the tentative agreement to the membership, and "we got standing ovations and support," she says. "So the lawyer was not happy at the end of the day, but we were."

Maybe it was their persistence at wanting to join the CAW, maybe it was about their tenacity during the strike, but in 1994 they finally got the okay to join the bigger union. Bryden was elated. She went to larger meetings and began to take more courses and eventually began instructing education courses, which she loved.

"But things happened in the union that took the shine out of the whole thing," she says. "It didn't matter how active you were or how hard you worked. It was all so political. You'd see all these male reps getting hired."

She wanted to be a national rep and devote her life to the union.

> I wasn't doing all that activism to get a job, but I just knew that I wanted to do that full-time. It was frustrating to watch reps get hired that didn't have a clue. They were poor at representing workers. But they were good drinking buddies [with the area director] and others. I just never clicked, ever, with the director.

Bryden stuck it out because she never liked injustice. What sustained her was the membership support in her workplace and in the broader local union that included other workplaces:

> I remember when I decided to run to become president of the local. I was on the executive of the local. I remember an assistant to the national president saying to me, "You'll never win that election." I said, "Just watch me." So, the day I won the election overwhelmingly, I called him. I said, "Guess who's president of Local 2107?" "Oh, congratulations!" he said. "I didn't think you could do it."

> I didn't take the membership for granted when we were running. I know it's a small little local in Nova Scotia. But I went to every workplace. I stood outside the workplace. I made up pamphlets. I talked to people and a lot of those units were predominantly women and I had a lot of support.

Once elected, Bryden faced pushback from the financial secretary of the local union who had supported her opponent. For the next election she encouraged a woman that she knew she could work with to run for that position, and she was also successful. Her time as president was easier after that.

She felt that being involved in the women's programs of the union was crucial in helping name experiences in her life:

> If it wasn't for those women's programs there would have been no accountability in CAW. They would have just continued doing what they were doing. It was only by the women's programs that gave me the confidence and the strength to keep going. And it confirmed for me what I sort of already knew but couldn't name.
>
> And it was that camaraderie of all the other women, and hearing their stories and going through the same thing that I went through, right? That helped me so much. Learning to fight back, it gives you the strength. As women, we always underestimate what we can do. I needed these programs to tell me that I could do just as well as men or better. For me having the camaraderie of other women confirmed it, and they gave me strength.

Bryden eventually did become a national staff representative but wanted more independence in that role. "I don't think we get any recognition for knowing what we're doing. That used to frustrate me so much at the bargaining table. I needed to be able to push that little bit further, to get what we needed to get for the membership."

She remembers one round of bargaining where she knew she could get more from the employer but the area director went behind her back and settled with the employer for what she believed was an inferior agreement. "I'll never forgive him for that for as long as

I live. There's nothing worse as a national rep. They wouldn't have done that to a male national rep, but they did it to me."

She found that she was isolated when she openly supported Carol Phillips, running for secretary treasurer:

> It's very difficult sometimes to stick to your principles. But you've got to, because it eats away at you if you don't. And it did me, it ate at me. I'll never forget sitting at the table when Carol went up to speak [to the national staff]. "You are the most amazing woman I've ever met in my life," I thought. The strength she had was friggin amazing.

But she also remembers being advised by a national officer even before she was on the staff of the union: "You better pick your friends, and not to be hanging around with certain women." They were all the women that she respected most.

She retired early, feeling burnt out and discouraged that she couldn't do what she wanted for the members. Service reps in the union carry a massive burden of workload and often juggle multiple rounds of bargaining at once in addition to all their other work. Bryden felt, "I was always being cut off at the knees, and being honest with the members, I just couldn't do it anymore. It was terrible because I love the union and I really didn't want to go. But I knew for my health I had to. It just wears you down."

Carla Bryden remembers getting calls from one of the most senior women in the union insisting that she wrap up bargaining for a small unit that she knew needed more time.

> Her calling me giving me shit over that tiny little unit, just makes me sick. She should have been supportive and knew what was going on. I had done most all the other bargaining, and to pick on this one little thing. . . . So I knew that was another sign. That's how it feels, like you feel like you're being monitored and watched.
>
> Still, to this day I would totally believe in the union. I just don't believe in all that other bullshit, and I think the union can do so much.

Diversity Rising

The decade of the 1990s had started with the hope generated by the fall of the Berlin Wall, but also with the gut-wrenching focus on violence against women. The events of Dec 6, 1989, sparked a renewed focus on gender-based violence that laid the groundwork for so many initiatives that improved the lives of women. The union rose to the challenge, responded to women's demands and began to further transform itself.

The CAW had, mostly through mergers, extended its representation into many new sectors and its membership was becoming diverse. Still, it was a male-dominated union with a macho culture. But as it had in decades before, led by feminists in the union, it would join with the broader women's movement to press for progressive legal and social change. It would also face pressure internally to increase the space for women and their issues. This pressure would lead to constitutional changes in the union, and significant and innovative gender equity gains in collective bargaining.

At a time when the union faced massive challenges in layoffs, plant closures, work reorganization, and technological change, the CAW fought to defend its members, expand its reach in the Canadian economy, and pioneer significant changes to build solidarity based on its growing diversity.

PART II

CAW Women Diversifying Their Union

Chapter Six

Contradictory Progress, 2000–2014

Economic Woes, Job Losses

By the end of the 1990s, anti-globalization protests were heating up. Wherever the World Trade Organization and other similar organizations met, there were mobilizations that drew thousands of protesters. They were met with large numbers of police and military.

The effectiveness of anti-globalization initiatives to take the focus away from the official talks between governments and to place it instead on poverty, job loss, and the erosion of social programs came to a head in Seattle. Activists were hopeful that they could pressure governments to go in a progressive direction.

The Battle of Seattle in 1999 saw a huge clash of activists from NGOs, labour, and others joining together to launch a massive pushback against trade liberalization and public sector cutbacks. The Third Summit of the Americas in Québec City in April 2001 was met with huge protests under a cloud of tear gas.

Then everything seemed to change. The attacks by Al Qaeda against the United States on September 11, 2001, sparked a major US-led coalition invasion of Afghanistan that lasted twenty years and initiated the global war on terrorism. Security and military concerns took priority. Right-wing talk radio exploded, and Islamophobia was on the rise. An angrier tone began to emerge. Some things seemed to change in the union as well, but it was contradictory. The national leadership seemed more cautious; the political landscape seemed to narrow. The task force on working-class politics in the CAW seemed to lead members away from voting for the NDP with greater support for the Liberals to oppose Conservatives.

Contradicting those trends, organizing by women and other underrepresented groups seemed to open more opportunities. As the numbers of CAW members in traditional manufacturing continued to decline, the union continued to boost its membership numbers mainly through mergers. While in line with the vision of former President Bob White to build a larger Canadian-based union movement, mergers then also helped stem the loss of other jobs.

As during World War II, offering to address women's concerns in the union was an enticement for women to join the union. Only this time around, the union's woman's programs were making great strides. Men still dominated leadership positions, however. Power sharing was a tougher nut to crack.

Long-standing frictions with the rest of the labour movement, going back decades, exploded when the CAW tried to win over members of the Service Employees International Union (SEIU). This move was bitterly opposed by SEIU's top leaders and the CAW was consequently ejected from the Canadian Labour Congress on July 1, 2000.

Manufacturing jobs in Canada fell by over 500,000 positions between 2003 and 2009, according to the Future Skills Centre. They further attribute 300,000 of the net decline occurring before the Great Recession of 2008–2009 with little job growth since in the sector.[1]

The impact on the auto industry was severe; companies were at risk of bankruptcy and the potential for job loss was massive. The Obama government in the United States provided huge bailouts to the auto sector, and Canada under Stephen Harper followed suit. In exchange for the bailouts and presumably jobs, governments pressured unions for concessions. Union leaders focused on job security and in exchange gave concessions to the companies. This was a painful period in the CAW where retaining jobs was essential but came at a very high price. The union struggled.

Solidarity in Diversity Roadmap: Gains for Women

Alongside this new cautious, defensive position, the women in the union nevertheless continued to make significant progress on equity issues. From the anti-violence and employment equity measures pushed by women for the 1991 constitutional convention, to the calls for a long-gun registry, to renewed calls to increase the number of women on staff, the union was in the forefront on key initiatives. The key policy document *Solidarity in Diversity* had laid out a roadmap for greater inclusivity and a changing culture. With unrelenting pressure from women, people of colour, Indigenous, and 2SLGBTQ+ groups there were significant gains.

The CAW was mainly focused on the challenges of trying to save jobs, and Hargrove continued to lead mergers with other unions and made building the union a priority. Two of the largest groups of new members in this period to join were the Retail, Wholesale and Department Store Union (RWSDU) in 1999 and the bitter organizing campaign of members to move from the Service Employees' International Union (SEIU) in 2000. These two unions in relatively new sectors for the CAW, would bring in thousands of new members, a large number of them women, thereby continuing to change the face of the union.

Christine Connor from the RWSDU was the president of what became the largest CAW local union, overtaking the dwindling membership of the giant auto local unions. Connor's membership, however, included a large number of part-time and lower paid workers. When it merged with CAW, the RWSDU had 23,000 members, of which 38 per cent were women. "There was a lot of excitement among members to be joining this much bigger union, one that had many more resources to help the members," says Connor. "We especially appreciated the education programs and support in collective bargaining."

Nancy McMurphy was the president of a large former SEIU local union for twenty years. The CAW won the support of approximately fifteen thousand SEIU members in 2000, 80 to 85 per cent of them women. In 2001 McMurphy was elected as the first women president. McMurphy remembers, "For many of us, while we were concerned about the fit with the CAW, we were desperate for representation by a Canadian union as opposed to the international."

She says many questioned the fit of health care workers in an auto workers' union, but they soon realized the support they would gain. Because the SEIU women had been dominated by male leadership for many years, she says, they appreciated having a voice with a dedicated women's department that could relate to the challenges women faced. "That brought a lot more engagement from members than we had previously seen."

Julie White: Living a Different Dream

Julie White started working for 3M in London, Ontario, right out of high school, at the age of nineteen. She knew it was a unionized plant but didn't really know much about unions at the time. A lot of other young people worked there, some who she knew. It was a small workforce of 300 people and most everyone knew everyone else. It was a friendly atmosphere. "I had a little red sports car, and I was living the dream, life was good."

Not long after she was hired, the workers went on strike, the first strike ever at 3M. "We were just a bunch of feisty young kids on the picket line. Most of us didn't have the financial responsibilities that workers with children and families had, so we just had a lot of fun." It was during those long days on the picket line during an eight-week strike that she began to learn about the union. Once the strike ended, she decided to attend a union meeting at her local. It was 1974.

White's father was in the military, and she'd grown up on a military base. She had a somewhat stable family, but she remembers family violence in the neighbourhood and the chaos that it would produce. She saw it often, but no one ever spoke about it the next day. It was considered a family issue.

She also remembers when she was about thirteen years old, her mother coming home one day from her job as a waitress in just her full-length slip, under her trench coat. She wondered why she was home so early.

She recalls her mom telling her that her boss was always touching her, and she couldn't take it anymore; it wasn't part of her job. He was the boss so there was no one to make a complaint to. So she just quit, took off her uniform, and threw it at him as she walked out.

White said that always stuck in her mind. "I thought about how women had some pretty awful experiences—at home and at work—and those memories stayed with me when I began to get involved in the union." She credits these experiences for shaping her commitment to fighting for women's rights.

When White realized there were issues about the wage rates for women in her plant, who were paid on a lower scale than the men, she understood the unfairness. White worked on a small assembly line, but felt she worked as hard as the men. There was also sexism and co-worker harassment in the plant and, in general, the environment could be toxic. Women couldn't use their seniority to post into certain areas of the plant because they were deemed areas only men could work in, which meant women were laid off out of seniority.

"They said it was too heavy and too dirty for women, but if it was too heavy and too dirty for me, it was too heavy and dirty for the guys, So that's where I started to challenge." White posted for one of those jobs and was successful with the help of her union to be the first woman to be awarded the job:

> The work wasn't bad, but the environment was. The guys didn't want me there. Many had less seniority than I did so when a lay off came, women could now exercise their seniority rights over the men. It was tough at times. They wouldn't help me with anything but they would help each other. They just watched as I struggled to learn the job. I thought, "Fuck you, I'm going to do this." And I did.

That job was no harder than the jobs that women were doing out on the line. In fact, in many ways it was much easier but there was a huge difference in wages between the jobs, something she knew she wanted to change.

This meant getting involved further. So in 1985, White was offered the opportunity to attend a four-week paid education (PEL) course in Port Elgin:

> I remember that because I was a single mom and they had no childcare at that time, and I had a four-year-old son. My friend at work, Jo Ann, said to me, "Julie, let me watch Derek." So for four weeks, I would drop off Derek on Sunday night and pick

> him up Friday afternoon. I couldn't have attended PEL without Jo Ann, and I reflect at times if this would have set me on a different path in my working career.

Upon her return, White ran and was elected as the first woman on the bargaining and in-plant committee in 1986 and, ironically, was elected in the same area that women had been banned from working in earlier. The area was predominantly men where she won her election, but the outcome was close.

Even after the election, times were tough. Many men did not want a woman representing them, so lots of nasty things followed. "I remember doing my rounds in the morning and there on the bulletin board was a white cloth dabbed with red marker with a note that said 'Julie is on the rag today.'" It was difficult at times, but she just took it down and went about her day:

> There was one guy in the plant who was particularly nasty with me during the election. And guess who I had to represent in the first grievance I brought against the company? But after I won that grievance for him, he became an important ally for me, even challenging some of the sexist comments from men in the area.

Her long-time plant chairperson of the bargaining committee, named Jim, could be a "crusty guy at times," but he supported her and also became her ally. "He really knew the collective agreement back to front. Looking back, I might have stepped away from the union if it hadn't been for him. He helped me through some of those rough patches in the early days and educated me on the collective agreement."

During White's first set of bargaining talks, she knew she wanted to level the playing field when it came to wage rates between women and men; she understood the unfairness. One of the key bargaining demands was to negotiate a single production rate and to move women's wages up to that higher rate, which they got in the end:

> That was my way of settling pay equity early. We took all the lower paying classifications that women were in and moved

> them up to the highest rate in the plant where men worked, and at the same time maintaining classifications. Our members still used their seniority to get the job they wanted, but women got a huge wage increase in addition to the annual increase, something that was long overdue.

When she first got involved as an activist in the local union, childcare wasn't offered, and she was a single parent:

> I used to take my son Derek to general membership meetings. Before the meeting started, I would take him downstairs where our local had a bar. He would get a bag of chips and a Mountain Dew and then sit at the back of the meeting with his colouring books. It was difficult; most of the meetings were held after supper so it meant bringing him with me to meetings that would last for more than a few hours. It didn't win me parent-of-the-year award.

It was at those meetings that White learned about opportunities for involvement on local union committees including the women's and political action committees. As a member of the women's committee, she learned about CAW women's conferences where she connected with other new young activists looking to get involved. A whole new world was opening to her where she connected with some kick-ass feminist leaders who were willing to bring her along and teach her the ropes.

White's role model at Local 27 was Beulah Harrison, out of the Northern Electric unit in London. "She was a mentor to me. I don't know if I ever told her that, but I used to watch her at general membership meetings. She was always so prepared, effective, and always challenging." There were not a lot of women at the membership meetings. Most of the workplaces were manufacturing plants where most workers were men. Harrison was chair of the women's committee, and she encouraged the young women to get up and speak or to put a motion on the floor of the meeting.

Julie White remembers one particular frustration:

> The guys always supported the recreation committee. It drove

> me nuts. They gave money to hockey and golf tournaments, but there was never any money left over to give to women's shelters in our communities. It wasn't a priority for them. The women's committee took it on, and eventually the guys got it. They either supported the motion, or we'd stack the next meeting with more women, so they learned pretty early on that it was important to support our motions. We taught them pretty good, I think.

Local 27 had no shortage of women leaders. Edith Johnson, the first person responsible for women's issues on the UAW-Canada staff, was from her plant and had been the first woman financial secretary of the local union (see chapter 1). After years as a committee person, White ran in 1996 and would become the second woman to hold the position of financial secretary at the local union. Although they had never crossed paths, Julie knew she was standing on Edith's shoulders.

Julie White decided to run for Local 27 president in 1999. There were two caucuses, and after the election the local union executive was split between the two. She had to learn quickly to work across those differences on behalf of the membership. "I grew up in a military base, and it could be quite difficult at times. I learned to pull up my socks, get in there, and get the job done."

The frosty relationships eventually melted, and the leadership learned to work together. White was struck by the impact her election as Local 27 president had on women in the union. She became aware that women were watching the outcome when Cathy Austin from Local 88 called to congratulate her. "I remember Sister Austin telling me she had a women's committee meeting after my election, and it was packed. Sisters were encouraged that a large local with a GM component just elected their first women president." Not long after, Austin would go on to be elected as the first women president of an auto assembly plant in the CAW. It was seen by many as another barrier in the patriarchy smashed.

Thinking back to those days, White is struck by how far the union has come. She is acutely aware of how the struggles both in the workplace and in the community led to the current structures in the union, driven forward by sisters and activists who came before her, ultimately becoming crucial resources for women in the union:

> You really see the impact of progressive structural gains, such as the women's department, women's committees, and conferences. Throughout my career, whether it was in the workplace, the local, or at the national union level, relationships I built with women became so important to me, and especially when times got tough as they often do when you're in a leadership position. It was those sisters that helped me through the rough patches.

White also recognizes the role of male allies, such as her plant chairperson, Jim, but also her national rep Al Seymour, who had supported the Fleck women through their strike and helped them achieve a first agreement:

> He was a guy that got it. He understood. And when we fought for same-sex spousal pension and benefits at 3M, Al was the guy that was right beside me. We shut down bargaining for two days, waiting for the company to agree and they finally did. Those were exciting times to be involved in the union.

In 2001, Hargrove named Julie White to head up the union's women's programs. Peggy Nash had pushed for an increased role in collective bargaining and felt that she needed to make that her priority. Simultaneously Nash—along with Julie White, Carol Phillips, Cheryl Kryzaniwsky, Anne Davidson, and others—argued that the union needed a full-time dedicated women's director, rather than Nash doing those programs off the side of her desk. White was the perfect choice as a respected leader in the union, president of her large local, and a national executive board member. Most importantly she was a feminist who strongly supported and was involved in the union's women's programs.

Julie White looks back with pride at the work of the women's department and believes the women's advocate program is one of the best programs in the union. In the women's advocate training program, she encouraged the advocates to see the bigger picture when they were helping others. She helped them understand the broader societal changes that were needed, such as gun control, better access to shelters and transitional housing, and childcare, as well as higher wages and pay equity. These issues went beyond the workplace and required political engagement.

One moment White recalls was when a brother stood up at a convention to thank his union for negotiating the women's advocate program. His daughter was in a violent relationship and the women's advocate helped his daughter find out about community resources. "I think it was a catalyst for men to think about the program and how it could help a family member," says White. "We spoke about the program at every major union meeting."

She also cites the example of a woman in Atlantic Canada who wanted to move to get away from a violent relationship. She moved across the country, and in every community the union was able to link her with a women's advocate if needed.

Gun Control

One highlight for White came in 2009, when a very determined group of women's advocates, along with local union leaders and feminist activists worked together to help win a vote in parliament to stop a Conservative minority government from destroying the national long-gun registry. The union knew the importance of the registry, which had been a key demand stemming from the Montreal Massacre. The union worked closely with the Coalition for Gun Control and the Canadian Labour Congress to generate support for the registry and to lobby MPs to oppose the bill.

The key focus of their lobbying was the NDP because some of their rural MPs were on the other side of the issue. NDP leader Jack Layton was allowing his caucus a free vote. With the intense pressure that was put on enough NDP MPs to reverse their position along with the Liberals, the Conservative bill was blocked. White saw the importance of coalitions:

> For me the best win was the defeat of the Bill C 391 to kill the long-gun registry. We understood the importance of the registry in saving women's lives. We register our car. We register all kinds of things. Why couldn't we register long guns? And we knew that women were being murdered in their homes, and destroying the registry would only make it worse for women.
>
> It was important to reinforce our support for gun control.

> The registry was in place, and it was protecting women. With the leadership of the CLC women's committee along with the support of secretary treasurer Sister Barb Byers and the support of our national union, we joined with a coalition of labour unions, like-minded people in our communities, doctors, police, nurses, parents, and others to fight to save the long-gun registry, and we did. And our union played an integral role in the outcome.

Some in the labour coalition wanted to lobby Conservatives, which White insisted was a waste of time. She knew they needed to focus on the NDP MPs, the votes that they may be able to influence. Which they did. And in the end, they won by just two votes. White remembers, "It was an incredibly emotional moment, because we

Julie White marching on International Women's Day. Photo: CAW.

were there with the survivors, and with the families of the women that were murdered during the Montreal Massacre."

Unfortunately, it was an outcome that would be short-lived. In the election that followed, Conservative leader Stephen Harper went on to win a majority government. As he promised he would, with one stroke of his pen, he scrapped the long-gun registry.

White sees victories behind the loss:

> Nevertheless, the ability to mobilize our members to work with other labour unions and our community partners to delay the destruction of the registry saved lives and empowered supporters of gun control.
>
> An unexpected outcome in the gun-registry lobby was the connections it built among women activists across the country, who we could call on anytime, anywhere to protect or advance women's equality—eager young activists who now understood the power of their voice, the power of their actions. So when the Abortion Caravan rolled into cities and towns across the country, women and CAW activists were united and ready to protect a women's right to choose.
>
> You see, the women's department became more than one woman as the result of the women's conferences, programs, campaigns. It provided the tools and skills that resulted in a network of women who understood the power of political action. Kick-ass feminists who were ready to protect and advance equality for all women and leave a legacy of their own for new activists to follow.

When the Fleck women went on strike and second wave feminism took off, women in the UAW/CAW had frameworks they could build on. There were so many milestones—from Lorna Moses to Edith Johnson and others being appointed to the national staff, to Roxie Baker joining the national executive board, the equity document adopted in 1991, gains in collective bargaining such as the union's policy on sexual harassment, to the national campaigns for childcare, gun control, and reproductive choice, with many steps in between. The uniting and partnering with the broader women's movement in communities across the country was the key to the growth of the women's movement in the union. Even without a critical mass of women in the union, they were able to make progress.

The union's education programs, conferences, and leadership courses were pivotal in bringing women together to motivate them to greater involvement. Campaigns involving local union women offered them a sense of purpose, belonging, and building. The campaigns linked the women to the broader labour and women's movements in communities large and small across the country.

Union women learned about the resources and tremendous work in the community and that these issues are also union issues. Women from community organizations, such as women's shelters and childcare coalitions, learned about the power of unions and their ability to make concrete changes for their members and impact on the broader community. The success of those women united has been a driving force of women's success in Canada.

2SLGBTQ+ Rights

By the end of the twentieth century, there was more openness to the struggle for 2SLGBTQ+ rights. Activist Harvey Milk, the first openly gay politician, had been elected to office in 1978. Even though his life and political career was tragically cut short when he was assassinated, he was hugely popular, particularly in his home of San Francisco. NDP Member of Parliament Svend Robinson was the first openly gay Canadian politician who came out while in office. He was elected from 1979 to 2004. The Bath House Raids in Toronto in 1981 provoked a huge backlash and was a turning point in favour of 2SLGBTQ+ rights. In 2005 Canada legalized same-sex marriage. The world was changing.

In spite of a strong macho culture, especially in giant manufacturing workplaces, the CAW saw gender diversity rights as a human rights issue early on. At CAMI Automotive and Nortel (also know as Northern Electric and Northern Telecom), they negotiated same-sex benefits and pension provisions before the law allowed them. Julie White and her CAW Local 27 bargaining committee negotiated similar gains at 3M. As national staff rep Al Seymour says,

> We held them up in negotiations for two days. I remember that that was the last issue. They wouldn't put it in the collective agreement, so we got a separate letter of agreement. And it wasn't until the law was changed that then things started to move along because unions were negotiating it.
>
> But that we accomplished in bargaining. And we went to the membership, and when we presented that to the membership, there were still some guys out there that were being smart-ass about it. But we settled it in 1995.

Lisa Kelly: Rights Don't Just Belong to One Person

In 1990, while Bob White was still president of the CAW, he hired labour lawyer Lewis Gottheil to set up a legal department at the CAW. Gottheil brought one articling student with him, Lisa Kelly. "It was one of those weird circumstances of totally changing your life," she says. At age twenty-five, she was suddenly in the middle of this formidable union culture.

The legal department was set up on the top floor of the union's low-rise building in North York. As an open concept office, on the same floor as Bob White, Hargrove, and others, they would wander into her office to ask questions or just to chat, and she enjoyed the access to the leadership. "Bob White fostered this culture of openness to challenge. When faced with a challenge, he had principled instincts that he would always go back to and were almost always right."

White and others would ask her about human rights issues, and it was a learning experience for them. "Long before coming out, I was active on LGBTQ issues," she says. She was not only knowledgeable but she was an advocate, working for change.

She found that as a woman who looked very young, it was difficult at that time to gain credibility with some union locals. That, combined with the very long hours and gruelling workload, were a deterrent to some other women who started in the legal department but didn't remain. She says,

> There were a lot of barriers in the union to people who had child rearing responsibilities, and women were still the small minority. So that was still seen as "you wanna play with the boys, act like the boys." I still really internalized that message that you have to be unencumbered. You have to be devoted to the cause, and you need to work out whatever that home stuff is, because that's got nothing to do with the workplace, even though we're fighting for those rights for our members.

Kelly credits the strength of the allies:

> And it was putting issues of the equity agenda as working-class politics that I think really made that breakthrough. Then allowing the space for people to talk through and say, "Yeah, I actually do have a LGBT family member," and they realized they were working with people who were affected by these changes.

In the early 1990s the union was not going to wait for the law to change to ensure members got the benefits they should have been entitled to. They began bargaining LGBT rights with employers. They bargained benefits for same-sex partners at Nortel and CAMI Automotive in 1994.

About the same time, Julie White remembers negotiations with 3M:

> At the time, one of our members was being denied not just benefits, but pension benefits as well. The law at the time defined spouse as opposite sex. We took it to the bargaining table and were able to successfully bargain it after waiting for two days, because the head office for 3M was in St. Paul, Minnesota. So we actually got benefits, and we also got pensions, even though the law said the person had to be of the opposite sex, we got a silent letter on it. This means it is part of the collective agreement and would be respected, but wasn't formally printed in the agreement. In essence it was hidden. So 3M in Canada recognized it.

She adds with a smile, "I don't think St. Paul really ever understood what was done at our plant at 3M."

The union adopted a policy on "Gay, Lesbian, and Bisexual Rights" in 1997 at its constitutional convention. The union's national leadership played an important role in creating the space to expand members' rights. Kelly recalls a member of the national executive board, who was president of a very large auto parts local, took the mic at the next council meeting and said same-sex benefits were against his religion, and he was not going to bargain it. Kelly says, "Hargrove shot back, 'Well, if that's against your religion, then you need to step down as a negotiator. If you can't set that aside and negotiate the mandate of the union, if that's interfering with your job, you should step aside because this is your job.'"

> We made the case that the rights don't just belong to one person. That as a union we fight for working-class rights. And LGBT workers, who might not yet be in our workplaces or haven't come out yet or are part of that fight. I think that made space when people saw their leadership taking the mics and saying—This is what we're fighting for, this is what the issue is. This is the mandate of a trade union, to fight for working-class rights, to work for a different society and not just be fighting for individual responsive rights. Why would we let the employer deny someone their benefits or their rights?

Then others got up and spoke in favour of the policy of bargaining the benefits.

"This is how change happens," Kelly says. "This is the mandate, and the leadership is serious about it. And people share individual stories, so they humanize it."

Stephanie Johnstone: Excuse Me, Are You Gay?

Stephanie Johnstone worked for thirty years at the General Motors warehouse beginning in 1984. It was a workplace of about six hundred people, in Woodstock, Ontario. She got involved with the union by joining the women's committee and at the first meeting she said "Listen I'm a woman, but I'm also a lesbian." At the local union she joined the human rights committee.

She had been engaged to be married and called the wedding off two weeks before. "I just knew something didn't gel, and that was in 1968, and John was more like my best friend than a partner." Then about almost ten years later she ran into John again, and "nothing had materialized in my life." So they ended up getting together, and he's "my daughter's father."

But it was right after Johnstone's daughter was born that she came out, realizing what was missing in her life. She met somebody and they ended up together:

> It was that whole search thing of not knowing where you fit, where you sit in the world in relationship to everybody. The things they were doing or were interested in did not interest me. I'm a very political person. I like the deep conversations. I like exploring all those things. I had so many friends that didn't want to talk about politics, didn't want to talk about social issues, whereas to me they were a driving force within myself.

Getting active in the union opened so many doors for her. By the 1990s, there was a desire to set up area caucuses for LGBT members. Much of this organizing took place by word of mouth, with CAW members who knew other members who were gay, lesbian, and gender diverse. She was asked by the national union in the early 1990s to write some LGBT principles, something she had never done before, and they were adopted by the union.

Stephanie Johnstone addressed a conference in Port Elgin at the union's education centre. Getting up behind the podium at the front of the room was intimidating.

> I spent the whole night there trying to come up with some notes. I'd never spoken to a large group of people like that before in my life. But I did it. Some people were upset that I was gay and I was speaking to them. But the meeting came around.

The union decided to hold its first national LGBT conference in Port Elgin in 2000. Normally for a conference, a national call letter would be sent to all the local unions. However, there was fear of outing members who were not ready to come out about their sexuality. So the union decided to include allies. This meant someone could attend without risking themselves.

It worked. About 100 delegates gathered at the education centre in mid-April.

The conference was a tremendous boost for gender activism in the union. Soon the unions had pride delegations and floats in pride parades across the country. The union sent out CAW pride flags, pins, and posters. The first poster was a lovely and striking portrait of Local 4451 member Pam Diggs with her son.

The activism spread, and a few years later the Canadian Labour Congress held a Pride Conference. They were expecting about one hundred delegates. Over three hundred attended. Then there was no turning back. At a recent Unifor convention, Johnstone was honoured for her activism. They also held a Drag Storytime that was met with resounding applause. Activists matter; they do make change.

Johnstone later became a union discussion leader, delivering union education programs, a turning point for her:

> What I learned with paid education leave was a turning point for me. I absolutely loved it. I loved teaching it. I loved opening people's eyes so that you got that glimmer, and you knew somebody just finally realized what you're saying. And to me that was the greatest thing on earth. I love the fact that they brought in the 2SLGBTQ+ issues. That was instrumental because it was something I could totally relate to when I had people in my class and they questioned certain things.
>
> I told them, when you have straight people that sit around on a Friday night, get drunk and decide to go over to Church Street and bash gay people, I just wanna guarantee you, we don't sit around on a Friday night and do that. We don't say, let's go over to Yonge Street and beat up all those straight people.

But there were repercussions in her own workplace:

> We picked parts, so I drove a big box lift truck called a Selector. It had a box on the back for picking parts. We wore a harness and a belt to keep us safe when we were high up picking parts. So I've been running around for an hour picking this order, and I get off. Somebody has written on the back of my box "I'm

> gay," or something like that. Now that box has to be shipped on through to a dealer. Your clock number goes on everything, every part that's picked. They know who put together that box.
>
> There was the big push on, not having the pinups in the workplaces. They would cut out all these Sunshine girls, or whatever they were, and say they cut them out for me. "Not interested. Don't you understand? You know I'm not here to exploit people." So they would say, "We did it for Steph because she's gay."

She was the only out person in her local so she bore the brunt. But she was asked to form an LGBT caucus in her area. She knew you couldn't just walk up to people with "'Excuse me, are you gay?' Because you would probably get clocked." Johnstone talked to gay people in the bars, found out where they worked, and invited them to join the caucus:

> So coming through the gay bars into a position where they were already out and established, they were fine with it and felt safe. That's how I built the caucuses. I went to Windsor one time by myself. I had our big banner that takes two people to carry the banner, and I finally found a guy. I said, "Will you help me carry this banner because it was our union banner, and at the time it still said 'Gay and Lesbian.'" Now it says 2SLGBTQ+.
>
> We had to go through several name changes with that banner as the name changed to include everybody. So this guy ran by me, and he had a flag, like a gay flag, tied around him, and he stopped and turned around. He said he was CAW. I said, "Don't go away, get back here." And so I actually was able to talk to him and get him involved on starting up a Windsor caucus.

She felt she was flying by the seat of her pants, trying to find people to get these caucuses started. It culminated in the first CAW LGBT conference April 14 to 16, 2000, in Port Elgin. "We had people from all over because of the element of opening it up to allies. So there was people there from the West Coast, they came from everywhere. We must have had at least four to five workshops, so probably a hundred participants." She remembers the dates because it was her fiftieth birthday.

Stephanie Johnstone and fellow CAW member Dave McLean worked on her computer to come up with the first black and pink triangle pin. "We were the ones that designed it, and the national union got them made." It was built from the ground up and not from the top down. As Johnstone says:

> The changes in the union have been beautiful to watch. We relied on the women's committee. We relied on human rights committees to help carry that message through. We needed those allies to help us get that door open. We always talked about getting the foot in the door and keeping it open for the next sister that came through. I'm blown away by how free they are now and how much more understanding the union has and saying, we support our brothers and sisters of sexuality differences, you know. That's key.

Pam Diggs: How to Be Myself Fully

Pam Diggs joined Standard Automotive in Stratford, CAW Local 4451, in 1994, becoming active in the union. They had only been there maybe about six months, when they approached their union representative, Bonnie Henderson. Pam Diggs says,

> [Henderson] had been the most approachable union representative for my issue, which was that I was working alongside some people who were making derogatory comments. I felt uneasy not only for me, but also for a few of my co-workers and I wanted that to stop. As a new employee I was a little afraid coming forward. So I asked Bonnie and she handled that situation. After that experience I got to know Bonnie very well. I learned of her advocacy and I was so impressed with her experience that I started to talk to her a lot more. And she became basically one of my first mentors in the union.

Henderson got Diggs involved in union meetings, the women's committee, the human rights committee and eventually workers of colour. They were getting as much education as possible in human rights issues and understanding what was happening within their community, inside the plant, as well as globally. Diggs enjoyed feeling like they were doing something other than just going to work, pounding out the product going home, and living in their own little world:

> Through the women's committee, I met Stephanie Johnstone and they and others in the surrounding CAW locals formed the first CAW LGBT committee, which I was proud to join. Then the committee worked with the national union on developing the first LGBT Pride Conference at the Port Elgin Centre [held in April 2000].

Diggs's son Cory designed a poster for the first conference that featured a photo of Diggs and Cory entitled "CAW/TCA Showing Pride and Diversity in Our Community and Our Workplace." Pam Diggs came out openly later in life at age thirty-two, "I placed my sexuality last as on my list. This seems like a strange comment, but it was my reality." With the priority always for their two boys for whom they had shared custody, providing for and raising them in a safe home was all that mattered:

> Things weren't always easy for me as a woman of colour, a single mother, and a lesbian. This union supported me and gave me strength in ways I did not realize I needed. It really wasn't until I became active with the union that I felt empowered, comfortable, and safe enough to come out without fear, and be myself fully. The education and experiences I have had with the CAW have truly helped shape the person I am now.
>
> The most challenging for me was not knowing how to be myself fully and integrate into London. So I would walk my kids down to the park to a festival, people were swearing at me from their porch and saying the "n" word and I'm walking with my kids. I always fear for my kids. So I just would walk really quickly. It wasn't late at night, and it was brazen. And these guys felt emboldened to do it. I don't know if they realized I was a woman cause I get that a lot. Ninety per cent of the time I don't even try and correct people. It's part of my identify as "they" because I don't feel like I fit in one box or the other. I dress androgynously most times. I'm not an

Pam Diggs and her son Cory in the poster he designed for the first CAW Pride Conference in 2000. Photo: Pam Diggs.

outgoing person, so I sort of—I'm always guarded with how I'm perceived.

I do drag and we've been performing as the Gutter Boyz since 2000. One of the most memorable times that we've ever performed was at the CAW conferences because of the numbers of people that were there, and the people who just enjoyed our shows.

I think education is the cornerstone to understanding why we need unions. A lot of young women don't get that opportunity to experience that because they're held back by certain people, maybe in their locals, that don't think that they should be able to go to those things. I always held the education part of the CAW as a pinnacle.

Dana Dunphy and Kim Crump in Conversation: There's Still Work to Be Done

Dana Dunphy: I was hired at the Windsor Casino in 1994. There were a lot of injustices that I didn't like, and so in 1995 we certified the union. I started out as an alternate, got elected as a steward in 1998 for a short stint, and then I was elected committee person for nine years. I ran for chair, lost my election, went back to the floor for three years, then I ran in the election again. I won, and I was chairperson for ten years until I came on [the national] staff in May 2023.

Some of the challenges really were—there was like a length requirement for women's skirts, and they used to make women get on their knees so they could measure their skirts to make sure they weren't too high off the knee. Those who dealt with money weren't allowed to go home until they balanced, whether that was five hours after your eight-hour shift, and people were walked out [of the workplace] for variances. So one day you have a variance of two hundred dollars, and you're walked out. You were put on investigative suspension and fired if they couldn't find the money. It was horrible. We had bartenders fired for twenty-five cents, cashiers because of the variance policy. The crowds were so big back then that the servers had to carry the trays over their heads. Our first agreement was a three-week strike. We're not shy of strikes at the casino. Our last strike was sixty days.

Kim Crump: I have spent time playing at the Windsor Casino. It's not often that you'll interview two people where somebody can talk to you from the perspective of a consumer of the product that our members are putting out there.

Before the casino opened it was at the [Windsor] Art Gallery, and it's now recognizable the influence that Dana and a lot of the union activists and leadership have had at the casino. The changes they've made, on women and uniforms and tray carrying, and the abuse that, in particular, women dealers faced at the table.

Dana Dunphy: Most of the members are women and they weren't allowed to wear pants. We took that whole pant issue to arbitration. They're predominantly in housekeeping and serving, cashiering.

In the casino industry, there was a ton of harassment. We made sure the employer followed harassment policies and did proper investigations, and we put a lot of pressure on employers to kick out patrons that harassed. It's predominantly the women in serving, bartending, and tables as dealers. And the dealers, they can't go nowhere. They're stuck on their table. They can't just leave. Over the years, I think harassment has lessened in this industry because of the union putting pressure on the employer. But it still happens. And the problem is, the more money they spend the more they can get away with.

Kim Crump: I started in 1989 at CAMI Automotive. I wasn't really involved in the union. We had a rich history at CAW Local 88 of strong progressive women in in our local, women like Cathy Austin, but there were others. Cathy was a huge influence.

My first instances of activism in the union were strictly motivated by the things that were going on in the workplace. My first women's conference was in response to the stripper issue at the hall. We had our monthly membership meetings at the local union hall on a Sunday, which also happened to coincide with the date of the Super Bowl. So after the union meeting in January 1997, all the women left the hall, and they had a men's-only Super Bowl party where they invited strippers. We complained. It was big in the press. It was big everywhere. It became really bad on the [shop] floor. The men involved were predominantly [union] leadership men. They put letters out on the floor, trashing all of the women that were involved in the complaint.

It was Cathy Austin who took the brunt of it because she was in leadership, as well as me and others. They put out a letter on the floor and called us the Fat Ass Dyke Committee, which is kind of weird because I was the only lesbian, and I wasn't on the women's committee at the time. So it's just very bizarre.

My activism just grew, and I got more active in the union around queer issues, but being queer at my local was never my drive. It was from more of a feminist perspective than as a queer activist. What was driving me were the things that I found oppressive as a woman working in a predominantly male environment. I was out when I started at CAMI, and I know that there are people, there are women and men that I worked with, that were still in the closet when they left thirty-two years later. So it was different for me.

Cathy's influence on our local can't be understated. She was committed to building a strong activist base with workers of colour and Indigenous members and queer activists. Anytime something came across her desk, she would make sure that the proper people got it or were exposed to it. She encouraged me relentlessly, like irritatingly so, to become more involved. She sent me to the first Pride Conference in 2000. Then I went to four-week paid education leave (PEL) in 2001.

Sue Carter from the education department had taken the PEL participants aside that were at the Pride Conference and encouraged us all to run for the four-week PEL human rights committee. Each committee brings a resolution to the final week of the program and Sue suggested we take forward the resolution that we would strike a pride caucus at each four-week PEL. So that was our resolution.

What a nightmare.

So we have mock convention in the last week of [the four-week program], and when the resolution to strike the pride caucus was announced, the mock resolutions committee recommended non-concurrence. [They were opposed.] The debate became so ugly that they had to stop the convention and take a break. I was extremely upset, as were members of the committee, as were members of the queer community that were there. There were also queer discussion leaders.

One particular man on the resolutions committee recused himself from the stage, came to the floor, said, "You know, give queers an inch, they'll take a mile," and he went on and on about how we don't need to give you any space for your depravity. It was just ugly. And so, instead of kicking this guy's ass out after four weeks of union education, when we all came back in and reconvened, the guy got up on stage, held a piece of paper and read, "For the words I said, that may have offended the gays in the group I apologize." And he got a standing ovation.

In my opinion it went from bad, to get me the fuck out of here,

’cause I can’t believe this is happening. That’s how it ended, and I think that that was on the very last day.

I don’t think that they [the staff] had any expectation that it would turn into such a shit show. I think we were ill prepared. It was not great at all. But you know those are the growing pains that you have to suffer through in order to get progressive change I suppose.

Kim Crump: We’ve had two strikes. In 1992, we at CAMI Automotive went out on strike for five weeks for several things, and one of the things that we were able to negotiate was same-sex benefits. We come back for a ratification meeting. [The leadership] they’re up there reading through the gains, and one of them was same-sex benefits. And the collective “Boo!” that went through my local when that happened, and here I am sitting there ready to cheer, instead I’m like, “Whoa!” Just sort of sink down in my seat. It was very ugly, and you know people are like “We’re on strike for five weeks for queers to have same-sex benefits.”

Kim Crump: More rights for me doesn’t mean less rights for you. Just because people are in positions of leadership doesn’t mean they’re at the same place that we are. However, I do think that it’s important for them to at least behave as if they do.

Must be very different for you at an amalgamated local too, Dana, trying to find space to get your voice heard. Especially a local amalgamated with auto, the rulers of the whole free world.

Dana Dunphy: Yeah, I think what really helped me at the end of the day was the women in my life. Pam Leach was a local vice president, a very good, strong woman. It’s tough for today, now that I’m not at the local in an elected role, for the people behind me to have a voice, because they’re kinda like treading their own path and having to build their own relationships, whereas I had that right coming in. It’s very different for them than it was for me.

It should be an unwritten rule that they’re gonna have some space, and some respect after thirty years of being unionized, but they have to learn their own path, and they have to build that relationship.

Kim Crump: The experience of gay women is very different in auto than the experience for gay men, and the experience differs sector to sector. I'm extremely proud of the fact that the CAW really never had a presence in London pride before Julie encouraged and supported us. So you know the ally component can't be understated in any of this conversation.

Dana Dunphy: I think what has made me very proud, is I've done a lot of work with our local unions. And now, when I call, they come. We go from a stage where we go to our pride event and there's ten people, to now there's three thousand people, and there's a lot of local leadership. Whether they wanna be there or not, they're there. And I think that makes me very proud.

I've been very fortunate in my tenure, whether it be in my workplace or with my local. I think my biggest challenge is when people say they support you and then they tell gay jokes behind your back or in front of you. My biggest challenge is trying to figure out or manoeuvre how to approach those people because those people are well-respected, elected officials in our union.

And that's a challenge. This is still a challenge for me. Where do you find that balance to take them on or not take them on, call them out, not call them out, should you? Shouldn't you. And I think that's still my challenge, today, after thirty years in our union.

Kim Crump: Most of my things that I would consider accomplishments don't have to do with queer activism. They have to do with the long-gun registry and choice. The proudest moment of all of my activism is the long-gun registry which ultimately, we lost anyway. But in the moment, that was the thing I will always look back on as my proudest moment.

Dana Dunphy: Irene Friend [see chapter 5] who was the equity coordinator out of the Windsor office at the time asked me to attend the women activists course. It was a two-week course back-to-back, and that course changed my life. It taught me that my voice was okay. And it taught me that my opinion was okay, whether people liked it or they didn't like it, and it taught me that it was okay to talk about scars in your life. When I came out of there, I felt like a changed person.

I could, if I really wanted to be like a crybaby, and cry for the next hour. I could talk about something that affected me every day in that two-week course, but different every day. And I still talk to people today that I met and made connections within that course. And I think that's the most important part about going to Port Elgin. I've taken a ton of courses, but the two-week women activists course was by far the best course ever.

Kim Crump: And if I hadn't had the experience as a participant, I wouldn't have been the activist I was, and I certainly wouldn't have been the leader I was in the local. I certainly wouldn't have been the person doing the tapping women in my local on the shoulder, saying, "This is for you. You need to do this. The fire that I see lit in you will just grow and grow and grow."

[When I instructed the PEL course] they included the Jackson Katz video, *Tough Guise*. After the video, there was the part where they asked the men in the room "What do you have to do when you leave the house to make sure you're safe from sexual violence?" And the only thing the men can come up with was, "Don't go to prison." And then it's turned around and we say to the women, "Okay, sisters, what do you do when you leave the house to make sure that you're safe from sexual violence?" There are pages and pages and pages on the whiteboard full of things that women do, and there's a clear click in the minds of the men. You can see it happen in the classroom. From the front you can see the shift in the men going: "Holy shit," especially the men who have daughters. They're crucial. Those courses are crucial. I see them as foundational building blocks for activism in the union, and without them I don't know where I'd be. I think we're truly privileged to have them.

Women's Caucuses: Violence Against Women

From the earliest days of the Canadian union, it was clear that the structure of having one or two women on the national executive board was not a great recipe for success. For Roxie Baker, as the lone woman for the first several years, it was hard for her voice to make a difference. Baker began to hold mini-caucus meetings for women in her room at the union's education centre during national executive board meetings. She worked closely with other women national executive board members as well as the senior women staff who attended those meetings. There they began to strategize to get women's issues on the agenda and get them adopted.

As women's numbers grew, especially at CAW council meetings, they pushed for a separate women's caucus luncheon, paid for by the council. "Why do you want to meet? What will you discuss? Who will chair the meetings? Why can't women get their own lunch?" These were some of the questions women faced. Baker was a solid advocate of this structure, and eventually the leadership agreed.

These lunchtime meetings were mostly reports from the women's committee and delegates. But increasingly women used them to encourage women to get to the mics and speak about issues. When Buzz Hargrove decided to take up the issue of gun control as a recommendation from his council report, he wasn't ready for the fierceness of the opposition. None of the women had understood how divisive and explosive the gun control issue was.

At council, each of the president's recommendations would be debated. Nash recalls, "When we got to gun control, delegate after delegate got to the mics to oppose. Hargrove adjourned for lunch and called me over. 'See if you can get some of the women to speak up,' he suggested."

At that women's caucus, the women spoke about the Montreal Massacre, about CAW women's conference recommendations, about the incidence of gender-based violence where guns were used, and about the importance of the union taking a stand. The gun-registry cause drew the women together to use the power of their voices to win this.

After lunch, women flooded the mics and told the kind of emotional stories everyone had now heard before. Even a few gun owners spoke in favour of the motion. When the vote was taken, the recommendation passed. Women were jubilant. Hargrove's office was flooded with angry messages denouncing the decision. It was an issue that would continue to percolate for years to come.

Women's caucuses however would continue, and today they are huge with hundreds of delegates. Later workers of colour and Indigenous workers, 2SLGBTQ+ members, youth, and members with disabilities formed caucuses. The ability to get together with others who understand the issues and can join in common cause was key to the union making progress on equity. These caucuses continue to thrive today.

Just as the union's caucuses and women's committees were opportunities to share experiences and develop ideas, so were central labour body women's committees. The Canadian Labour Congress became a centre for activism, especially with the leadership team of Bob White, Dick Martin, Nancy Riche, and Jean Claude Parrot in office.

Former CLC officer Byers recalls there was an important cross-fertilization that occurred when union women got together at the committee. There was also some competition between unions that women used to their advantage to push their union to act.

This was important for focusing on gender-based violence on December 6. Byers says,

> If Julie [White] hadn't been there on the guns issue, we wouldn't have been able to push it to other places. But it became, not a competition, but other women were able to say to their union leadership "Hey, this is what's happening in such and such a union, so we need to be there." Even though their male leadership may not have been there. So it was really important when we did the campaign "15 Days 15 Ways to End Violence Against Women." It highlighted the effects of domestic violence on the workplace.

Byers told the CLC president that she would speak at every CLC council meeting to report progress on the violence issue and push union leaders to negotiate language on violence and women's advocates. "Sometimes you had to make the boys feel that they were in quiet competition with each other."

Former CLC women's staff representative Sue Genge remembers when women sparked the "15 days and 15 ways" campaign. It had been fifteen years since the Montreal Massacre, and the

CAW had focused extensively on issues related to gender-based violence. Genge says,

> I remember Julie coming to me, saying it's fifteen years we have to do something big and significant. We put our heads together, went to the women's committee and came up with this idea for a campaign. I've never seen so many organizations outside of labour that have taken that kind of approach on violence against women. So that was quite significant. The important thing is I was able to go and say, "This is what the affiliates want us to do."

What they came up with was a series of fifteen postcards, each one on a topic related to women's equality that would give women more independence to reduce gender-based violence. They covered everything from childcare to gun control to pay equity. Each card had an analysis of the issue, the change that was required, and an action item that women could take part in. The campaign raised the economic reasons women stay in an abusive relationship addressing the age-old question "Why doesn't she just leave?" It engaged local women across the country and was a tremendous success.

Save the National Gun Registry—Bill C 391

While gun control laws have existed in Canada for several decades, it was the bill passed in 1995 by the Liberal government, in response to demands following the Montreal Massacre, that required, among other provisions, that all guns and gun owners be registered, that sparked a backlash. They made some amendments, but the opposition continued. It was during this time that the CAW stepped up and supported gun-control measures.

Subsequently a private member's bill introduced during the minority Conservative government in 2009, would have abolished the requirement to register long guns not already registered.

Many Canadians were outraged that the Conservative government had set its sights on the destruction of the long-gun registry. The union had a strong track record of work on this issue and was the first union to support the Coalition for Gun Control. Given all the progress in the union making gender-based violence a union issue, taking on the issue of gun control made sense. It was a key goal of the families of the Montreal Massacre victims and of the CAW women's conference from 1991. The Coalition for Gun Control, led by Wendy Cukier, was persistent in demanding action from the federal government.

Julie White led the CAW campaign to pressure the NDP MPs to vote against the Conservative bill. It was the campaign she was most proud of. "We worked inside and outside the labour movement, allied with the Coalition for Gun Control (CGC), victims' families, Canadian Labour Congress (CLC), police, doctors, community leaders, feminists' organizations, and individuals from across the country."

She mobilized CAW activists and, with the help of CLC, put pressure on those opposition members thinking of supporting the bill because of the prevalence of gun owners in their riding. The bill to kill the long-gun registry died at the committee stage, so it was not passed. This was a huge victory for not only the labour movement but Canadian women and their families. However, once the Conservatives won a majority government in 2011, they abolished the long-gun registry early in 2012. (See also Gun Control under Julie White, earlier in this chapter.)

Abortion Rights

The union had supported a woman's right to reproductive choice since the 1970s. UAW members had joined those protecting the Morgentaler clinic in Toronto, and from the OFL to the CLC, labour, at the insistence of women and with the support of some male allies, had been on side. (See chapter 2.)

Cathy Walker, who joined the CAW staff with the CAIMAW merger in 1992, was part of the 1970 Abortion Caravan. The caravan was a group of seventeen women who drove across Canada to the House of Commons in Ottawa, about 4,500 kilometres. Their goal was to decriminalize abortion and to gain recognition of women's right to control their own bodies. (See also Cathy Walker in chapter 5.)

At that time, Canada was a staid, conservative country. Legal abortion was highly restrictive, and nineteen out of twenty women who sought abortions were refused access by their doctor.

The 1970 Abortion Caravan in Ottawa. Photo: Cathy Walker.

Backstreet abortions flourished, and women died as a result. As the women drove across Canada, they garnered support and heard heart-wrenching stories about women's lack of access to safe, legal abortion.

In Ottawa, they joined four to five hundred women to march on Parliament Hill and to demand a meeting with Prime Minister Pierre Trudeau.

When no one from the government would meet with them, furious, they marched to the prime minister's house and deposited a black coffin on his front lawn. Next, forty of them snuck into the House of Commons. In parliament's visitor gallery, they chained themselves to their seats and shouted out their demands. Pressure grew with the Morgentaler clinic in Toronto, but it would take another eighteen years until the laws were changed to open up access to abortion.

This important piece of women's history was documented by Karin Wells in her 2020 book *The Abortion Caravan, When Women Shut Down Government in the Battle for the Right to Choose.* Walker became the CAW national occupational health, safety, and environment director and led bargaining on these issues.

Cathy Austin: Good Out of a Painful Situation

Cathy Austin speaks in a low-key voice, any disappointments and frustrations mediated by a calm thoughtful demeanour. She grew up in a farming community. Her husband got hired at the General Motors Warehouse in Woodstock, and she got a job at CAMI, the GM/Suzuki joint venture in Ingersoll. She just had to get through the training program and probation. They put her on the assembly line, on the truck side where there were about one thousand workers. "This was really my first exposure at an extremely male-dominated workplace. And so, I was on a huge learning curve."

Another fifteen hundred workers would later be hired for the CAMI car side of the plant, but she thinks only about 10 per cent of the workforce was women, that is those who made it through probation. She found that the men didn't tell her the little tricks to avoid getting hurt on the assembly line in a bid to push her out. "I just kept thinking, I need this job, I need this job. I had to learn constantly."

She later transferred to the car side where there were a few more women, and she found that in contrast to the approach of the guys in the truck side, women were more likely to speak out to say that the jobs were unreasonable for them to do. "I started going to union meetings out of curiosity because I thought I either needed to use the union to fix things or I would get fired. Simple things like getting water when the workplace was too hot, took a struggle."

When another woman, Kim Yardy, joined her team, they began to speak up more. She ran for a position on the committee. As she campaigned, all the material she posted would be torn down. So women had to work harder in elections. They had to order more leaflets and put them up again and again. Austin didn't win her

Cathy Austin at the G20 protest, June 2010, in Toronto, Ontario, advocating for maternal health care that includes abortion. Photo: Kim Crump.

first election, but she put together a team of supporters and allies to make change happen.

She was a great organizer. "We decided to help people plug into their interests, see how they could pursue that in the union. If you're an environmentalist or if you like history, or you're passionate about childcare, let's bring that into the union. You work on that."

"We began to speak about power. You needed power to get the decisions you needed." They began creating an unofficial slate, encouraging people to run strategically for key positions in the workplace and their local union. Austin ran for the position of committee person, "because I was a shop floor person and that's how I wanted to be in the fight."

Once she got elected as a committee person, she had to learn survival. On the shop floor, management pushed hard, but she pushed back. She got a reputation so that people said, "Don't fuck with Cathy."

But the union leadership gave her an even tougher time. At one point they moved her desk out into a hallway and threw her confidential files out all over the floor. "They always made fun of me big time, because I believed in taking notes and keeping records."

She recalls a guy who at that point was a junior member of the executive. He was shocked by the treatment Austin was receiving but didn't know what to do:

> But he learned from that and he grew and became an ally. Sometimes something good can come out of a painful situation.
>
> I knew in the plant, if I was ever seen tearing up or crying, I'm finished 100 per cent. And so I always used to plan around that. If I knew I was going to be in a super-heated meeting, I'd have an escape plan all worked out, because I'd be finished if I was ever seen to be crying. It would reinforce that, "Yeah, she's a woman. She can't handle it. Told you so."
>
> The pressure was relentless. I can remember just saying, "One more hour, one more hour, and if you can get through the day, that's an achievement."

She never considered stepping away because she knew that's what they wanted. Her husband wanted to help, but she knew she couldn't be "rescued." He would serve her scotch when she was in the bath when she got home. She also had allies in the plant who supported her and helped her see the benefit of her struggle.

She later ran for and won a trustee position and then ran for vice president. She was substituting for the president who was often absent, and then she ran for the president and won. In 2006 she was the first woman to get elected president in the CAW auto locals—a major achievement. She remained in office as president until 2009.

Austin loved collective bargaining:

> Women are natural negotiators. And we decided as a local, Mike Van Boekel was plant chairperson, that there would be a requirement that all bargaining committees would include a woman.
>
> I can remember in bargaining where I was totally excluded, although I was the president. Not once did the guys ever ask me out when they were having dinner or lunch or anything, and sometimes I just used to take a sandwich and eat in my car.

And here you are, the president of an automotive local having a sandwich in the car because the bargaining committee didn't even invite you for lunch. That was part of the drill, not being included. It was Cathy Walker—she noticed this and she just said to me one day "Would you like to go for lunch? I'm starving," and my heart just went, "Oh, my God! She just asked you out for lunch, but she's a national person, and I admire her so much." I watched Cathy for years. The work she did was just so amazing. And she just asked me out for lunch. So we ate lunch. That was the first time ever I had lunch out at bargaining with someone, and it was wonderful.

And so like something as simple as that was a huge moment for me, and then Mary Shortall, again a wonderful sister. After "stripper gate" at Local 88 [when men in the local had strippers at the union hall during the Super Bowl game], although I had nothing to do with it or with bringing forward the complaint about it. She said to the women who were lodging the complaint, "I said you're gonna bring forward this complaint, but you know that I'm gonna pay the price for this, because I'm going to be the lightning rod on this one."

They said, "Yes, but we have to do this, Cathy, this is not right." I said, "I know that, and I know you can't sit on it."

So one of the things that national union decided that Local 88 committee people and executives should have a mandatory week-long human rights training. I was the only woman there and it was excruciating.

Mary Shortall, the discussion leader, could see that. She did her best to protect me. Once at a break I went out to my car, and I was throwing up because the pressure was so bad, and she come over and she said "Cathy, do you mind going out for a cup of tea with me after?" And I said, "Oh, that would be wonderful." It was just personal and touching.

Sari Sairanen: Why Can't It Be Sari's Job?

Sari Sairanen has a calm assuredness about her that inspires confidence. She doesn't dither. As the assistant to the Unifor national secretary treasurer, she is one member of the top leadership team. She is a problem-solver and a senior role model in the union.

Sairanen comes from a Finish family with a union background. "My parents got engaged when my dad was on a picket line," she says.

She joined Air Canada in the Winnipeg reservations office in 1994. Having studied economics and labour relations in university, she got involved in her workplace as a health and safety rep. She was concerned that senior people at work were taking painkillers or they couldn't lift their arms because of pain related to their work. She wanted to make improvements in ergonomics to prevent these injuries and pushed for, and won, better chairs. She also opened people's eyes to the possibilities of going home whole at the end of the workday, pain-free, without medication.

Later she ran to be the local union vice president of the western region:

> I went to the airport with a box of doughnuts, and people would ask me "Who are you?" And I said, "Well, I'm running for the (Local 2213 Western Region) VP position." And I was told, person after person, "That's Gary's [Pryce's] job. Why are you going after Gary's job?" And I'm thinking, "What do you mean Gary's job? Why can't it be Sari's job?" I was quite naive. I had no campaign manager, I had nothing. It was just me going out there and just introducing myself and I won.

She went to a weekend school for CAW women on public speaking in Winnipeg delivered by Cheryl Kryzaniwsky, who was her local president. There were a few people from her call centre in the course, but mostly women from other local unions:

> Not having been involved in other CAW activities, looking back, I probably appeared very naive. The call centre work would be considered white collar work. And there were a lot of women there from industrial settings.
>
> But it was also about the challenges that they were having in our workplaces, and I thought to myself "Holy Moly, I don't experience any of that. I go up to the supervisor, and I say 'this is not working,' and they go, 'Oh, okay, well, what should we do differently?'" And so it really opened my perspective on what

> you have in collective agreement language, and how that dictates and controls a lot of your work environment. That includes how appreciated or valued you are in the workplace. Its about respect. You are contributing to the workplace and you want it recognized.

Then Air Canada and Canadian Airlines, the second-largest Canadian carrier, merged in 2002:

> I ran for bargaining rep, and I remember the Canadian Airlines local president, Anne Davidson, trying to talk me out of it. Same thing with Gary Fane (the union's staff airline director) trying to talk me out of it. "What do you mean, I can contribute. Why would I wanna step aside?" And I didn't.
>
> I became the bargaining rep and I guess I never looked at myself as a woman in a man's world, or woman in any kind of world. It was just I had a skill set. I had a voice. I had convictions, and I never thought of it that way. And then, when I was bargaining rep when Anne Davidson went on staff, I ran for president. There were seven candidates, six of them men. It was about the vision that you had. How you believe that people should be treated. Your membership, the relationships building with employers. I thought I had those skill sets.

Sairanen beat all those men, winning the presidency twice, both times with a man running against her. The majority of the members were women, and so she was surprised that apart from Cheryl Kryzaniwsky, most of the leadership were men. She wondered how they would know about the challenges most of the members were facing with respect to harassment, childcare, family responsibilities:

> I had good people around me. That you're a woman, that never entered into any of the discussions. Of course, people would be saying "Do you have bargaining experience?" And so that translates into male. Probably because few women took on those responsibilities because they were being played as being a big hardship. And you gotta have a big brain to be able to

> do that. I remember Cheryl talking about that, in that public speaking course. It's not about you having extraordinary intelligence. It's really breaking down the subjects, finding others who are subject matter experts, and having people around you. You just have to be strategic in how you're thinking and how you're tackling issues.

Sairanen came onto the CAW staff in 2006 after having been elected twice national president of that large local union. She succeeded Anne Davidson. Then she joined the national executive board of the union. At one of the national executive board meetings, Cathy Walker indicated that she was going to be retiring from her position as health and safety director. Sairanen told Buzz Hargrove that she would be interested, and she got the job. When she joined the staff, she was immediately made director of the department, much to her surprise. There were two other staff reps in the department, both men, who were not happy about that.

The hardest part of coming onto the staff in the health and safety department was not having her colleagues supporting her. "One of them apologized to me for how poorly he treated me. But you know that's sixteen years after." She just focused on doing the best job she could for the membership. And she found other colleagues that she could develop a relationship with. "You have those moments when the veil comes down, and you can share some of those stories. You gotta find your tribe, as they say, those who are your trusted people." Sari Sairanen is proud of the support she was able to give local leaders to be able to take on issues in the workplace, and of lobbying governments on violence and harassment in the workplace.

Growing Diversity, Growing Power

The economic pressures and political insecurity the union faced at the beginning of the new millennium also offered the opportunity for other transformational changes. Representing new sectors of the economy, mainly through mergers with other unions, meant the CAW had greater diversity in the membership, including larger numbers of women. From the early days when women numbered about 5 per cent of the membership, they were now over 30 per cent with greater racial and gender diversity.

Consequently, women demanded greater change. The union continued to advance progressive policies and programs, while campaigns led by the women's department built the capacity of local union women to organize and develop leadership skills. Every woman who pushed for change in her workplace, every woman who spoke at a mic during a leadership meeting, and especially every woman who was in a leadership role encouraged other women to expand their vision of what was possible in the union. If some women could get elected, others considered the possibility. "Why can't it be my job?"

The future would hold more opportunities but also more roadblocks and challenges.

Chapter Seven

The Privilege and the Price of Change

The women interviewed for this book all value how the union had improved their lives. Many said their activism gave their lives meaning and allowed them to develop new skills and confidence. Having the protection and support of the union was a tremendous benefit. Being able to take on a bigger role—an educator, organizer, or an elected leader—for most felt like a privilege.

They also spoke of the barriers they faced, especially with their personal lives. Like many working women, lack of childcare was a major impediment, compounded by long hours and an unpredictable schedule. Personal relationships often were strained.

Some women faced additional challenges. Some felt called to higher leadership and found the glass ceiling in the union was firmly in place. Others tried to advance gains for women, such as pay equity, that called for the union to do more than just develop a policy or create education programs. Others found that they faced additional barriers because of their identity, language, or geographic location.

The women in this book tried to leave a legacy of improvements in the union that would benefit others. Most succeeded; not all were happy with the outcome.

Challenging Racism

In our economic system, employers have benefited by treating some groups of workers differently, from the slave trade, to indentured labour, sheltered workshops for people with disabilities, to gender and racially segregated jobs, to temporary foreign workers, and immigrants. Pitting workers against each other can save employers money but undermine union organizing and solidarity.

Employers control workplace hiring, and some employers hired only men, some only women. Some hired newcomers whose English skills were limited. The union doesn't choose who gets hired but works with those in the workplace. Employment equity initiatives have tried to break down those racial, gender, and ability barriers by requiring employers to hire a diverse workforce.

From the early years of the Congress of Industrial Organizations (CIO) through the UAW's organizing efforts, to the CAW, leaders in the union believed that dividing workers by race or gender was against their principles and weakened the union. Unions fought for non-discrimination laws, as well as pay and employment equity. However, workers reflect society and often come with attitudes toward differences in our society that don't always follow those principles.

While the first woman hired on the staff of the UAW/CAW was Lorna Moses, an Indigenous woman who remained there for many years, there were few other Indigenous staff,[1] and few Black or racialized staff. Just as in the early years when women often found that they were the only woman in the room, Black or racialized women often found that same situation until very recently. Some just rolled up their sleeves and got on with their jobs. Some who were ambitious found that they had no chance of advancement and eventually moved on. Some organized, helped build opportunities, and opened doors for others. They all tried to make a difference.

Georgina Anderson: Unintimidated

Georgina Anderson came from a union family and attended meetings with her father. When she got a job at Bendix, an auto parts plant, part of Local 27 in London, Ontario, she got active in the union, even though she was a single parent.

Anderson, a Black woman, was in a workplace of men and women in equal numbers, but it was not racially diverse. With an affable manner, strong union principles, and a persistent work ethic, she won the respect and support of her fellow members. In Jason Russell's history of Local 27,[2] Anderson says she didn't face

Georgina Anderson, of UAW Local 27, during the Boycott Eaton's campaign. Photo: UAW.

overt discrimination, but nevertheless she and other union women had to challenge established practices while not being intimidated.

She fought for women's equality and was a member of the first UAW/CAW women's committee for many years. Anderson co-instructed the first CAW women activists program, which was game-changing in the union. For emerging leaders like Ena Morris and Josephine Ebanks she was a role model.

Anderson was active in the union until Bendix closed, and when she got another job at a CAW plant in Stratford she was also active in the union.

Elaine White: More First Nations Women

Elaine White never had the chance to meet Lorna Moses, the Indigenous woman who was the UAW/CAW's first woman organizer, but they would probably have had lots to discuss as pioneers and organizers in the union. White joined the staff more than two decades after Moses but, while many things in the union had changed, White also had to blaze her own path.

White steps up to a challenge in a way that brings other people in and inspires confidence. She is modest but courageous, not afraid to challenge but at the same time, she's a relationship builder. This made her a strong in-plant union representative and a successful organizer.

"I had the power within me to leave my abusive ex-husband, which was the big first step of my activism." She's from an Indigenous family but grew up off reserve and had difficulty relating to her heritage. But she wonders if her Indigenous heritage might have inspired her connection to nature.

White worked at the Chrysler plant in Ajax, where she sewed trim for the interior of vehicles. Her plant was 80 per cent women. In about 1990 she transferred to the Chrysler plant in Brampton because the trim plant would be closing. She also wanted to leave the plant where her ex-husband also worked. "It was the best thing I ever did in my life."

In Brampton, she was assigned to the paint shop, in the sealer area where they worked with many chemicals. She got elected as an alternate committee person, raising health and safety concerns, and fought for better protection.

At first going to union meetings, she was afraid to speak. But she remembers seeing a guy go up to the mic:

> He was big, a tough auto worker, right? And he got to the mic, and he was holding a piece of paper, and his hands were just a shaking and I thought, "Holy Jeez, I'm not the only one afraid. This guy is scared to death." I thought, "If he can do it, I can do it." So whenever I had a paper, I held it with two hands so they wouldn't shake."

Then Elaine White got elected to CAW council with the support of her in-plant committee, and her local union, which were predominantly men. "They didn't try to step on me to get their positions at council. They supported me."

After about a year, she was named the women's advocate for her plant. She feels the women activists program and women's leadership classes were a game changer that transformed women and gave them the confidence to run for positions. "It was the best thing that I ever did, the best course I ever took in the union." She also got involved with the council women's committee and the Toronto West women's network.

Her local president, Vince Bailey, wanted her to get involved with the workers of colour and Aboriginal workers committee, which was a supportive environment. There workers identify what their struggles are, some of the obstacles they face, and the importance of getting elected to positions and making change. She did that for a time until she could recruit another Indigenous woman in the local union who she felt was more qualified. "I'm happy now with Unifor, that there are more First Nations people involved."

White was later thrilled to be hired to organize for the national union, talking about the union to workers. Then she got an organizing contact from the Casino Rama. "I think I got [assigned] because it was a big one, and it was almost impossible."

She asked her old local union in Ajax that serviced a casino in that area for resources. There, she partnered with a Mandarin-speaking casino dealer, and they went to the Casino Rama four days a week for eleven months, talking to workers. They found harassment was a big issue, and there were many Indigenous workers, mostly women. Most of their seventy-five organizers were women. It was a huge campaign and they won. "It was a good feeling," she says.

One year, Elaine White was on a panel at a CAW women's conference on the topic of violence. She had to speak in a packed conference room with hundreds of participants:

> "I'm gonna talk about something here that I've never talked about before."
>
> Yeah, that was a profound moment. Nancy Diamond was on the stage, and she was the mayor at the time where I grew up in Oshawa, and that's where I experienced my sexual assault issue. I'd never talked to anybody about it before or after. The only way I got through it was to just not let it drag me down.
>
> I just kinda went by the seat of my pants without notes.

> I think I felt safe in that environment and it all came out. Afterwards I thought, "What the heck did I just do, oh, my God. I can't believe I said this. But I don't wanna keep it in me." But it was very empowering for the women in the room to hear that they weren't alone.

One of the proudest moments of her life, she says, was when she became the chair of the council women's committee. Elaine White made area women's networks a priority so that women's committees could connect with others in other locals and get new ideas for motivating women to get involved.

Denise McMorris: Community Builder and Educator

In 1988 Denise McMorris was hired by American Motors (AMC) in Brampton and then moved to a nearby Chrysler plant in Bramalea. The old plant was a product of a different time with few women, let alone Black women.

McMorris is Black, tall, and elegant:

> It was a challenge back then on different levels, because women on the shop floor didn't have a voice at that time, and I'd never worked in a shop floor environment before. I remember in that old area, I was putting on door handles, and I was the only woman, a woman of colour at that time in that area. The men embraced me if I didn't question anything. If I asked, "why are you late giving me my break? So why are you giving me this (work), and not the other person?" The minute I pushed back, that was when I saw the inequity comes into play.

She remembers that back then breaks were twenty minutes:

> I saw everybody going on break, and no one came to relieve me. So, I kept working, and then a person came to relieve me when the break was over and I said, "Well, I'm gonna go on my break, no matter what." He says no. I says "Well, I'm gonna go." And the girl beside me, Lisa, said to me, "Denise, call your union rep." I didn't even know what a union rep was at the time. "You let them know what exactly happened," said Lisa.

So McMorris called her union rep who told her, "No, no, you come right now. She's going on her break right now." That got McMorris thinking about the union.

She thought eventually, though, she would quit when she faced constant criticism from a supervisor. She felt it was racism because she was always told to speed up, work faster. By that time, she had bought a house and the money was good, but she couldn't take the constant chirping from the supervisor. The women she worked with were very supportive. They told the supervisor to back off and they urged McMorris not to quit. They sent her to the union.

With the transfer to the new Chrysler Bramalea plant these struggles continued but now she knew about the union. She was often at the union office complaining about the treatment she was facing, and then she met Vince Bailey, her Local 1285 president. Bailey was also Black and a member of the union's national executive board. He sat her down and after a long conversation, he told her he'd like to send her to the union's education centre to learn more about the union.

She attended the union's new women activists program. She had never been to a union meeting before:

> I [learned] I was standing on the shoulders of women in the union. One of the key pieces in that program was that you have to get involved in the union. You have to go to union meetings. You have to let your leadership on the shop floor know who you are. You have to be part of your union if you want to have a voice. The union has carved out space for us, but it's for us to take the mantle and run with it.

She felt energized and empowered. That course got her involved in the union and she started feeling stronger. There were not many women in her local union and few women of colour so she still found it intimidating. She still wasn't sure there was space for her, and felt there was no way she would get elected to any position.

Nevertheless, she knew the union was key to fighting for equity and inclusion. And with each round of hiring, more women and more racialized workers were getting hired. She worked at the Bramalea plant for about fifteen years before attending the women's training program. It was then she got involved in community work for the union, such as in the food bank and volunteering at the Vanier women's prison. Bailey, who worked in the local union office would ask her to volunteer and she'd go. She credits him as a mentor. "I started going to union meetings now, but still not talking because I'm a very shy person, so I didn't go out to the mic and didn't say anything."

Bailey sent her again to Port Elgin to the education centre to attend a two-week course for workers of colour. "But I'm a single mom. I have a little son, and I won't have childcare during your course. He said, 'There will be childcare, so you can take your son with you.'"

She then saw the union through a different lens, how spots were mandated for women and people of colour. Bailey was the graduation guest speaker, and he spoke of his challenges and how he rose to leadership positions.

"That gave me strength," McMorris says. "It let me know that there's space in this union for me." She felt the courses gave her the tools to encourage others to see her as building the union and not as a threat.

On her return she got more active in the union, while there was some pushback in her workplace for being away on courses, she persisted. At Bailey's encouragement, she ran for and was elected to the position of community liaison, based on her community work. She also became a union facilitator and began teaching courses in the community and at the education centre. She was often able to include her son, and he was so proud of her.

And she was proud to call herself a trade unionist and a feminist. "I wear the banner proudly."

Through her work in the prison, she saw firsthand the discrimination against First Nations' women, having their children taken away, and being thrown in jail for very minor offences. She also saw the impact of homelessness by volunteering at Sistering, a women's support organization in Toronto.

Then the national President Buzz Hargrove invited her to be a coordinator of the union's legal services program. She readily accepted. McMorris was the first Black woman hired on staff at the CAW in 2005. Later there was an opening in the union's education

Denise McMorris facilitating at a CAW women's conference.

department, and she moved to the union's education centre in Port Elgin. She would only last a year.

As the first Black woman on the national staff, she didn't get the support she needed and the experience was difficult. The broader community of Port Elgin was conservative, and her son was the only Black child in the town. While the school and the teachers were kind and supportive, the broader community often was not. In local stores he was treated with suspicion. Sometimes there were direct racist comments. He badly wanted to get out of there, so McMorris sent him to her mother's place near Toronto.

Denise McMorris returned to Toronto to escape racism and the unwelcoming environment. She now faced a choice—return to being a coordinator or go back to the plant. She saw the coordinator's position as a blessing. While she was assigned to legal services, she would spend most of her time instructing human rights, women's, and workers of colour courses. She was happy to be with her son and back in Toronto and she stayed there for six years until she retired.

Looking back, she had wondered if at times in the plant she was just a crybaby. It took her a long time to get past that. She credits her faith with giving her strength to deal with the challenges and continue. She also points to Elaine White, another leader from her local who was a role model for her. But it was the education programs that gave McMorris strength and helped her find her voice, and the union who saw her as a leader.

Ruth Pryce: You Didn't See People Like Me High Up in the Union

Ruth Pryce has a kind manner and doesn't mind taking on a challenge. When her health care employer was taking advantage of workers, herself included, she decided to do something about it. After growing up in Antigua in a union family, she came to Canada and worked in Kitchener for Rivera, a private health care provider. She became a union member in 2001, but she felt their union at that time wasn't representing the workers. The employer moved them to Kitchener to a new facility and was overriding seniority provisions. So, when Marilynne Lesperance from the CAW met with them, they decided to change unions and go to the CAW. Lesperance later encouraged Pryce to run for the position of chairperson of the bargaining unit. (See chapter 5 for Marilynne Lesperance's story.)

She had two small kids at home, but she ran and won. "I didn't like to see the employer taking advantage of people and, growing up, I learned that if you want something done you should do it yourself."

There were about 130 members in her workplace, about 65 per cent were immigrants. She decided to work the midnight shift to have enough hours to go full-time. Once that happened, she bid on the day shift:

> As the chairperson in negotiations, I had to make sure that everyone was treated with respect and treated equally. As a Black person, I had to fight for everything, especially to get the hours we worked recognized. I didn't call everything racism, but I had to examine everything. We were written up a lot and we were accused of things that we didn't do, so these are the things that I had to fight. That was really hard; it wasn't easy.

She got a call from Raj Dhaliwal, the head of the human rights

Ruth Pryce at a Toronto *Why I March* demonstration in 2017, one day after President Trump's first inauguration. Photo: Candice Basara.

department, asking her if she would like to attend a human rights course. "My activism just took off because I got the opportunity to attend these education courses."

Her local union was splitting in two to better serve the membership, and she was encouraged to run for a position on the new executive. At first she said no, because her children were still small. Then she decided to run for a trustee position, which would be for three years. During that time, after the split of the local union, she got more opportunities to attend courses and meetings. Then the local president encouraged her to run for the position of vice president.

That was a bigger position and she had to campaign for election. But she won and held the position for several terms, for about ten years. She got elected as co-chair of the CAW council workers of colour caucus and later she was elected to the national executive board.

Pryce noticed what she believed was favouritism in terms of staff appointments and promotions. She challenged the then-national president at a women's conference to have more diverse representation among his assistants. "'How many Blacks were assistants to the president?' I didn't get an answer. You didn't see people like me high up in the union. I don't think it was right. Now it's changing a little."

Pryce wanted to see more diversity throughout the union, including in the top leadership. She felt they were held to a higher standard:

> Let us screw up if we want to be a screw up. How many other people out there screwed up a lot, and they're still there. It's a struggle we're fighting and it will take generations. What's happening in the world is, it's in our union.

Denise Hampden: Trailblazer Who Left Disappointed

Denise Hampden's political activism comes naturally, being from a family connected to South African activists and musicians. She remembers them handing out anti-apartheid flyers:

> I didn't really understand it. My parents didn't talk to me about apartheid per se. I was way too young for that, but I understood that we were doing something important, and my mother talked to me about how important it was to stand up to injustice. And when you see things that are wrong, you have to say so. And maybe they don't change. But at least you said so. And, basically, that momentum will gather.

She began work at VIA Rail in 1987 and became a member of the railway union. Her local union had very diverse representation and she became the recording secretary. She attended the workers of colour and women activists programs in 1995. The latter program was not a happy experience. She had serious criticisms about the course and learned that she could be disappointed in other women.

She was the chair of her local union when they merged with the CAW. A senior staff rep from the CAW, who was overseeing rail for the union, set up a structure that led to all white men representing the sector, which infuriated Hampden. She points to the history of the predecessor union that represented the sleeping car porters who were Black railway workers in Canada. And yet somehow now they are represented by all white men. "There's not one Black face to be seen at the bargaining table for railway today and a tiny number elected to major leadership positions."

When a man from the local took the local's women's committee seat, that was a step too far. She complained to the national union, and he was forced to step down. Hampden says the women's committee then was free to act on behalf of women, but the overall rail council structure was not representative.

Hampden got active delivering education programs. She got so busy that she was at the union's education centre almost every week of the year. She felt as though she had no life to speak of because she was giving her all to the union. After so many years of doing this work for the union, the director of the education department led her to believe repeatedly that not only would she be appointed to one of the three education jobs soon to be open on the union's national staff but that she would be appointed the next director.

That didn't happen. She got none of the jobs. She felt she sacrificed her personal life for the union, and then was insulted by the promise of a job that did not materialize. She knew, because she had seen it happen many times over the decades, that if she had been a man in the union, travelling across the country, delivering education to thousands of members, representing the union in so many ways, that her appointment to staff would not have been a question. And it would have happened decades earlier.

She had seen it dozens of times. Barrier-free paths had been laid down for men in the union for years. This was not a consideration available to her—a woman, who isn't white, in the union.

She was furious and left to go and work for another union as an education officer. She still seems broken-hearted to have left her union, her employer, her life, for something new. Respect is essential, as nourishing as food for someone who is passionate about making a difference.

Hampden is very proud of her education work, where she overcame her insecurities to become a sought-after instructor:

> The biggest challenge for me was translating my political principles into facilitation. I always felt like I wasn't good enough. It probably comes from spending too much time with blow-hard men. It's hard to be a trailblazer, because when you look up, you don't see yourself. You don't think that you have the fire that's

> needed to blaze that trail, but it took me a long time to get to the place where I thought, "No, I can. I can actually do this."

Denise Hampden also piloted the Handkerchief Project for the union, an initiative to commemorate the Montreal Massacre. The idea was to ask not only women, but primarily women, to send her a handkerchief or a piece of cloth or a piece of fabric that was significant to them, along with a note about how they felt about gender-based violence:

> We were twenty years after the Montreal Massacre and we needed to broaden the public discussion. We needed to make sure that people who were nineteen years old knew when it happened that day. I had a conversation with my nephew, and he didn't know that that person had separated the men from the women.
>
> I was going to school in Montreal on that day. I was at McGill, and my father called me, freaking the hell out. So I really wanted to do something meaningful. By the time of the CAW council meeting in December, they flooded the lobby of the Sheraton Centre in Toronto with all of the handkerchiefs that they had received from all over the world. It made a real impact.

She's proud of that work as well as leading a Unifor education conference on truth and reconciliation in 2018. She had also put tremendous work into the Aboriginal and workers of colour leadership program and, before she left the union, she offered what she felt was her most successful course ever. She learned so much about Canada's history.

Denise Hampden helped shape the union, but she left disappointed. It is a direct example of having to work twice as hard to get half as much. And even then, you may end up with nothing. Working as a staff member in a union is an enormous honour. But it is clear to her that only a select chosen few are afforded that honour.

Bhupinder Sanghera: Once Your Plant Closes, You're Gone

Bhupinder Sanghera landed in Canada in 1975. It was a very different country then; much less diverse. She got hired as a sewer but quit when she didn't get the wage she was promised. Then she got hired in a UAW workplace, which closed. Finally, she got into another called Hudson Bay Die Casting, and she became a member of Local 1285.

She and her husband had to fight with the University of Toronto to win recognition of their teaching degrees. Both had master's degrees, but were told they would get credit for the equivalent of grade 12, and that they had to do the degrees over. A person from England, she recalls, only had to do a short course of eighteen days. They fought back and eventually got their degrees credited properly. Her husband had returned to teaching by then, but Sanghera was active in the union and didn't want to switch.

The local union sent her to a paid education program at the union's centre in Port Elgin in 1988. She remembers being the only woman and one of three people of colour. "I felt very intimidated at first. Honestly, I was feeling so isolated." But that didn't stop her from being vocal and from being motivated.

When she returned from her first education program, she ran for the local's women's committee and became the chair. In 1992, her local sent her to the women activists course program. The course motivated her to want to run for the position of chairperson in her plant. The local leadership were not encouraging. She agreed to support another candidate, but she pressed them to support her to become a council delegate. They did.

She also made sure that the local sent women to conferences and courses. She remembers always taking five other delegates with her when she went to a conference, to build more activism in the local. "It was a male-dominated society. Our executive was almost all white and male. So it was not just hard for women of colour, it was a challenge for white women to get involved at that time."

Her plant closed in the mid-nineties. She had been helping the union with organizing and tried to get an organizing job from the union but was unsuccessful. She was told by the leadership that if she were still in the union there might have been something, "but once your plant closes, you're gone."

Her heart was in the CAW and she still loves the union, but she had to get another job. A friend helped her get a job in another union. The CAW lost a real leader when Bhupinder Sanghera's plant closed. Today Sanghera is Canadian director of Workers United Canada Council of the International Workers United Union, which is affiliated with the Service Employees International Union.

TCA-Quebec Women

Women in English Canada in the CAW often looked to Quebec as a more progressive place. The René Lévesque government, elected in 1976, introduced anti-scab legislation. Quebec was the home of the ten-dollar-a-day childcare program. And it was the Fédération des femmes du Québec that initiated the World Women's March.

However, in the CAW, or in Quebec called the Travailleurs et Travailleuses de l'Automobile de Québec (TCA), it was more difficult for women. The Quebec section of the union has had autonomy over its affairs. The membership of the union was much smaller than in English Canada, and the percentage of women was even smaller than the rest of the country.

The union has a proud history in Quebec. The occupation and brutal repression of workers at United Aircraft in Quebec led the Lévesque government to bring in the anti-scab law, and the labour minister at the time, Bob Dean, was from the Canadian UAW, then called les travailleurs et travailleuses canadiens de l'automobile (TUA) in Quebec.

The airline and hotel union mergers brought in more women members to the union in Quebec, joining with women in industry. But they struggled for representation. An early advocate was Paule Ange Neron from Local 956, who was the first woman elected as a delegate to the Quebec council. She never made it to the executive, but she did encourage other women to get involved and would hold a caucus meeting of women delegates during the council's meetings. She was not shy about raising issues on the floor of the council.

Peggy Nash was often tasked with addressing the council on behalf of the national president. She recalls giving a speech to them about violence against women, as she stared out at a room of mostly men. They were always respectful and friendly, but women's programs there lagged behind the rest of the union. The smaller numbers of women in the Quebec section of the union meant a greater uphill battle to have a bigger voice in the union.

Diane Mimeault: Few Women in Quebec Membership

Diane Mimeault started working in the 1990s at CMC Electronic, a small plant in Montreal with about equal numbers of men and women. At age thirty-one with two daughters, she was looking for a challenge and more of a sense of community, so she got involved with the union organizing drive.

After they were certified and joined Local 2889, she was elected into the bargaining committee of three people, one woman and two men. She got involved in health and safety, which she loved. Mimeault worked there for twenty-five years and became the president of the local. She also did stints at the Fédération des travailleurs et travailleuses du Québec (FTQ), and the Montreal labour council.

Mimeault was also a trainer in the Quebec women's programs, delivering the women activists course. She said she never had the goal of joining the staff because she found the work hard. "But because when we had the women's caucus, the women talked and said it's important to have a woman rep. In Quebec, we worked for that." She thinks she was chosen because she had done everything, bargaining committee, health and safety, local president, organizing, training. She was the first woman hired as a service rep on the Quebec staff. Her children were then fourteen and ten years old. She was on the Quebec staff for twelve years.

"Some men in the union were not okay with this," she says. "Some said I couldn't do the job. Some units and some locals didn't want to have a woman rep. But my colleagues in the office were very good. I had a lot of support." She says it was sometimes tough, but "I'm a person who likes a challenge. So, in my mind, I said, I will show you."

She thinks back to pioneers like Paule Ange Neron. She would call a meeting for the women delegates to inform them about the campaigns in the union and encourage them to speak during the council meeting. Mimeault remembers Neron as a pioneer who was happy for her when she was appointed to the Quebec staff.

Mergers didn't increase significantly the number of women in Quebec. And because women carry most of the work at home, fewer women tended to get involved. Mimeault asked the men on staff to encourage women to come to council, "But in my experience most of the reps did not because they want the power. In Quebec, there were some women involved, but not too many."

It was difficult for Quebec women to attend the women activists courses. Port Elgin was far away in Ontario, and for many there was a language barrier. It was difficult to get the Quebec leadership to sponsor a course just for Quebec, but they did run it occasionally. Similarly, when there was a push for a Quebec women's director, the response was that there simply weren't enough women members in Quebec. New organizing tended to focus on male-dominated jobs.

Still, Mimeault feels that in general the CAW was for her a second family, frustrating sometimes, but it was a big family.

Sandra Cormier: Quebec's Bumpy Road

Sandra Cormier came from a union family. "I remember my first job," she says. "I worked at St-Hubert, a barbecue chicken place. We managed to get the union in but I hadn't signed a card." She was eighteen and unsure:

> So my dad and my mom sat me at the table and they said, "You have to meet the organizer. Listen to her, if you don't agree, that's fine, but you can't run away from this." So I sat down, listened to her, signed my card, and from then on I understood what a union was.

In 1980, she started working at Aeroplan, the Air Canada rewards system, and there was no union for the first three years. "I was getting very frustrated with the way it was managed." So she got involved in the organizing, and she knew the more you got involved, the harder it was for them to fire you. "So I was very vocal about people signing cards. There were only twenty-five of us back then."

Cormier became a CAW leader in the Quebec section of the union. She was elected for three terms at Aeroplan for the first eight years they had a union. The unit grew from 25 to 350, about 65 per cent women. She later served as the local union's vice president in that region. Aeroplan had always been part of Air Canada, and when they organized, they were just integrated into the Air

Canada collective agreement. However, "there was a big battle to integrate the seniority. That was tough," says Cormier, "but in the end it turned out wonderfully [and they got their full seniority]."

In all her elections she had to run against men, and usually won. She later got involved in the union's education programs. She attended the paid education leave (PEL) program in 1990. There was a group of twenty-seven from Quebec and she was the only woman. "They protected me. I was twenty-eight or twenty-nine. Still, I felt isolated as the only woman."

She later taught PEL and the union's family education program. Women's programs were difficult to conduct in Quebec. The union wanted her to adapt the women activist programs for Quebec. They had no women's department in Quebec, and she felt she had no idea what she was doing.

She says they even put a guy in charge of the women's caucus in Quebec:

> He was not a nice person. He was a womanizer, and he oversaw the women's caucus. I told him one day, "Get out of here. We don't want you here. Why are you here? You know we don't need that babysitter." He was very upset with me. I wasn't very polite when I told him.

From her time in the union, she feels that Quebec was twenty years behind the rest of the union concerning women's programs:

> I can't speak for today; it might be a little better. There were few women around. For organizing drives you should have women, at least one or two women, but they would always pick men to do organizing. We were so much further behind in Quebec. But the biggest locals in Quebec were much like the local from GM, mostly men. Early on, men were in charge, even in our local, even though there were more women.

She had a dispute with the Quebec leadership over their selection of a woman staff rep. Many women wanted Cormier, but the administration preferred someone else. "She was a lovely person and I wasn't opposed to her. We just didn't like them telling us who it should be." She got along well with the staff rep after that, but the leadership took Cormier off the education programs. She was penalized for her opposition.

"After a while we started seeing more women getting involved in the union. Early on it was about 5 per cent but then it went up to about 18 per cent." She credits the education programs, especially the family education program.

As Sandra Cormier looks back, she thinks her biggest success was winning full seniority for the Aeroplan members in the Air Canada collective agreement:

> I fought for the seniority for four years before they recognized that. There were layoffs at Air Canada and people were allowed to transfer into our workplace. So twelve people transferred to our workplace, where we were about twenty-five to thirty people, and they all went ahead of us because they had more seniority. Oh, man, that really upset people. Eventually they gave us seniority. You have to respect the time that people have been working. She saw changes being made as time went on but felt there still weren't enough spots for women.

Pay Equity

Before and during the Second World War in Canada women fought for equal pay with men, while employers often saw them as a cheaper source of labour. Unions trying to organize women workers took up the equal pay struggle. In 1951, Agnes Macphail, the first woman in Canada elected to the House of Commons and the first woman sworn into the Legislative Assembly of Ontario, successfully pushed for Ontario's first equal pay law in 1951.

Employers got around this by creating separate classifications for women workers or "girls," with separate seniority lists. This meant that women could be laid off before men, even when they had more overall seniority. It was the women of UAW Local 222 at General Motors Canada who got this changed in 1970 when the human rights code was amended to prohibit sex discrimination. (See whole story in chapter 1, "Women's Committee Victory over Seniority List.")

However, in subsequent decades it became apparent that there were jobs which predominantly were filled by women and jobs predominantly filled by men. The latter were almost always paid more. This was a continuation of the undervaluing of women's work. For example, a childcare worker could be paid much less than a parking lot attendant. A personal support worker could make less than a janitor.

Pay equity was first introduced in Ontario in the late 1980s, but was strengthened by the NDP government in Ontario in 1990. The goal of equal pay for work of equal value, or pay equity, is to examine jobs worked predominantly by women or men in an employer's workplace, and compare or rank them in categories like skill, effort, responsibility, and working conditions. Then based on the ranking, to increase women's wages. Decreasing men's wages was prohibited. Once this comparison was done and the pay adjustments made, the equity plan had to be updated and maintained so that inequities didn't creep back in.

Despite challenges and limitations by subsequent governments, ultimately the courts have sided with women's rights to be paid fairly. The law has been upheld many times, resulting in women collectively receiving millions of dollars in pay increases. Other provinces have followed suit as has the federal government.

Pay equity is not automatic. It depends on workers, through their unions and with employers, to develop a pay equity plan to correct the underpayment of women workers.

Colette Hooson and Theresa Farao: Pay Equity Heroes

"What ticked me off was my boss was an ogre, and he was picking on the women in the next department that he also oversaw," says Colette Hooson. "So my job then was to come in and defend them. I didn't know it was a grievance; I just thought it was unfair."

Because of this she was encouraged to run for the bargaining committee in her workplace, Green Shield Canada, and later was elected president of her local union. She was the first woman president of the local of predominantly women. "We developed leaders in the local because one thing we know as women, we're not afraid to share power. When you share power, you bring people along."

Theresa Farao, from the same local but a different workplace, says that an example of Hooson opening doors for others was the creation of childcare for Local 240 members, so they could attend local meetings. Theirs was also the first local in the CAW to have a youth delegate with voice and vote on the executive board of their local union.

Hooson comes from a strong working-class family in Liverpool, England. She left during the Thatcher years when she saw how the Conservative government was attacking working people. Her family was always political and always pro-labour.

Farao came from a family marred by spousal violence. Her mom was generous and always helped others. She didn't come from a union background but, coming from Windsor, she saw how unions played a large role. She organized her workplace, the Canadian Automobile Association (CAA), and they joined the CAW. She volunteered to take a leadership position in 1995 and was elected chairperson of her unit. When Hooson joined the union's national staff in 2004, Farao was elected local president in her place.

But earlier, in 2002, she began negotiating pay equity. "My first pay equity was in 2002, and we just finished bargaining with CAA, and Colette said, 'You know what? We're gonna hit 'em with pay equity.'"

The CAA had a predominantly female workforce. "When we bargained the first collective agreement," says Hooson, "a woman that had been there like twenty-five years, Joyce was making $1.50 less than a woman that had only been there two years. So, it was just a matter of making sure that everybody was paid the same rate."

Hooson and Farao were very creative when they turned to bargaining pay equity. For example, when an employer wanted to remove a male comparator job (driving instructor) because it no longer existed, they insisted on keeping that "ghost job" as a pay equity comparator. Every increase in the collective agreement was applied to the ghost job so that the female-dominated jobs could compare to it.

When they bargained a new pay equity agreement with an employer, they would do their best to go back and find former women employees so that they could get paid retroactively. If someone was deceased, the money would go to their estate. If they couldn't find them, the money would go to a women's shelter or a food bank.

Farao remembers the time when they were in the middle of bargaining at CAA, the employer decided they were going to change the hours of operation on a Saturday and go from three hours a day to eight hours a day, and the people would work every other Saturday. There were a lot of women, single mothers, so daycare was an issue. "Believe it or not, those extra five hours had a huge impact on some of these women. So we filed a grievance."

Hooson encouraged them to do a fightback campaign. They got their local union executive to give them some money and they bought T-shirts and buttons that read: "Our time is precious. Family before profit."

One week in June, instead of their very official looking uniforms, they wore the buttons and the T-shirts in the Windsor CAA office:

> They [management] were pissed off with us. The human resources person from Toronto called, and said "If you wear those T-shirts in the Chatham office [as was planned for the next day] then they are going to shut the office and sue for the lost revenue."

So Farao talked to the women in Chatham and Windsor:

> The next day every one of them wore the T-shirt, and the buttons. Mid-afternoon, the employer called to say, "Okay, if we promise not to do anything, can you please not wear the T-shirts again tomorrow?"
>
> So that's what ended up happening, and nobody got disciplined. We got to wear our T-shirts and our buttons to make our little demonstration and it was kind of fun.

Hooson recalls that one of the toughest situations she had to deal with was a strike by a union group who weren't from her local union but had been adopted by her local. She says she did have to rally the other locals in Windsor, but she was more experienced and knew which locals had a large number of members that they could pull out for support if it was needed.

Hooson recalls,

> I remember me and the chairperson Linda Craig, standing in front of a semi (truck) to stop him from getting in [across the picket line] and all the other women were absolutely terrified, and Linda Craig was terrified. And I just said to her, "He's not gonna run us over with this many witnesses." And he backed off. And then the cheers went up. But, God Almighty! I was terrified. It was all bluff and bluster. But I had to keep my strength about me to keep everybody else strong.

She said they got served with papers, an injunction that said they would need to pay a million dollars if they kept up the picket line:

> And I just said, "Does anyone here got a million dollars? Well, don't worry then."
>
> I had to dig deep on that strike, and it wasn't even my local. But those women ended up leaving the other local and coming into ours.

She recalls a group of women who worked on the cosmetic counters:

> We used to call them the Cosmo queens. They're all dolled up to the ninth degree. And they all come on the picket line with tiny little summer sandals, faces full of makeup or false eyelashes. And I just said to them, "You'll be lucky if you last a day. Get your running shoes on and get the makeup off," because it was the middle of the summer and the makeup would've just melted straight off the face.

Farao recalls another strike at Beech Grove Golf and Country Club, a very high-end club in Windsor. They had a no-noise by-law ordinance:

> So we got pink whistles, in support of breast cancer awareness because they were predominantly women that were on the picket line. And they blow the whistles just when somebody was gonna swing playing golf. When the police came, we told them that the whistles were for breast cancer awareness, as well, as if there's an emergency, or they need help. 'Cause they were

> trying to run us down with cars. And so, the police allowed us to blow our whistles, and it really pissed off a lot of men. Men were doing whatever they could, climbing fences, trying to go through the picket line, just to get to the golf course.

This group of workers had belonged to another union, the Service Employees International Union (SEIU). When they left that union to go to the CAW, there was a twenty-four-hour window where the collective agreement didn't apply. So the employer clawed back up to four dollars of their wages. Then they locked out the workers who wanted to get that money back. The workplace had done pay equity but when they clawed back money from the women's jobs, they were no longer pay equity compliant. Farao says they agreed to only a one per cent pay increase and went back to work, but then immediately filed a pay equity complaint with Ontario's Pay Equity Commission that led to bigger pay increases.

One of Hooson's best pay equity success stories was when she got a $9.74 per hour increase for a group of health care workers in Northern Ontario. She always argued that this money was owed to women, and the union had an obligation to go and get it. She served as the union's pay equity expert, and inspired Farao to join her in the pay equity struggle and then take over from her when she retired.

Farao knew that when you did a pay equity plan, you would see how much money was there, and how many women's lives were changed because of it. Initially the union dragged its feet on pay equity. With a majority of male staff reps in the union, it seemed complicated, difficult, and not worth the trouble:

> I've been told it's not a real thing. I've been told that it'll mean lost jobs. I still get backlash today about the federal pay equity and from people within our union. They don't see it like they see men's work, which drives me crazy. Men's work is so much more valued than the work women do.

When there was a freeze on public sector wages, they could still bargain pay equity. Hooson told people in the union, "Pay equity is your way around the freeze." She says the pushback was tremendous. A senior union rep who came out of the health care sector was concerned that if the lowest paid workers got more money, then they would replace some of the higher, more qualified workers, which Hooson says never happened.

Farao is now a national rep in the union. "I service twenty-seven-plus bargaining units, and I continue to do pay equity provincially." She assists other staff reps when they seem unable to negotiate pay equity. "I don't know what it is. but they just cannot even negotiate basic language on it. They say they're just too busy." She wonders whether they are a bit embarrassed that they may have agreed to contracts in the past that were discriminatory, even if they didn't realize it at the time, but she says they inherited a system "where women got screwed."

And sadly there were no consequences for the staff who failed to bargain pay equity. Staff were told it was their responsibility, but if they failed to bargain it, nothing happened.

Farao adds,

> The last of several resolutions was passed in 2014. Part of that resolution was that the staff were to report on whether the units they represented had a pay equity plan in place. Only fifteen out of sixty-five reps did it. But things are changing. When Lana [Payne] sends out a letter on pay equity, they respond. New staff training now includes pay equity.

Hooson says,

> If we treated health and safety with the same disrespect that we treat pay equity, we'd have workplace fatalities left, right, and centre. This is a piece of legislation that we've fought for and we're not using it to its fullest capacity so that pisses me off beyond belief.

She points out the connection between domestic violence and the economic independence of women:

> The more money that you put in the hands of women gives them more rights or more power to be able to get out of a domestic

> violence situation, to be able to have the money to get their own apartment. But it's one tool that as a union we could use, just one little step we could give a woman.

Farao emphasizes the role of leadership as role models and how their behaviour trickles down to the membership. If the local union leaders, who are still mostly men, don't show anti-sexist behaviour, then she feels nothing will change. If they make little sexist jokes in small groups, that sends the signal that the union's policies aren't worth supporting. It undermines the union and it can confuse or silence young members who aren't sure how to behave:

> They would start off with stupid jokes, or they would say things with sexual innuendoes. And because it was a smaller group, people thought it was okay. I would call them out on it. 'Cause it's not okay. If you accept it, then nothing's ever going to change.

Farao and Hooson took a lot of heat from men when they called out sexist behaviour, but they felt they couldn't let things slide or they would never change. Farao continues,

> Because we do it, I'm a bitch, instead of being assertive, because I challenge or get you to think or not accept comments that you're

Theresa Farao, CAW president Local 240, and Colette Hoosen, CAW national staff, at CAW leadership meeting in Windsor, Ontario. Photo: Gord Gray.

> making. Our union, unfortunately, is not always as progressive as we believe it to be.
>
> Unfortunately, not all the women on staff were feminists. Not all sided with women. They were used to deferring to men or they were ambitious and thought that siding with men was the ticket to promotion. It was easier not to rock the boat.

"But," says Hooson "There are some that will do what needs to be done, because it's the right thing to do, regardless of the consequences."

Opportunities, Obstacles, Allies, and Outcasts

Many of the women we spoke with still felt the pain of the barriers thrown in their way. Women's progress in the union has often been a game of snakes and ladders. The privilege and the joy of representing workers, of taking on a bigger role in the union, often meant falling into line with the male leadership while eking out progress where possible. Failure meant getting blocked or squeezed out.

When some women were appointed to a staff position, the union could give them assignments that the women believed were designed to see them fail. Marilynne Lesperance, a former school bus driver, had to prove she could win the confidence of male rail workers and the respect of the tough rail companies. Some expected her to fail.

Some women were isolated and had to figure things out on their own and find support and advice wherever they could. Diane Hollingshead was parachuted into a mess of an assignment with no office, no staff, no organization. Many would have bailed, but she stuck it out. Some women found that being the woman or the only Black woman, was isolating and undermined their full participation. For Denise McMorris, even though she loved education, seeing her son subjected to racism was just too much.

Most of the women interviewed loved the union and recognized the positive change it had made in their life. Women were inspired by the power of the auto bargaining units that could bring industry to its knees. They could bargain key breakthroughs on childcare, gender-based violence, or international solidarity. Yet that power brought with it a strong male culture born out of the earliest organizing days. While striving to be progressive, that culture could also resist sharing power, especially with women.

Some women decided when they clashed with that culture that their love of the labour movement was not worth sacrificing their principles or self respect. Some women refused to compromise to win a position. Some joined the staff and then left or stayed but harboured resentment. Some were unhappy, others just swallowing their own views in bitterness.

The union's culture could also foster competition and envy among women because there were so few spots open to them. It was a system that could undermine a woman in a leadership position, cutting her off from other women. Many women learned that the only way to survive was to organize other women, to gain in numbers, and open more spaces for women. This was a building process that took many years. Eventually the leadership recognized this feminist force as a source of pride and lauded women's programs in mergers and organizing drives.

Sometimes however women's leadership was inconvenient when it challenged male power or the male image of power. Some women became outcasts in the union when they disagreed with the leadership or when they pushed for advancement but were blocked. Women who pushed to get ahead were sometimes seen as disloyal or not supporting the administration, that is, the leadership. This branding ostracized them.

Roxie Baker, the first and only woman on the CAW national executive board for many years, rose to the position of vice president of the CAW council. This position was usually a stepping stone to the presidency of CAW council. But Baker was asked to step back so that a male leader could take that spot. Despite her leadership in her local for decades, she lacked the boisterous bluster that the union's culture prized at that time. Baker says,

> I felt that at the point when we were changing officers at Canadian council and normally as vice president, I would have moved into the role of president. But that didn't happen now. I can't say it was done on purpose, but I felt that wasn't normally what was done. No one spoke to me about it, and I

> didn't make no fuss about it, either. I was given the position of secretary treasurer, and I was willing to carry on and do what I was asked to do.
>
> I felt let down somewhat. I didn't think it was right, but I wasn't a kind of person that stood up and stomped my feet and thumped my fists on the table.

Later when president of her airline local and long-time national executive board member Cheryl Kryzaniwsky did make the jump to become president of the council, she irritated the top leadership. Her style was completely different from past leaders. She had independent views that challenged orthodoxy by insisting, for example, on having an agenda for council meetings that she would chair. She refused to see herself as a prop and demanded respect. She was strongly "encouraged" to take a staff position as the director of education where she would need to enact the decisions of the leadership, a decision she regrets.

Annie Labaj, who was a pioneer in her GM plant and a fighter for employment equity, insisted on including women in education and international programs. She was dismissed as a bureaucrat without the workplace credentials of her male co-workers. This of course disregarded the fierce sexism she and other women faced in the plant and in the union.

Colette Hooson was labelled a "pain" because she fought relentlessly for pay equity and raised this at every meeting she could. Fitting into the Windsor community was difficult for her and others who worked outside of the auto sector. Hooson often butted heads with the auto leadership in Windsor and was eventually ostracized and isolated by some for speaking out on issues like choice, an issue that had long had the support of the union.

The national leadership labelled Julie White as "trouble" and sometimes warned new staff to steer clear of her. As a former member of the national executive board, she would reach out to new women joining the board only to be told to her that they had been warned not to be seen with her if they aspired to play a bigger role in the union.

Carla Bryden's voice still vibrates with pain and anger at how she refused to fit in with the "boys club" in Atlantic Canada. She was passed over repeatedly for a more senior staff role in Atlantic Canada in favour of more junior and less qualified men who were drinking buddies with the director there. These stories are not new, and while they occurred at the staff level of the union, they were replicated in many local unions.

Peggy Nash had a senior position in the union but had to push her way in to represent the president in bargaining in sectors such as hotels, health care, and airlines. When the president decided to reassign the latter two to a male colleague, she argued that as a woman, she should keep those female-dominated sectors. He refused. "So I told him if gender was not a factor, I wanted to work with the auto sector."

Caught off guard, he told her it depended on the auto leadership, that if she could gain acceptance from the union leadership at one of the auto companies then she had his support. The Ford group agreed. She would be the first woman assistant to lead auto bargaining from the national union. She worked hard to be firm but not blustery, to gain their respect. The strong economy in 2003 helped them negotiate a strong collective agreement. Her counterpart in bargaining, the head of human resources at Ford Canada, was also a woman, Stacey Allerton Firth. These gender anomalies across the bargaining table made the front page of the *Toronto Star*.

Late in the presidency of Buzz Hargrove there was unrest in the union and a lot of speculation about who would succeed both him and Jim O'Neil, the secretary treasurer. Some felt it was time for a woman in one of the top positions. Getting the nod from the current leadership was essential to be elected to the new top leadership team. Nash knew that challenging the system at that time was highly unlikely to succeed. But she had spent decades urging women to push for a greater role, so she tried to step up.

She made the case privately to the leadership that it was time for a woman to be considered for one of the top two leadership positions. She was shut down. "The union is not ready for a woman leader," they told her. She pressed, but it was evident the union was not going down that path. Clearly, the top leadership was not ready for a woman.

Having been an assistant to two national presidents at the CAW, now with the guarantee of a third all-male top leadership,

Peggy Nash during an International Women's Day march in Toronto. Photo: Peggy Nash.

she knew it was time to move on. She also struggled with the union's push for strategic voting. Jack Layton had asked her multiple times to run for the federal NDP. She had created leadership programs in the union to encourage women to step up, to run for positions. She now saw that would not be possible for her in the union. She loved the union and did not want to leave. While she always felt the union was her real home, she would fight for a place in parliament. Hargrove said she was crazy to leave. She felt that for her own self respect, sadly, she needed to move on. It took her two elections, beginning in 2004, to win in 2006. She found running for elected office and being an MP was a rewarding experience, and she wished she could have achieved that kind of organizing success in the union.

Carol Phillips: Time to Move On

Carol Phillips chose a different path. In 1989 Phillips co-chaired the successful campaign for Audrey McLaughlin to become the first woman leader of a political party in Canada. In 1990 she was on the election planning committee that resulted in seeing the NDP elected government in Ontario. She joined the inner staff of the premier's office shortly after. "I was extremely reluctant to leave the union, but President Bob White said it was an opportunity that I should accept." Given responsibility for appointments to agencies, boards, and commissions, Phillips was able to implement affirmative action on a much broader scale. After two years though she was uncomfortable with the direction of the government, and Bob White asked her to come to Ottawa as his assistant, as he became the president of the CLC.

She returned to the CAW in 1994.

As the then-assistant to the president after Nash was elected as an MP in 2006, Phillips, with her vast experience in the union but also in the Ontario government and the Canadian Labour Congress (CLC), was renamed to the assistant's position. Phillips had pioneered affirmative action programs, the social justice fund, and revamped the union's paid education leave program. She had bargaining experience and was a former local president. She decided she would run for the position of national secretary treasurer against the administration caucus.

Phillips had wanted to change some of the long-time structures in the union:

> We all knew it was bullshit, that the national executive board were the ones who chose the candidates and made the decisions. It was the front office, a small cabal of strong men who would sit around and decide where the union is going, who's going to run, who will get the nod. The union was changing. There were a lot of younger people coming in, a lot of women workers of colour, and 2SLGBTQ+, who were not only coming in but coming onto staff, but in very narrow areas of influence. So, there was a lot of window dressing going on, but the fact of the matter was, where the change happened was in this small group of men. So, I just decided it was time.

She consulted with some others in the union and in 2008, knowing that there would be some leadership changes in the union, decided to run for the position of national secretary treasurer. She would run against the leadership choice of Peter Kennedy, who had been the assistant to the secretary treasurer. There was nothing she had against him personally but knew he would just carry on the same as before and not challenge anything.

She had been excluded by the leadership from the decision-making process about that election. "It was an assumption, that I was part of that inner group. For the longest time I had been part of that inner group in the Bob White days, now I was part of the window dressing."

She says she was barred from a meeting where a small group of men were deciding the future leadership. Phillips was furious. She responded: "You can take your fucking assistant's job and shove it where the sun doesn't shine. I've had it. This is absolute bullshit. I'm being kept out of key meetings. You guys don't trust me. I don't like the decision-making structure."

She had been angry since the decision of the union to support strategic voting and "the way they handled that and rammed it down the throats of so many good activists."

So she started phoning around the union for support. Certainly, there was some support, but she was shocked by the opposition, which was ferocious from some of the auto locals. They wanted to support Ken Lewenza who was tapped to run for president and Kennedy would be his running mate. They saw her run as an attack against Lewenza who was from auto. "All of a sudden, they decided that I had just been a figurehead all along, cause you had to have a woman. So, it was thirty years of work in the union. Gone. It was a misogynistic attack."

She says they decided her Achilles heel was to threaten what they would do to her supporters. They started naming women staff who were going to be punished for defying the leadership. "It was vicious, and it was unrelenting" she says. "They hated my questioning of the structures of the caucus system, of the fact that there was this pretend decision of the national executive board."

She went to the national executive board but decided not to ask for an endorsement but to run outside of the caucus . She felt that most of the board had made their decision and were locked in before the discussion began; she knew the system. Since the formation of the CAW, the NEB never wavered and had always supported the president's recommendation for the positions, and as always with a show of hands.

Then she went to the union's staff meeting where the staff would also vote on the candidate. They allowed her to speak from the podium. As she looked out on the rows of familiar staff faces, faces now frozen in disapproval, fear, or defiance, she spoke about democracy, invoking UAW founder Victor Reuther:

> I believe I'm in the best traditions of the CAW. Victor Reuther rejected a structure that he thought was top down when he supported the CAW to leave the UAW. Did anybody in this room think that was a betrayal of trade unionism or their union to reject the international union? No, we didn't, because we knew it was time to move on to new structures.

She says it was not friendly.

"Oh, my God! [Bob] White was livid that I had invoked Victor Reuther," she says.

Some supporters from the staff, Mike Shields and Kim Yardy, were brave enough to speak in support of her. Phillips's run was essentially over after she failed to sway the staff. They would ensure the vote went the way the administration wanted.

Former staff rep Carla Bryden will never forget Phillips's bravery and strength when she got up to speak. Phillips was "Friggin amazing." (See also Carla Bryden, chapter 5.)

However, Phillips did speak at a women's conference before the convention. She recalls staff were sent there to intimidate the delegates and report back on who was supporting Carol. Women did support her at personal cost. Their support was held against them, but not against most men who supported her.

Bryden remembers, "I'll never forget the women's conference where some staff women were spying for the leadership around Carol's decision to run. They were there to report back what was happening. It was unbelievable."

After the convention Phillips remained on the staff as an assistant to the president. "So I was there till December, though they kept trying to fire me, but they just ground me down." Meanwhile Julie White was threatened with firing for her support for Phillips. White told Phillips, "Let him go ahead and try." she was confident she could rally women around her. Other women staff like Annie Labaj also paid a price for her support of Phillips.

Annie Labaj says,

> Suddenly everything I did was being questioned. They tried to get me moved out of the international department, back to education, and have another staff appointed as the international director who had been in the department only a few months. So lots of it was rough times afterwards, for a lot of people. Well, for the women especially, once they sort of found out who was supporting Carol. They didn't know who was supporting her until they got a list.

Some senior women in the union had opposed Phillips and were vicious toward her, seeing the opportunity for their personal gain. "But I fully understand the whole issue of being victims of our own oppression, which I learned pretty early," Phillips says. "We can't help ourselves sometimes in identifying with the guys because they're powerful."

But Phillips believes the guys were misreading the room, that the world had moved on, the union had moved on. A lot of the women in the union had moved on, and even a lot of the men, who had grown up with feminism:

> They'd misread totally how much fundamental feminization of thought happened among activists, how radical a change. They still thought that they could do whatever the hell they wanted and just bully their way through. They didn't get how radical those programs were in the scheme of things and how radically they changed the thought process. They just didn't understand that. The approach people took to being more engaged in having an open mind around patriarchal structures and what they had done and how they needed to change, and how the union fit into those patriarchal structures.

Phillips's challenge to the leadership was a bold and courageous move that inspired many women. Ultimately when Carol found she could not count on enough support from the union staff, who then

Carol Phillips at a GM Oshawa childcare rally, with Julie White and Barb Byers, Canadian Labour Congress vice president. Photo: Annie Labaj.

played a political role in the union, she stepped back and did not launch a broader campaign. Eventually she left the union and took a position with the Ontario Labour Relations Board. Nevertheless, her bold initiative got women thinking that change was long overdue. There needed to be women at the top of the union.

Some Black and racialized women also found that their path in the union was limited. They were offered opportunities that they loved, delivering education programs or organizing. But others found that no matter how much dedication they showed to the union, there was always a male leader who needed to be taken care off and their opportunity did not materialize.

While the union supported anti-racism work, there was not the support and opportunities to women of colour that would have helped them succeed. Encouragement alone was not a plan. Some talented Black and racialized women left the CAW and found leadership positions in other unions.

The leadership did respond to demands for progress, but

they had difficulty sharing power. They underestimated how fast women wanted change and how frustrating it was to be told to keep waiting their turn.

Stickin' with the Union

The rise of second wave feminism was able to take advantage of structures built into the UAW from the war years. What helped make the labour movement women's programs so successful in Canada was the ability of labour women to join with their sisters in the community to fight for change. Whether in strike support, fighting for abortion rights, childcare, or against gender-based violence, they forged a relationship that made both groups stronger.

When this growing movement conflicted with the impact of neoliberal economics on the lives of workers, especially in manufacturing, it could have stalled the progress being made on equity issues. Nevertheless, CAW activists (and many in other unions) pressed on and made progress. These initiatives shone a light on how entrenched the dominant cultural norms were, in manufacturing in particular, but in female-dominated sectors as well. This tension between the traditional workplace and the feminist movement was real in the lives of women, racialized, and 2SLGBTQIA+ workers. They loved and appreciated their union, called on their union to defend their rights, but still sometimes found the union leadership or culture pushing back or blocking their way.

Perhaps not surprisingly, some women bought into that traditional culture and served to reinforce it. When a significant opportunity opened up to get behind an activist feminist leader, some women clung to the old ways. They failed to see that the world was changing.

What is impressive, though, is the number of leaders from diverse groups who developed during this period before the creation of Unifor in 2013 when the CAW joined with the CEP (Communications, Energy and Paperworkers Union of Canada). The numbers of racialized and other diverse women in the CAW were rising, and they were organizing. There was a new confidence and the space that the union had created, going back to the war years, was stretched, expanded, and filled with a new generation of activists eager for change. The CAW merger with the CEP to form

Unifor would help to accelerate the inclusion of new and more diverse activists.

Change can take a long time and it doesn't happen on its own. The top leadership of the CAW had been mostly supportive when women and human rights activists pushed for policies and programs to foster greater equity and diversity. Women were frustrated by the lack of diversity in the very top leadership of the union.

The women in this book tell stories that show that gains don't just happen but are the product of organizing and struggle, courage and leadership, over many years. Each of the people we interviewed for this book showed leadership, each struggled to make a difference. The men we interviewed are examples of allies who supported and assisted women and 2SLGBTQIA+ activists in their efforts. Allies can be essential to making progress. But ultimately, activists pushed for and achieved change.

Epilogue

The Future Looks Feminist, Lana Payne, President

The pandemic that shut down much of the world beginning in 2020 reminded us of the value of work. Essential positions such as nurses and other health care workers, grocery and food production workers, educators, childcare workers, firefighters, and police officers were the priority—not financial manipulators or real estate flippers. To their credit, some governments provided the economic support to help people ride out the collapse of the economy, but it was service workers and essential workers that made sure we could all survive.

Newly elected Unifor President Lana Payne's victory speech at the convention had squarely focused on unity (see Prologue). It was a pivotal moment in the history of the union. Since the election, Payne has built bridges, restored relationships, and regained the confidence among members. Despite the lingering disappointment of some, they grew to understand, regardless of their differences, the time had come to move on, a signal first sent by the national president in her acceptance speech.

People loved the union, whichever candidate they had supported to become president. Payne knew that meant not being vindictive with those who didn't support her leadership. Some staff were ready to retire, and this gave Payne the chance to hire new faces, new energy, and new ideas. Payne also immediately set about touring dozens of workplaces, meeting members, listening to them, and hearing their concerns.

For example, when she toured Fort McMurray and listened to the concerns of energy workers, she spoke of the need to rebuild the battered Canadian manufacturing sector and how essential

Quebec Unifor members marching in solidarity with striking workers, led by newly elected President Lana Payne, left Daniel Cloutier, Quebec director, right Gavin McGarrigle, western regional director, front left Roxanne Dubois, executive assistant to Unifor national president. Photo: Unifor.

energy workers were to that process. "Workers were never the problem," she said. "And often they know what the solutions are for their sector if someone would just listen to them."

One energy sector member told her that listening to her remarks: "It felt like you were in my head."

In the new post-pandemic phase, there was a window for workers to make progress and Payne's goal was to increase members' expectations.

CUPE Education Workers Strike

The Doug Ford Conservative government offered Ontario workers the perfect opportunity to test their strength. With its Bill 124 in November 2019, the government aimed to hold salary increases for broader public sector workers, both union and non-union, at 1 per cent a year for three years. This move infuriated workers and their unions as it overrode their right to free collective bargaining.

The 55,000 Ontario education workers in the Canadian Union of Public Employees (CUPE) were an early test of the new law.

These frontline workers included educational assistants, school secretaries, custodians, and early childcare workers. Predominantly women, these workers were some of the lowest paid in the public sector. Their collective agreement had expired at the end of August 2022, and the following month they voted 96.5 per cent for a strike. The major sticking point was pay, especially for low-wage workers.

When the union issued a strike notice in October, the Ford government responded with Bill 28, the Keeping Students in Class Act, to pre-empt a strike using the notwithstanding clause of the Canadian Charter of Rights and Freedoms to override collective bargaining. The law would punish strike action by CUPE members by fining them up to four thousand dollars a day. The union could face a fine of five hundred thousand dollars per day.

Reaction was swift and furious. The union announced that they would strike regardless, and that they would challenge the fines and pay them on behalf of the workers, if needed, to ensure that the workers would not be paying out of pocket. Human rights and civil liberties organizations joined the broader labour movement in condemning this overreach by the Ontario government.

Laura Walton, president of the education workers union local, and other leaders had done an outstanding job organizing and mobilizing their membership. The role of the rest of the labour movement was to support them. When you shut down the education system you get the attention of parents. They were exhausted from home schooling during the pandemic, but they understood the value of the work CUPE members performed. And these members understood the value of their own work. Many parents came out to the picket lines and shut down the streets around the provincial legislature, Queen's Park, Toronto, and communities across Ontario. Canada's largest province became occupied by thousands of regular people, many of whom had never before joined a protest. It was solidarity that Ontario hadn't seen for many years.

Payne said, "You don't let moments like this pass you by." She told Doug Ford, "You've got a big problem here."

This was bigger than one union or one round of collective bargaining. Taking away the right to collective bargaining is a direct attack on all unions.

Doug Ford wisely backed down.

This flexing of labour's muscle and the subsequent victory added more wind in labour's sails and reinforced Payne's belief that this was indeed a moment for workers. The CUPE strike had helped all workers. It reminded them that it was they, as workers, who had helped society through the pandemic, and now they as workers needed to get recognized.

The Metro Strike

Later that year, Unifor's members working at Metro stores and warehouses (a large grocery chain) began collective bargaining for a new contract. Most grocery-store workers, predominantly women, make very low pay, but they masked up and went to work during the pandemic, ensuring people were able to get food. During the pandemic, all major grocery employers had given the workers hero pay of an additional two dollars an hour for the risks they were taking to provide essential work. At the end of the pandemic, employers took away this pay while prices were skyrocketing. These high prices and resulting big corporate profits put the grocery chains directly in the line of fire of politicians and the union. In bargaining, the members were determined to make big gains. They wanted back their hero pay.

Unifor had developed a mobilizing and bargaining plan for the sector. The goal was to establish pattern bargaining, the same system that helped auto workers achieve good wages and benefits. With pattern bargaining in a multi-employer sector, the union negotiates an agreement with the company where a good contract seems most likely. Then the union takes that pattern to other employers and tells them that it is a floor that they have to match or improve on. Such a plan was long overdue in the grocery sector.

The union's Metro bargaining committee had strong membership support. By July 29, 2023, there were 3,700 workers at twenty-seven Toronto area stores on strike.

"We have members who can't afford to shop in the stores where they work," Payne told the media from a picket line rally: "There is something happening in this country right now. These workers have set a fire to the labour movement, standing up, fighting back against corporate greed. We deserve justice, we deserve good jobs, we deserve decent pay."

The bargaining committee brought a tentative agreement to the members with unprecedented wage increases. But it was rejected by the members. A second tentative agreement offered an immediate $1.50 with an additional $2.00 to follow soon after. These improvements were unprecedented. The union set a new bar for grocery workers and then succeeded in taking the pattern to match wages at No Frills, which is part of the Loblaw chain.

Then a sister union, the United Food and Commercial Workers, with a much bigger footprint in the grocery sector, took the pattern and used it for their bargaining. The job of a union and its representatives is to improve life for the members; whatever works is valuable in collective bargaining.

Auto Bargaining

Payne's biggest challenge was to be in bargaining for Unifor members in the auto sector later that year (2023). Traditionally, workplace leaders are tested in their workplace and local elections to secure a place at the bargaining table. Then the real test is in standing up to the employer and winning a strong collective agreement, taking on the employer with a strike if necessary. Certainly, there were lots of women who had bargaining experience in other sectors, but the large industrial locals that were the traditional backbone of the union were still heavily male dominated. Rarely had a woman risen to the higher levels of these organizations.

Payne had proved herself in the fightback with the collapse of the cod fishery where she demonstrated her strategic, organizing, and bargaining skills. She had been elected secretary treasurer and then president of the Newfoundland Federation of Labour, where she had led a successful fight to bump up the provincial minimum wage. And she had been elected as Unifor national secretary treasurer, where she had wrestled the union's finances under control. All of this took smarts and boldness.

Unifor represented workers in some twenty-five economic sectors from health care to telecommunications. Nonetheless, the auto sector was still a key to bargaining breakthroughs because of the large numbers of workers under one roof with the power to shut down the industry and because of the power of pattern bargaining.

This was also the first auto bargaining in the post-pandemic

Lana Payne and leadership in auto talks, 2023. Photo: Canadian Press.

period. Like many other workers, Unifor members had made sacrifices during the pandemic, and then saw corporations rebound quickly while they languished with high inflation and a crisis of affordability. The members were primed for collective bargaining, and they gave their bargaining committees at Ford, General Motors Canada, and Stellantis a 98 to 99 per cent strike mandate. This vote is intended to be a signal to the company that the members are behind their union and ready to take a strike to defend their contract proposals.

The union decided to focus on Ford of Canada with a strike deadline of September 19, and then took the unusual step of extending the deadline by twenty-four hours to reach an agreement. Payne agreed to the extension when it became clear that Ford wanted to settle and that the union could use that opportunity to maximize their gains. "We went with Ford because we had a number of things that we wanted to do differently, to be able to set down our own path, which was really important."

The Unifor-Ford agreement offered the 5,600 workers a $10,000 "productivity and quality bonus," plus an almost 20 per cent increase over the life of the agreement, more for the skilled trades workers. In addition, the union was able to reinstate its cost-of-living allowance (COLA) which added to the pay increase. The three-year agreement meant the Canadians would be back at the bargaining table in 2026. It also compressed somewhat the pay grid, whereby newer workers increase their pay based on their time with the company, from eight to four years to reach the maximum hourly wage.

The union said some members would receive between 50 and 70 per cent wage increases. Payne called it "life-changing." But members' expectations were high, and the Ford ratification vote was surprisingly low, at 54 per cent.

By mid-October, the 4,300 workers at General Motors Canada ratified the pattern agreement, following a short strike, by 80.5 per cent. By early November, the 8,300 Stellantis members at multiple locations had ratified the pattern agreement with some local improvements by margins of between 60 and 100 per cent. "I am proud," says Payne, "of our members for their support and solidarity over the course of these negotiations, including their brief but necessary strike action that helped make this historic agreement possible."

So much was riding on that year's auto negotiations. Payne was the first woman union president in the North American heavy-manufacturing sector. She took the unique step of forming an auto sector women's advisory committee to get good advice about the union's equity measures and to ensure fairness in other contract provisions. The support they provided was essential. Any woman in the public eye knows the negative power of social media. The women's committee also helped refute and shut down some of that ugliness.

But Payne says that the biggest gender challenges came from outside the union, from people who don't understand how the union works:

> Collective bargaining is about the collective. This is the whole point. It is not one person for sure. But as president, you have to set the tone, you have to set the frame for how this is going to happen. And then in the end, yeah, you pull the trigger. We had the first strikes in the auto industry in some cases in forty years. But there you go. Let's go guys. This was a turning point for us.

Payne said women wrote her letters after that deal. One was a single mom who said, "I don't know how to thank you but I want you to know. I can finally breathe." Payne says,

> One of the women on the Ford committee was crying because she was going to get a twelve dollar an hour pay raise. It's those little nuggets that you get that make it all worthwhile. It proves that collective bargaining is the most powerful tool working people have. It can change lives.

Lana Payne: Ask Big Things, Build Big Things, and Do Big Things

It's hard to overstate the significance of Payne's election as president of Unifor. From the earliest days of the United Auto Workers, this is a proud union that has been powered primarily by men and male energy. They built a powerhouse of a union that not only created the conditions for working people and their families to live good lives but they also created a political movement of working-class power that acted in the interests of workers. Along the same timeline, women have played an important role, eking out some space in that male energy. Women used that space to organize and to press for change.

The union lost talent when women were pushed back into the home in the 1950s. And some women chaffed against the limitations they faced. They were not fully able to contribute or use their potential creativity and power because men were not ready to share power with them. Some women just gave up and left the union. Looking back at some of the demands from the 1940s, it is worth noting that, while gains have been made, some goals like universal childcare and equal representation in the union still seem a long way off.

That's why the hopes for Payne are so high. Decades of feminist working-class women organizing paved the way for her get to her position as the head of the union. Her election is the opportunity for the union to not only regain lost ground but reposition itself to appeal to the working people of today, to new Canadians, to young people, to the enormous diversity that is Canada.

She is a tough working-class feminist, and she is clearly on the left politically. The kind of foundation she's trying to lay right now is to build worker power rather than suppressing it. She says that has to be a very deliberate action, which means sometimes doing things a little differently than they were traditionally done in the union.

And the union will look different. Payne has ensured that women are much better represented and that workers of colour are in all the "spaces and places. Already, the union looks a lot different in two years, so imagine what it's going to look like in ten years."

Lana Payne was the keynote speaker for an International Women's Day event at Unifor Local 636 in Woodstock. The local is one of the oldest locals in the old auto union where former President Bob White was once local president. There were several long-time activists there that day but the place was bursting with young women who were so excited about the union. Hearing Lana speak they were full of enthusiasm. Clearly, they see that they have a place in the union, and they are rising to the occasion.

Payne says: "It is the women that really carry you on their shoulders in so many ways. Not just the women that came before, but the women there now, and they are so proud to have a woman president."

The Unifor Local 222 hall is a large facility in an Oshawa Park on the edge of Lake Ontario. This is a storied local union that was once home to the largest auto local union in Canada, the workers at General Motors Canada. It fostered great leaders like former Ontario Federation of Labour President Cliff Pilkey and the women who fought successfully to change the Ontario Human Rights Code to ban sex discrimination.

GM's footprint is much smaller today, but it will be part of the new investment in electric vehicles. The local union is an amalgamation of members from many different workplaces including industries like Lear Corporation and St. Mary's Cement. But it also includes workers at Loblaws and Durham College. Today there are many more women in all those jobs, including at GM, and it's changing the union.

There were 250 to 300 women at an International Women's Day luncheon in Oshawa, once the largest local in the union when most members worked at General Motors. Payne tells the story of a long-time member who told her: "I just never thought I'd see this, a woman president of the union." And she said, "I've been dying to meet you in person."

A large part of the job as president is to inspire the people around you, to be able to take up the challenge and to feel good about their union. "If your members feel good about the union in this way, they will do anything to make sure that survives and grows and they'll fight for it," says Payne.

Progress is never smooth. She is making way for women and more diversity, and there will always be pushback about the pace of change. The goal is to make the staff reflect the membership of the union. And most people feel good about that.

"It's a path you're laying down and everything you are doing in terms of building worker power, bargaining great agreements, changing the culture of the union, the staff, everything is about setting down that path, and you're offering that path to young activists."

Women's Reaction to the First Woman President

Unless you have experienced the culture of a very male-dominated organization, you might not understand how groundbreaking it was to see a woman elected to the top post in Unifor. Women have been appointed to positions in political cabinets, in the miliary and the police, but in the union, you need to get elected.

Lana Payne's election was an earthquake that signalled major change in the union. For most women, this signalled a key breakthrough after decades, generations, of pushing for equality. There was excitement and tremendous pride that Payne could win.

For Maureen Kirincic, who comes from the days of being one of the very few women in a giant auto plant, it was unthinkable:

> Well, I was still shocked when we got a woman assistant [to the president]. I'm still at that. We really saw a lot of changes once the airline group came in. Look at how far we've come. And then a women president. I never thought I'd see it in my lifetime. Never in a million years. It's a good victory.

The presidency of the largest industrial union in Canada brings with it power. The power to shut down a key sector of the Canadian economy and to open doors in prime ministers' and premiers' officers. It offers the blunt power of a strike but also the soft power to influence.

Carol Phillips who ran unsuccessfully describes it this way:

> She's the highest-profile trade-union leader in the country. I had to smile when I saw her in the *Globe and Mail* business section with business leaders talking about the next year and, there, smack in the middle is Lana Payne. It used to be Bob White, and then it was Buzz Hargrove. But now they want to know what Lana Payne thinks. Partly because she's head of the union, but it's also because she's incredibly articulate. She speaks about social justice and economic justice in a way that we've come full circle back to social unionism. So she has re-embodied that social union history in a big way. It's wonderful. It's inspiring. It makes me feel great about the union and having been part of it over the years. It makes the awful times worth it. It's terrific.

There was just outright jubilation on the part of many women. Mildred Skinner from the FFAW in Newfoundland said,

> Oh, that was tremendous! The day I heard she was running for president. I cried, and I had no doubts that she was going to win. When I arrived at the FFAW inshore table in 1996, Lana was the only women there, you know, and I knew right away when I looked at her, that she was responsible for getting me there. She was our voice for a long time. I've got so much admiration for her, like many, many of us have. She's smart and she's made a huge difference for women of the union, me included. So yeah, I'm proud to call her sister.

Elaine White said,

> She broke the glass ceiling along the way, then she just broke the whole damn ceiling right out of the building. She really did it with a lot of support from a lot of people, and it wasn't just women supporting her. It was men supporting her as well. And

> I think that really shows that we were ready for change. She had the heart of the workers. Payne is a feminist, and women expected her to be transformational, meaning that she would wield power differently and inclusively. While it is hard in a big organization to make meaningful institutional change, Payne has shown a different kind of leadership. But she has been no less tough than her predecessors when it comes to fighting for the membership.

Denise McMorris,

> When I first heard that she's going to run, I questioned it. From the perspective of where I came from [a large auto assembly plant], a woman could never win, and I felt that she's going to be devoured by the Boys Club. There was such a huge turmoil in Unifor at the time, I had my doubts to be honest with you. I said to myself, "Why on earth would Lana do this?" It took a lot of guts, a lot of courage! Not all the women supported her. I was very surprised. But I said to myself, "Lana stands on the shoulders of powerful of giants, and so, Lana will do this with the support that she needs."

Symbolically, the election of a woman to the top position at Unifor signals that society has changed. A real gender barrier has been broken. It also means that feminism is entering a new phase. Women generally in society may still have to fight to get their issues addressed and, in many organizations, women still have to fight for any space to play a leadership role. However, Payne's win shows it's possible in the right circumstances for the right leader with guts and strong principles.

As Kim Crump says,

> In that moment, I was euphoric. Overwhelmed with joy. But most of all I was filled with hope. Our fierce, courageous, sister/friend had put it all out there and smashed through the glass ceiling, and I know she'll do all she can to bring the sisterhood along with her.

Lana makes connections of the heart, and she feels things deeply. This is what made her the best candidate in the election, and this is what makes her such a great leader. She truly believes a better world is possible—for women, for workers, for society, and because she invests in building genuine relationships and continues to win the hearts and minds of our members. I believe it's possible, too, because I believe her.

Change is possible if you fight for it. That is a beacon for the next generation of feminists who are learning how tough the struggle has been. And it has been a very long struggle for them to continue.

Afterword

Advice for New Activists

We asked the women interviewed for this book to offer their advice for new activists. Here is some of their advice based on the collective experience of decades of women's union activism.

Lana Payne: This is your union. Don't give up on it. Make it yours, and some of the ways you do that is you always have to organize. It was Madeleine Parent who said, every moment is an organizing moment. And for a young activist, you've got to find your people. And obviously organize around what it is you want and what you think the union should be doing.

If you're feeling discouraged, because that can happen, have good friends and sisters and brothers and allies around you. It's so critical to how you get through the rough times.

For young activists, you have an opportunity to transform this union, too. You have an opportunity to use this as the most powerful tool to change, not just your conditions of work, but the conditions of the world. That is what can happen when you use your union effectively, be part of it and participate in it.

Carol Phillips: You just have to go with what you believe in. Sometimes we're really forced. We're really pushed and encouraged to fit in to learn the ropes and fit in. But for the most part, most of us have our own unique talents, and sometimes you won't fit in. That doesn't mean we don't just keep pushing ahead.

The other thing is really relish the feeling of solidarity, really enjoy it, and really cultivate it, and embrace it because whether it's solidarity as workers or solidarity as women, that is the most rewarding part of this whole thing.

We have to stop fighting for the crumbs. We have to bake our own cake.

Roxie Baker: If you want to become a leader, take advantage of the education courses in the union. I got as much education as I could, and I sent as many members to courses as possible. All the knowledge that I gained, it's only because I went to education programs offered by our union.

Attend as many one-day programs in your local union as you can. There, you will have an opportunity to learn and grow as an activist. It's important for everyone, but especially for women to gain knowledge on equity programs, learn about the union's current campaigns, meet other activists, often from our community. Women's programs, conferences, and equity programs are one of the best things that a new activist can do for yourself as you begin your activism. It will give you the opportunity to grow and use your newfound skills once you return to your workplace.

Denise Kellahan: Attend every meeting that you possibly can. Spend some time, researching the history of your organization or union, to know the history. Because to go forward, you have to know where you've been.

Get involved, and don't be afraid to run for positions. Choose the areas that you think you really want to make a difference in, whether it's on a health and safety committee, or whether it's serving as shop steward.

Approach your local to see whether there are opportunities to attend courses or conferences or workshops. Put yourself out there to learn as much as you possibly can.

It always helps if you have support of your co-workers, so be respectful of your co-workers and let it be known that you're interested in things Don't be afraid to ask, would they support you or nominate you for something? With each job that you do, you are going to make a difference, whether you're sitting as chair of the health and safety committee. Each thing you do you will make a difference in your workplace, and it will probably be one of the most gratifying things you ever do in your life. Because feeling that you can make something better for somebody else is a pretty darn good feeling.

Cheryl Kryzaniwsky: Don't give up; don't ever give up. Reach out and talk to another woman who might be going through what you are experiencing. You need never be alone. Then when you have a victory, reach out and say "I'm available." Don't ever be too busy to talk to another woman and encourage her and always always reach back. Never pull up the ladder that helped you reach your pinnacle. We don't need to protect our space; we need to always be expanding.

Elaine White: Do it from the heart, get involved for all the right reasons. Get more people involved with you. It's not about having your position. It's about getting support from everybody. So build your support system around you and get involved. But make sure that you include other people along the way.

Be strong. Sometimes you step outside of your comfort zone, you gotta do it. Take some courses and educate yourself on the principles of our union. It's about how can you make change. The courses up in Port Elgin are critical. If you can't take them in Port Elgin, sometimes they have area schools. Just go to meetings and get involved and mobilize other people.

Laurell Ritchie: Just get in there and do the stuff that you think needs doing. And sometimes that will mean creating new organizations. That's how we started the Coalition Against Free Trade. That's how we started the Equal Pay Coalition. Sometimes they're big coalition efforts like that. Other times, they're small projects that may be particular to a local. But if there's a project or an issue that needs attention, whether it's a one-time petition or something with a little more staying power, just get in there and do it.

Denise Hampden: Find your lane. Find the thing that you are most passionate about and talented at. If you are talented at web page design, offer up your services to whoever needs them, and design the hell out of those web pages. If you are talented at writing, offer up your services.

Take your course. It's what I say about the calls to action for truth and reconciliation. Take your corner of the planet and do something.

Find what's going to bring you satisfaction. Don't rely on the union for satisfaction, 'cause you will get nothing but disappointment if you're relying on the union for that.

I would say to young women, do not forgo having a family or doing things you love—going to the theatre, taking up ice skating. Don't forgo that because you think you're needed elsewhere. I still think I was needed elsewhere. I really do. It's just there weren't enough of me.

Sandra Cormier: I'd say not to give up, to stay in the machine, to continue to work within the boundaries and just chip at them once in a while and never stop. It's challenging. It's hard. It's not an easy road to go through. But it changes. Little things change. Sometimes there are little steps, but most of the time you have to have faith that things will change and they do, and they do it better than it was.

There are so many beautiful memories that I have of the union. We wouldn't do our work if we weren't optimistic.

Cathy Walker: Women still have to work harder than the men in the union for our role to be acknowledged. Find a mentor. It doesn't have to be a woman to provide sound advice. For me, it was Jess Succamore, former CAIMAW secretary treasurer, who knocked some of the more extreme chips from my left shoulder. Jess always felt women were as competent as men and as worthy to become leaders. Find someone with experience to guide you through the rough spots and they will provide needed advice and support.

Peggy Nash: Your belief in building a better world will see you through the tough times. When you have to fight to make change, remember you are also making history.

Reach out to women in more senior positions in the union and ask for advice. Reach out to other women in your workplace and get them involved. Activism is about relationships. They build greater power. Whatever you decide to take on, make it a "we" action and not an "I" action. Build the union while fighting for change.

Remember to find joy and have fun. Life is too short to see everything as a chore. Resistance is joyful. Others will want to be part of it.

Julie White: Stand your ground, build your network, connect with the Sisterhood. It is a powerful source of support and advice as you begin your activism. When times get tough, and they will, the Sisterhood will be your touchstone, your support, your go-to place, especially during challenging times, even within the union.

Don't let fear send you running. If you are not successful, build support, find your allies, and come back to fight another day, knowing that silence is not an option. Change often takes time.

Don't be hesitant to challenge, to speak up, or to tell your story even when it makes some uncomfortable. And know that women are watching, listening, and supporting you even when it feels you are alone.

Attend women's programs and conferences—find your passion and then organize, lobby, demonstrate, and protest, and encourage other women to join you. Run for a leadership position even when it has always been held by a man.

Support progressive, feminist voices even when others are not. Some may call you disloyal to the union when you are pushing for change—don't listen to the gossip, don't listen to the noise.

Step aside, step back, and encourage a new activist to get involved, like another sister did for you. Share your knowledge and your power, and remember power with vs power over builds the union.

Take time to celebrate the wins, even the partial ones. And remember to always find time to celebrate those magical sisterhood moments knowing that the work you are doing together is building a better world.

Biographies of Interviewees

Jane Armstrong, in 1980, joined the staff of CALEA. After the CAW 1985 merger she organized plants in southern Ontario. Heavily involved in anti-apartheid solidarity with the SACTU solidarity committee (South African Congress of Trade Unions) in the 1980s, she continued with international union solidarity work until retirement. In 1991, Armstrong joined the CAW communications staff, and from 1994 to 2004 was CAW national communications director, the position she held up to retirement.

Cathy Austin, past president of CAW Local 88, was a feminist trailblazer, mentor, educator, and advocate for social justice and peace. Cathy began working at CAMI Automotive in 1989 and almost immediately became a member of leadership. She was elected for several terms as a workplace committeeperson. Cathy was then elected to the local executive board, where she first held the position of trustee, then vice president, finally becoming the first and only woman to ever be elected president of a large auto local.

Roxie Baker is a retired auto parts worker from Stratford, Ontario. She has been a proud member of the UAW, CAW, and Unifor for thirty years and continues to represent Unifor retirees. Roxie was the former president of Local 1325 and was elected as the first woman to the CAW national executive board. Currently, Roxie is chairperson and benefits representative of retired worker chapter 1325, area council and CURC council.

Lynn Brophy was an educator, political junkie, and a social justice and human rights activist. She was the director of communications for CAW Local 2213 before joining CAW national staff working with the education and communications departments. Additionally, Lynn was auto-parts sectoral-training council co-managing director. And, she was a lover of many things creative and artistic.

Carla Bryden began her career in the banking industry and was instrumental in organizing the union at Bergengren Credit in 1987. Carla was a long-time CAW discussion leader until she was appointed as a national representative for the CAW in 2005. She always felt strongly about injustice and became active in the women's movement through her activism in the union. Carla retired in 2017 and now resides in Halifax, Nova Scotia.

Barb Byers is a feminist, socialist, activist, and trade unionist. She has worked in various levels of the provincial, national, and international trade union movement. Barb's elected positions include president of the Saskatchewan Government and General Employees Union, president of the Saskatchewan Federation of Labour, and secretary treasurer of the Canadian Labour Congress. Following her work in union positions, she continues to be engaged with the labour movement and is actively involved in her community. Barb was awarded the Order of Canada in 2015 in recognition for her service to the labour, women's, and social action movements.

Christine Connor worked in the Metro produce department for many years. As chairperson for her unit, she sat on the executive board of Local 414 as area representative. In 2004, she was elected as first women president of CAW Local 414 in its sixty-year history. She went on to represent retail workers on the national executive board from 2004 to 2017, when she joined the Unifor national staff.

Sandra Cormier began working at Air Canada in1986 in the non-unionized Aeroplan department. Once the department unionized in 1990, Sandra was elected the first district chair, a position she held until 1998. Additionally, Sandra was a CAW discussion leader, board of trustee, and CAW Local 2002 eastern-region vice president from 2005 to 2016. Sandra retired in 2018.

Kim Crump is a lesbian, feminist, and activist. She is a retired auto worker and proud member of Unifor Local 88. Kim served three terms as an elected member of the executive board as guide and trustee respectively. For several years, Kim worked full-time with the CAW education and women's departments as a curriculum designer and discussion leader.

Wendy Cuthbertson was director of communications for the UAW/CAW, 1977–1987, leaving the union to become a senior official at Ontario's new pay equity commission. A member of the OFL and NDP women's committees, she also sat on various NDP executive committees. She served as the president of the Canadian Association of Labour Media and worked for the Service Employees Union in Washington, DC. Her PhD thesis, "Labour Goes to War: The CIO and the Construction of the New Social Order, 1939–1945" was published by the University of British Columbia Press.

Anne Davidson is a former CAW BC and Alberta area director. Prior to joining staff, Anne worked in the airline division. With extensive bargaining experience through five airline mergers and union representational votes, Anne was elected president of the airline division and was appointed to the CAW national executive board. In retirement, Anne remains active and is elected to the Co-op Housing Federation of BC and Canada and is appointed to the board of the Agency for Co-operative Housing.

Starting on the shop floor, then working within the union, Annie worked to change the lens through which members saw their world. From being the first woman to be appointed as a national representative from General Motors to international director and overseeing the social justice fund, her twenty-eight years at the national union gave her many opportunities to interact with members, not only in Canada but around the world.

Pam Diggs first worked in housekeeping for thirteen years at the Holiday Inn in London, Ontario. She was then hired at Standard Products, an automotive parts factory where she became a member of CAW Local 4451. Pam currently works at Labatt Brewery and is a member of SEIU 2 Branch 1. Her union activities include participation on the women's, human rights, workers of colour, and the 2SLGBTQ+ committees. As a long-time member of the Gutter Boyz (drag king troupe), Pam participates in many fund-raising events for queer youth, PFLAG, and various pride events across Ontario.

Dana Dunphy is a Unifor representative servicing local workplaces in the Windsor and Sarnia communities. Dana has dedicated most of her adult life advocating for workers in her community. She was elected to various union positions for over twenty years and spent eleven years as chairperson at Caesars Casino. In her spare time, Dana likes to ride her bike and spend time with family, friends, and her dog Nova.

Theresa Farao is a lifelong union activist. She organized her workplace over twenty-five years ago. She has held various leadership positions, including twelve years as Local 240 president. In 2016, Theresa became a Unifor national representative. Theresa is passionate about pay equity. With twenty-three years of experience, workers have received hundreds of thousands of dollars through her efforts. Theresa has also been involved in developing pay equity education and training materials for committees and staff.

Irene Friend was one of the first local equity reps at the Big Three auto companies and the first full-time employment equity coordinator for the UAW at Chrysler Canada. Friend first worked at a small UAW Windsor plant from 1969 until 1976 when she heard that Chrysler was hiring women for the second shift at the van plant. She applied and was hired in the first group of women to work assembly at Chrysler in Windsor. Years later she became the full-time Chrysler employment equity representative until her retirement.

Sue Genge is a lifelong activist in the women and labour movements. She was an employee member of the Ontario Pay Equity Tribunal and a leader in CUPE Ontario. Sue was also president of her local at Metro Library in Toronto, chair of the CUPE Ontario division women's committee, and a member of the OFL women's committee. In her role with the CLC women's and human rights department, Sue led the work on women's issues including equal pay, employment equity, violence against women, childcare, and pride.

Denise Hampden is a long-time labour educator in Canada. The legacy of her ancestors in Africville and Sipekne'katik First Nation guides her work for social and racial justice. Denise only has two goals in life: to be a good ancestor and to get into good trouble whenever necessary.

Diane Hollingshead was first involved in the union representing workers at Air Canada, and then as a CAW national representative until she retired in 2006. Never one to step down from a challenge, Diane believes her role representing members and fighting for workers' rights and equality across a broad variety of sectors was both an opportunity and a privilege. It's work she remains proud of.

Colette Hooson was a women's activist, feminist, educator, and socialist who worked tirelessly for others. She began her career as a computer operator at Green Shield Canada and quickly became active in the local union, eventually becoming chairperson. She then became local union vice president and, in 1998, became the first female president of CAW Local 240. In 2004, Colette became a CAW national staff representative, where she remained committed to improving the lives of workers, negotiating groundbreaking language with an emphasis on bettering the lives of women.

Stephanie Johnstone joined the workforce at fifteen, becoming an alternate union representative with the United Steelworkers when she was just seventeen. Stephanie began working at GM in 1984 and held many different positions over her thirty years of service. Recognized with the Outstanding Retiree Award, Stephanie remains active in the struggle as the vice chair of the Local 636 retired workers council and the 2SLGBTQAI+ member at large on the retired workers council executive.

Denise Kellahan held elected union positions while working for many years in the service industry in BC. In 1992, Denise's union merged with the CAW, and Denise finished her working career as a national representative for the CAW. Grateful for all she learned in the union movement, Denise loves to share her experiences with younger workers.

Lisa Kelly completed her law degree and joined the CAW as an articling student in 1990, continuing as in-house counsel for over twenty years. She went on to be the education director and women's director before retiring in 2022. Her time at the union saw advances in 2SLGBTQ+ rights, the gender wage gap, universal childcare, paid domestic violence leave, and other equity initiatives.

Maureen Kirincic was hired at Chrysler in 1977 as a TPT (temporary part-time) student, making $6.39 an hour. In June of that year, she transferred to full-time status and worked there for five years. As a Local 444 member, she was active on several local union standing committees. She joined the UAW staff in 1982 in the organizing department. Maureen retired in 2007 and stays active volunteering in not-for-profit organizations in her community.

Cheryl Kryzaniwsky was hired at Air Canada in 1974, in a non-union department until she transferred into the reservations department and became a member of the Canadian Airline Employees Association (CALEA), later becoming a member of the CAW as the result of a merger. Cheryl was elected as president of CAW Local 2213 and, in 1995, she was elected as the first women president of CAW council, for a three-year term, before moving to director of education until she retired in 2005.

Annie Labaj, starting on the shop floor then working within the union, has worked to change the lens through which members saw their world. From being the first woman to be appointed as a national representative from General Motors to international director and overseeing the social justice fund her twenty-eight years at the national union gave her many opportunities to interact with members, not only in Canada but around the world.

Marilynne Lesperance was born in Windsor, Ontario, and after moving to Toronto she began to work as a school and charter bus driver. She was instrumental in organizing her workplace when the CBRT (Canadian Brotherhood of Railway, Transport and General Worker) union came calling. She became a business agent and president of her local union, before ending her career as CAW national representative after twenty-seven years of service to workers in both the CBRT and CAW unions until her retirement in 2004.

Denise McMorris is a woman of colour with over three decades of labour activism. Working at the Chrysler Bramalea assembly plant, CAW Local 1285, she was appointed CAW national coordinator for the legal services plan and as a national representative in the education department facilitating education programs. As a long-time volunteer at a woman's prison, Denise assisted inmates to reconnect with their families during their incarceration. In retirement, she continues to serve on various committees and boards in her community.

Nancy McMurphy was a long-term care worker and workplace chairperson for over twenty years. After her members joined the CAW, Nancy was elected president of Local 302 and remained in that position from 2001 to 2021, when she retired. From 2004 to 2016, Nancy was also the national executive board health care representative.

Diane Mimeault was a union activist from Quebec for thirty years. During that time, she held the position of health and safety representative for fifteen years before being elected as president of Local 2889. She was then appointed as a national staff representative for TCA-Quebec, working out of the Montreal office for twelve years, before she retired in 2019. Diane has two children, six grandchildren and has a passion for knitting.

Lorna Moses was hired to the UAW staff along with Edith Johnson in 1975, as a leader in her workplace, Northern Telecom, in Belleville, Ontario. She was the first woman staff organizer and organized the union in Fleck Manufacturing as well as many other workplaces. She went on to a senior staff position at the Ontario Federation of Labour and retired from the CAW in 2001. A member of the Tyendinaga Mohawk Nation she was taught to stand up for what she believed in, which led her to the union.

Bob Nickerson's history of trade unionism began in1955 at Duplate Canada, UAW Local 195. In 1961, Bob was elected plant chair and eight years later was appointed to UAW staff. In 1979, he became assistant to Bob White, the Canadian director of the UAW. When the Canadian section split in 1985, Bob was responsible for overseeing the successful transfer of funds to the CAW. Bob was elected the first CAW secretary treasurer and held that position until his retirement in1991.

Lana Payne was elected Unifor national president in 2022, becoming the first woman to hold this leadership position. Before her election, Payne served the union as secretary treasurer from 2019 to 2022. Payne brings three decades of leadership experience to workers, including through her previous position as Atlantic regional director. A proud feminist and activist, she found her home in the labour movement in 1991 with FFAW/CAW.

Carol Phillips began her labour career as an elected union leader in the 1980s. She then moved through the ranks of the Canadian Auto Workers Union (CAW) staff serving as a negotiator in various sectors (aerospace, auto parts, office and professional) to the director of three departments, international, education, and political action. Additionally, she was the assistant to three CAW presidents. While at the CAW, she established the innovative CAW social justice fund that has supported millions of dollars worth of development projects around the world. Since January 2009, Carol has been a member of the Ontario Labour Relations Board and continues to serve in this capacity.

Tina Pretty worked at FFAW-Unifor for forty-one years, including as the executive assistant to the president for over two decades. She is a proud women's advocate who went on to arrange women's advocate training for many of her union sisters in Newfoundland and Labrador and supported them in their role.

Ruth Pryce was born in Antigua and Barbuda. She excelled as a health care provider and union leader in Canada. She played pivotal roles in organizing unions, held various leadership positions in CAW/UNIFOR, and advocated for diversity and workers' rights. Ruth was the first Black female president of Unifor Local 1106 in Kitchener, Ontario, and was elected to the national executive board from 2013 to 2022, representing Indigenous and workers of colour members. She retired in 2022 and remains dedicated to union advocacy and worker education.

Laurell Ritchie began union work in 1972 with the Canadian Textile and Chemical Union. She was also a co-founder of the Equal Pay Coalition, board member of the National Action Committee on the Status of Women and co-founder of the Coalition Against Free Trade. In 1994 after the CTCU joined CAW, Laurell became a CAW national representative working in both the work organization and benefit departments.

Sari Sairanen is the executive assistant to the secretary treasurer of Unifor. Sari has a passion for meeting people, learning their stories, and building relationships in support of lasting, meaningful work adaptations for workers today and tomorrow. Sari comes to the national union from the airline division.

Bhupinder Sanghera is a trailblazing labour leader and the first South Asian woman to direct Workers United Canada Council. With over forty years of experience, she has organized across multiple industries and championed equity through initiatives for women and workers of colour, advancing justice in the Canadian labour movement.

Al Seymour began his career with the UAW in 1967. First appointed to the UAW organizing department out of Winnipeg, Manitoba, Al transferred to organizing in Kitchener and, in 1976, he was assigned to servicing in London, Ontario. In 1988, Al was appointed as the London area director of what had become the CAW and, in 1995, he became special assistant to the CAW national secretary treasurer until he retired in 1997.

Mildred Skinner was a long-time inshore fish harvester and FFAW science technician from Newfoundland and Labrador. She was the first woman ever elected to the FFAW executive board. Mildred is a trained women's advocate who continues to be active today working as sea field technician for the FFAW.

Cathy Walker started working in factories in the Vancouver area in 1970 and became active in her union. She held various positions in her local, eventually becoming president in 1973. In 1974, Cathy was appointed national staff representative and shortly took on the additional duties of health and safety, workers' compensation, and the environment. When Cathy's union merged with the CAW in 1992, Cathy was appointed director of the CAW health and safety department, a position she held until her retirement in 2006.

Elaine White worked at the Brampton assembly plant, where she was elected as an alternate committeeperson in the paint and trim area. Later as a women's advocate. Elaine was active in various women's committees and facilitated numerous programs and conferences. She eventually became the CAW legal services coordinator and a CAW national representative in the organizing department until her retirement in 2016.

Marilyne White was an Air Canada flight attendant for twenty-three years, holding several positions in her union, the Canadian Union of Public Employees (CUPE). Then she joined the staff as a national representative and for seventeen years, bargaining collective agreements and presenting grievances at arbitration. Born in Winnipeg, she was married to Bob White for thirty-eight years and currently lives in Toronto.

Terry Weymouth is a retired Unifor national skilled-trades coordinator and certified electrician. Terry promotes opportunities for people to engage in skills training and pre-apprenticeship programs utilizing her experience in both the industrial and construction sectors. Terry has become an adviser to government, industry, and academia. She continues to blaze a trail for apprenticeship opportunities for women.

Notes

Chapter 1: UAW, A Woman's Place Is in the Union, 1935–1978

1 In the first half of this chapter, for the union's history, we are indebted to historian Wendy Cuthbertson and her book *Labour Goes to War: The CIO and the Construction of a New Social Order, 1939–1945*, UBC Press, 2002.

2 Cuthbertson, *Labour Goes to War*, p. 94.

3 Cuthbertson, *Labour Goes to War*, p. 93.

4 Cuthbertson, *Labour Goes to War*, p. 147.

5 Don Taylor and Bradley Dow, *The Rise of Industrial Unionism in Canada—A History of the CIO*, Queen's University, Industrial Relations Centre, 1988; Nicole Greason, CIO's History Inspires Podcasts, *Labor Notes*, Feb. 23, 2024.

6 Cuthbertson, *Labour Goes to War*, p. 94.

7 Here's a short guide to the UAW/CAW structure:

- Workers decide to form a union to negotiate their workplace terms and conditions with their employer. This workplace union is called a bargaining unit. The workers (now union members) elect a small committee of their peers, called the bargaining committee, to carry out the negotiation and enforce the contract once it is agreed to with their employer. They also elect additional members, often called stewards, to represent them in the workplace with management to ensure their rights are respected.
- The members of one or more bargaining units elect representatives to lead their local union. The local union leadership may join in contract negotiations but usually plays a role in the broader union, joining in discussions about the union's policies, constitution, its community, or political activism.
- CAW council: A council brings together the national top leadership and the local leaders and other delegates elected to council to debate union policies and make decisions. The council would meet in between major conventions which might only happen every three years. A council would meet every few months.

- A smaller group of top national and local leaders would be elected to the executive board. This is like a board of directors and is charged with the most senior decisions and responsibilities of the union.
- Constitutional and collective bargaining conventions bring together hundreds of elected delegates from local unions. This is where top elections occur and where the elected delegates make the most important and binding decisions of the union

In the CAW the top elected officers were the national president, national secretary treasurer, and the Quebec director.

8 Cuthbertson, *Labour Goes to War*, p. 125.

9 Cuthbertson, *Labour Goes to War*, p. 131–132.

10 Minutes of the Canadian UAW Council Women's Committee, April 14, 1981 (riseupfeministarchive.ca)

11 Cuthbertson, *Labour Goes to War*, p. 71.

12 Cuthbertson, *Labour Goes to War*, p. 97.

13 Cuthbertson, *Labour Goes to War*, p. 144.

14 Christine McLaughlin, "Remembering an Extraordinary Struggle for Sexual Equality in Ontario," June 4, 2012 (activehistory.ca); Martin Glaberman and Ed Jennings, "Wildcat! The wartime strike wave in the auto industry," from *Radical America*, v9, no 4-5 (July-August 1975) (libcom.org).

15 See also chapter 7.

Chapter 2: Union Women Winning Victories, 1978–1985

1 Bob White, *Hard Bargains: My Life on the Line*, McClelland & Stewart, 1987, p. 134.

2 *Toronto Star*, 18 Oct 2011, Insight, "May 1978: Fleck women put fire back into feminism."

3 Constance Backhouse, "The Fleck Strike: A Case Study in the Need for First Contract Arbitration," *Osgoode Hall Law Journal*, v18, no 4 (December 1980).

4 Backhouse, "The Fleck Strike."

5 William Serrin, "U.A.W. Rebel: Bob White; A 'Superstar' For Canadian Labor," *The New York Times*, April 7, 1985.

6 Serrin, "U.A.W. Rebel."

7 Mike Moffatt, "Reforging Ontario: Given manufacturing's collapse,

can the province spark an economic renaissance?" *Review Canada*, December 2014.

Chapter 3: CAW Mergers Building a Sisterhood, 1985–1995

1 *Confronting Harassment in the Workplace*, CAW-Canada, 1987.

Chapter 4: Tragedy and Transformation, 1990–1995

1 Francis Fukuyama, "The End of History?" *The National Interest*, no. 16, 1989, pp. 3–18.
2 Garnett Picot and Andrew Heisz, "The Performance of the 1990s Canadian Labour Market," *Canadian Public Policy / Analyse de Politiques*, v26, 2000, pp. S7–25.
3 CRIAW-ICREF, Fact Sheet: Violence Against Women In Canada, 2013 (www.criaw-icref.ca).
4 See also chapter 7 for Georgina Anderson's narrative.

Chapter 5: Women on the March, 1995–2000

1 Nick Driedger, "What worked and what didn't: A history of organizing at Starbucks," *Organizing Work* (https://organizing.work/).
2 Carla Bryden was attracted to a BC-based union of women workers, the Service, Office and Retail Workers Union of Canada (SORWUC). It had been an independent union, established in 1972 by a group of 24 women who organized mainly women workers in a variety of sectors but who advocated for feminist issues such as equal pay, childcare, against sexual harassment, and gender and racial discrimination, but also for better pay and working conditions. However, they disbanded in 1986.

Chapter 6: Contradictory Progress, 2000–2014

1 Mike P. Moffat, "The big shift: Changes in Canadian manufacturing employment, 2003-2018, Full Report," Sept. 8, 2021 (Future Skills Centre / Centre des Competences futures).

Chapter 7: The Privilege and the Price of Change

1 See chapter 1 for Lorna Moses's narrative.
2 Jason Russell, *Our Union: UAW/CAW Local 27 from 1950 to 1990*, Athabasca University Press, 2011.

Index

Page numbers in italics indicate photos.

Abella, Rosalie, 55, 126
Abella Commission, 126, 127
abortion, 34, 184, 204–5
Abortion Caravan, 145, 184, 204–6, *205*
The Abortion Caravan... (Wells), 206
Acheson, Shelley, 30
adjustment programs, 149–50
Aeroplan, 232–3
affirmative action: CLC, 70–1; employment equity, 126–7, 144–5; FFAW, 97–8; at Ford Motor Company, 58–9; and Friend, 138–9; and Labaj, 90–2; and layoffs, 100; OFL, 61; "Solidarity in Diversity" slogan, 109–10
AFL-CIO, 7. *See also* Congress of Industrial Organizations
Air Canada: CALEA negotiations, 71–3; CALEA strike, 73–4, *73*; and Canadian Airlines, 163; and Cormier, 232–4; and Hollingshead, 154–6; and Kryzaniwsky, 110–11; and Sairanen, 210
Al Qaeda, 173
Amalgamated Clothing and Textile Workers Union, 56
American Federation of Labor (AFL), 6, 7
American Motors (AMC), 220–1
Anderson, Georgina, 41, *54*, 119, 216–17, *217*
anti-globalization, 173
anti-racism, 21
anti-scab legislation, 230
apprenticeships, 90
Armstrong, Evelyn, 28
Armstrong, Jane: biography, 275; on childcare, 134; on collective bargaining, 132; early retirement, 133–4; and harassment issues, 75; and Kryzaniwsky, 112; on media coverage, 130–1; and Nash, 71–2; on union leadership, 77–8
Arrow shirts, 56
Austin, Cathy, 180, 196–7, 206–9, *207*, 275

Backhouse, Constance, 39–40
Bailey, Vince, 219, 221
Baker, Roxie, *66*; overview, 66–7; advice for new activists, 270; biography, 275; breakthrough negotiations, 56; and childcare, 56–8, 83–4; and Cuthbertson, 45–6; and Kryzaniwsky, 114; on national executive board, 163, 200–1, 243–4; at UAW Canadian council, 23, 57; women's advisory committee, 53
Bank of Commerce, 164
bank workers, 26–7
bargaining units: affirmative

action, 138–9; and Bryden, 164–6, 167–8; and Davidson, 160–3; defined, 8, 9, 287n7; and Farao, 236–7, 239–40; and Hollingshead, 156–9; and Hooson, 235, 236–7, 239–40; and Moses, 24–5; overriding, 257; pattern bargaining, 258–9, 261; and Payne, 96; and Phillips, 67–9; and presidency, 261; and Pryce, 224; and Sairanen, 211–12; Starbucks, 144; and structure, 149; and women's goals, 127–31
Barlow, Maude, 100–1
Battle of Seattle, 173
Bauer, Larry, 84–5
Beech Grove Golf and Country Club, 238–9
Bell, Leroy, 79–80, 81
Bendix, 216
benefits for spouses, 187, 198
Benson, Kevin, 160
Bill 28, 257
Bill 124, 256
Bill C 391, 182–3, 203–4. *See also* long-gun registry
birth control, 145. *See also* abortion
Black women/workers, 119, 121, 153, 251. *See also individual workers*
Blair, Phoebe, 12
blockage, 15
Boekel, Mike Van, 208
Bowman, John, 144
Bread and Roses (Jobs and Justice) march, 134–5, *136–7*
breadwinners, 19–20, 24
"Break the Silence" campaign, 131
breastfeeding, 76–7
Brophy, Lynn, 119, 121–4, 275
Brotherhood of Railway and Airline Clerks., 160
Brotherhood of Railway Carmen (BRC), 150
Brown, Rosemary, 146
Bryden, Carla, 164–8, 244–5, 249, 276, 289Ch.5n2
Byers, Barb, 202, *251*, 276

Caesar's Windsor casino, 52, 195
Cameron, Stevie, 103–4
CAMI Automotive, 185–6, 187, 196, 198, 206
Canada-US Auto Pact (1965), 18
Canadian Air Line Employees Association (CALEA), 71–8, *73*, 110–13, 154–5
Canadian Airlines, 160–3
Canadian Association of Industrial Mechanical and Allied Workers Union (CAIMAW), 142–4, 145, 147
Canadian Auto Workers (CAW): bargaining 1981, 67–9; and BRC, 150; break from UAW, 59, 62–3, 73–4, 79; and CAIMAW, 142–4, 147; and CALEA, 74, 112–13; and CBRT&GW, 150; and CEP, 252–3; challenges with, 149; childcare (*see* childcare); constitutional convention, 108–10; and CTCU, 148; education camp/centre (*see* education centre); and feminism, 35; and FFAW, 92–3; first Black woman on staff, 222–3; first woman assembly plant president, 180; first woman assistant to president, 71; first woman president (*see* Payne, Lana); first woman

Quebec council delegate, 230; formation of, 59, 61, 65; founding convention, 65–6; history of, 10; human rights (*see* human rights); and RWSDU, 175; and SEIU, 174, 175–6; skilled trade program, 141–2; structure of, 287–8n7; and TCU-Canada, 160; vs. UAW, 54–5; website of, 133; women's committees, 105–6; women's conferences, 91, 106–8; Women's March (2000), 91–2. *See also* Hargrove, Buzz; Unifor; United Auto Workers; White, Bob
Canadian Automobile Association (CAA), 236–8
Canadian Brotherhood of Railway Transport and General Workers Union (CBRT&GW), 150, 151–2
Canadian Congress of Labour (CCL), 7
Canadian council (UAW), 9–10, 23, 53, 57, 287n7
Canadian Fabricated (Can Fab), 56–7
Canadian Labour Congress (CLC), 34, 69–70, 164, 165, 190, 204
Canadian National Railway (CN), 126
Canadian Textile and Chemical Union (CTCU), 148
Canadian Union of Public Employees (CUPE), 256–8
card check certification, 8
Carr, Shirley, 70
Carter, Sue, 197
Cashin, Richard, 92, 96
Casino Rama, 219
Cassidy, Dave, xvii
Chaplin, Ralph, 8
Charlton, Sheila, 37, 44
Charter of Rights and Freedoms in Canada, 54
checkoff. *See* Rand formula
Chernecki, Bob, 129–30
Chetwynd, Anne, 77
childcare: Canadian Fabricated, 56; CAW as leaders in, 35; Chrysler, 84; cost of, 134; and cross-fertilization, 35; Cuthbertson and UAW staff, 76–7; early 1980s overview, 53, 55–8; at education centre, 222; and executive board, 114, 115–16; and Farao, 235–6; and Fleck, 46; funding for, 83–5; Kryzaniwsky and council presidency, 113; and Nash, 130; Phillips and bargaining day, 68–9; poster for, 85; program closure, 92; in Quebec, 230; setting up, 85–6; and strikes, 111; and J. White, 177–8, 179
Chretien, Jean, 101
Chrysler: childcare, 84; and Friend, 136–9; and Kirincic, 46–51; and McMorris, 221–2, 223–4; pregnancy accommodation, 140–1; and tradeswomen, 141; and E. White, 218
CIBC Visa, 75
Clancy, Pat, 51, 70
class, 83
clothing, 195–6
Cloutier, Daniel, 256
CMC Electronic, 231
Coalition Against Free Trade, 271
Coalition for Gun Control (CGC), 204. *See also* gun control
cod stocks, 93

collective bargaining. *See* bargaining units
Collison, Robert, 62
common expiry dates, 67–8
Communications, Energy and Paperworkers Union of Canada (CEP), 252–3
communism, 7
complaints, 75, 81, 82, 125
Confederation of Canadian Unions (CCU), 142, 148
Congress of Industrial Organizations (CIO), 6–7, 13, 14, 33
Connor, Christine, 175, 276
constitutional convention, 108–10
conventions overview, xv
Cormier, Sandra, 232–4, 272, 276
cost-of-living allowance (COLA), 261
councils. *See* Canadian council
courses. *See* education centre
COVID pandemic, 255, 258, 260
CP Air, 159–60
Craig, Linda, 238
Credit Union, 165–6
cross-fertilization, 35, 55, 91
Crowther, Roger, 144
Crump, Kim, 195–200, 266, 277
Cuthbertson, Wendy: and affirmative action, 58–9; on Baker, 67; biography, 277; and CALEA, 74–6; CAW constitution, 63; on CAW formation, 63; on Equal Pay Act, 14; on excluding men, 44; on Fleck strike, 40, 44–5; on Ford strike, 10; GM talks, *46*; joining national staff, 21; *Labour Goes to War*, 6; and Nash, 76; on OFL women's committee, 28–9; UAW childcare, 56; on UAW vs. CAW, 54–5; women's committee, 45–6; women's committees, 53

D'Aquino, Tom, 100–1
"Daughters, Ourselves" (Cameron), 103–4
Davidson, Anne, 159–64, *161*, 211, 277
Davis, Bill, 41
Davis, Julie, 31
Days of Action, 148
De Havilland Aircraft, 4, 67–9
Dean, Bob, 230
Dhaliwal, Raj, 224–5
Diamond, Nancy, 219
Dias, Jerry, xvi–xvii
Dias, Leslie, 163
Diggs, Cory, 193, *194*
Diggs, Pam, 190, 192–4, *194*, 277–8
directors, defined, 9
divisiveness, 79–80, 81, 118, 122, 123–4. *See also* homophobia; racism; sexism/misogyny
Doherty, Scott, xvi–xvii
Dubois, Roxanne, xviii, *256*
dues, 8, 15–16. *See also* Rand formula
Dunphy, Dana, 195–6, 198–200, 278
Durham College, 90

Eadie, Mary, 69
Ebanks, Josephine, 119, 217
École Polytechnique de Montréal, 103–4
education: and Baker, 270; and Brophy, 121–2; and Cormier, 233–4; and Labaj, 90, 91; models of, 121–2; E. White on, 271. *See also* women's conferences
education centre: overview, 65,

100; activist course, 124, *125*, 199–200, 218–19, 226; and childcare, 222; diversity at, 229; Hampden's experiences, 226, 227; and Indigenous Peoples, 121; Johnstone's experiences, 189; learners based education, 121–3; McMorris's experiences, 222–3, 224; public speaking, 210–11; and Quebec workers, 232; racialized workers, 121, 222; Sanghera's experiences, 229; skilled trade program, 141–2; 2SLGBTQ+ workers, 121; E. White's experiences, 218–19; J. White's experiences, 177–8; women's only, 118–20, 123–4. *See also* paid education leave program
elections, xv–xix, *xviii*, 8, 113–14
employment equity, 126–7, 144–5. *See also* Friend, Irene; *specific groups*
equal pay: overview, 234; as Allied rhetoric, 12; Hooson and Farao, 235–42; in mid-nineteenth century, 7; in 1940s, 3–4, 10–12, 13–14, 59; 3M, 178–9; Union Station, 153
Equal Pay Act (1951), 14
Equal Pay Coalition, 271
Equality in Employment (royal commission), 126
ergonomics, 210
ESL (English as second language), 144–5, 149
ethical breaches, xvi–xvii

Fane, Gary, 211
Farao, Theresa, 235–7, 238–9, *241*, 278
Fédération des femmes du Québec (FFQ), 134, 230
feminism: overview, 262; and activist courses, 124, 199–200; and Bryden, 164; and Charter of Rights and Freedoms in Canada, 54; and Ferguson, 3; and McMorris, 222; men as allies, 29–31, 35; misreading, 250; and Montreal Massacre, 103; and Phillips, 70–1; second wave, 19, 64, 252; and traditional culture, 252; and women's committees, 35
Ferguson, Margery, 3–4
"15 Days 15 Ways to End Violence Against Women" campaign, 202–3
Final Offer (film), 62
fines, 257
Firth, Stacey Allerton, 245
Fish, Food and Allied Workers (FFAW), 92–100, *97*, 265
Fleck, James, 38–9
Fleck Manufacturing, 24, 36–45, *42–3*
Ford, Doug, 256, 257
Ford Motor Company: affirmative action, 58–9; equal pay, 4; post-pandemic negotiations, 260; solidarity for Fleck strike, 40; and Unifor bargaining, 260, 262; union security strike 1945, 15–16; wildcat strike 1942, 10–11, 59
free trade, 100–1, 126
Friend, Irene, 136–41, 199, 278
Friendly, Martha, 85

Gabelmann, Colin, 146
Gallagher, Deirdre, 28, 40

gender roles, 104, 127
gender-based violence: overview, 104, 105–10; CAW first addressing, 105–7; and collective agreements, 128, 130; and economic independence, 240–1; "15 Days 15 Ways to End Violence Against Women" campaign, 202–3; fishing industry, 154; Handkerchief Project, 228; "Our Daughters, Ourselves" article, 103–4; and E. White, 219; and women's caucuses, 200–1. *See also* Montreal Massacre
General Motors: affirmative action, 58, 59; and Bell, 79–80; *Final Offer* (film), 62; job insecurity, 126; and Johnstone, 189; and Labaj, 86–8, *87*; and McCloskey, 16; pattern bargaining, 261; seniority lists, 88–9, 234; strike mandate, 260; strikes, 6–7, 18, 60; trim plants and seniority, 18–19; union talks, *46*; wire and harness department, 88; women's employment numbers, 18
general strikes, 5
Genge, Sue, 34–5, 61, 202–3, 278–9
Gerard, Ken, 84
Gindin, Sam, 116
Gingras, Carole, 69–70
Gottheil, Lewis, 186
Great Depression, 5, 6
Great Recession, 174
Green, Mary Ann, 89–90
gun control, 182–4, 199, 201, 202–4
Gunnarsson, Sturla, 62
Gutter Boyz, 194

Hall, Marc, 125
Hampden, Denise, 226–8, 271, 279
Handkerchief Project, 228
harassment: and anti-harassment video, 133; Austn's experiences, 207–8; bosses, 176; Bryden's experiences, 165–6; and collective agreements, 128–31, 140; and complaint letters, 75; FFAW, 98–100; Fleck Manufacturing, 36; Ford Motor Company, 58; Friend's experiences, 137–8, 139–41; Johnstone's experiences, 190–1; Kirincic's experiences, 47–9; and learner-centered education, 124; Moses's experiences, 25–6; and persistence, 99–100; policy and procedure, 80–3; statistics, 106; and training, 140; by union leaders, 207–8; J. White's experiences, 178; at Windsor Casino, 196; workshop on, 72. *See also* gender-based violence; homophobia; human rights; pinups; sexism/misogyny
Hargrove, Buzz: and Canadian Airlines, 160–2; and childcare, 56, 83–4, 115; complaint letters, 125; gun control, 201; and Hollingshead, 156; and Lesperance, 151; and McMorris, 222; and mergers, 175; succession of, 245. *See also* Canadian Auto Workers
Harper, Stephen, 184
Harris, Mike, 127, 148
Harrison, Beulah, 41, 179
health and safety, 25, 146, 147–8, 210, 212
Henderson, Bonnie, 192
Hollingshead, Diane, 111, 154–9, *155*, 242, 279

homophobia: Crump's experiences, 196, 197–8; false support, 199; at Fleck, 44; Johnstone's experiences, 190–1. *See also* harassment; human rights; 2SLGBTQ+ workers
Hooson, Colette, 235–8, *241*, 244, 279
Hosek, Haviva, 73
hotlines, 26
human rights, 78–81, 90–1, 100. *See also specific rights*
Human Rights Commission, 126

identity politics, 83
Indigenous Peoples, 121, 216, 219. *See also* racialized workers
interest rates, 61
International Association of Machinists and Aerospace Workers (IAM), 161–2
International Women's Day Committee, 40
International Women's Day (IWD), 20, *183*, *246*, 263–4
International Women's Day march (1979), 44
International Women's Day march (2000), 135, *137*
Islamophobia, 173

Johnson, Edith, *21*, *31*; overview, 20–1, 180; and Fleck strike, 45; hired as staff, 50; women's committees, 46, 53, *54*
Johnson Controls, 56
Johnstone, Stephanie, 188–92, 193, 279

Katz, Jackson, 200
Kaufman, Carl, 76
Keeping Students in Class Act, 257
Kellahan, Denise, 143–4, 163, 270, 279
Kelly, Lisa, 186–8, 279
Kennedy, Peter, 247–8
Kennedy, Sharon, 41
Kentucky Fried Chicken, 142–3
Kirincic, Maureen, 46–53, 69, 80, 264, 279
Koeck, Moe, 30
Kryzaniwsky, Cheryl, *117*; overview, 110–18; advice for new activists, 270–1; biography, 280; and CALEA strike, 73; and Hollingshead, 155; and Nash, 76; on national executive board, 163; public speaking education, 210–12; style of leadership, 155, 244

Labaj, Annie, *87*; overview, 86–92; biography, 280; as dismissed, 244; and Phillips, 250; women-only workshops, 107
Labour Board or the Human Rights Commission, 75
Labour Goes to War (Cuthbertson), 6
Landsberg, Michele, 131
Lankin, Frances, 72
Laville, Marie, 131–2, *133*, *136*
layoffs, 48, 92, 100, 118–19, 126–7
Layton, Jack, 182, 246
Leach, Pam, 198
leaders: overview, 118–24; advice for new activists, 269–73; and affirmative action, 144–5 (*see also* affirmative action); in CIO, 13; as role models, 241; waiting to lead, 151; women as presidents, 243,

245. *See also* Payne, Lana; *individual women*
Lesperance, Marilynne, 150–4, 224, 242, 281
Lévesque, René, 230
Lewenza, Ken, 116, 248
LGBT workers. *See* 2SLGBTQ+ workers
Liberal Party, 134
lifting law, 146
lockouts, 153, 239
long-gun registry, 182–4, 199, 201, 202–4
Lougheed, Peter, 100–1

MacDonald, Marion, 164
MacInally, Helen, 88
MacKinnon, Dorothy, 28
Macphail, Agnes, 234
Maheux, Ken, 114
Malcho, Karen, *66*
management, 36
manufacturing overview, 62, 174
Massey-Harris, 3
maternity leave, 51, 55, 69, 76. *See also* pregnancy
McAnally, Frank, 106–7, 108, 116
McCarthy era, 7
McCloskey, Bev, 16–17, *17*, 19, 20, 88
McCurdy, Earl, 96
McDermott, Dennis, 12, 21, 36, 60, 70
McGarrigle, Gavin, *256*
McGregor Hosiery, 148, 149
McKinnon Industries, 3–4, 18
McLaughlin, Audrey, 246
McLean, Dave, 192
McMorris, Denise, 220–4, *223*, 242, 266, 281
McMurphy, Nancy, 175–6, 281
membership in WWII, 5–7
men as allies: overview, 29–31, 35; Austin's experiences, 208; and excluding men, 44; and Fleck strike, 43; McMorris's experiences, 221, 222; J. White's experiences, 178. *See also individual men*
mentors, 272
mergers overview, 174, 175, 231. *See also specific merged unions*
Metallic Roofing, 13
Metro, 258–9
Milk, Harvey, 185
Mimeault, Diane, 231–2, 281
misogyny. *See* sexism/misogyny
Mitchell, Margaret, 73
Montague, Rene, 39
Montreal Massacre, 103–4, 184, 228. *See also* gender-based violence
moratorium compensation, 97
Morgentaler, Henry, 34, 204
Morris, Ena, 119, 217
Moses, Lorna, 20, 21–5, 50, 281–2
Mulroney, Brian, 101
Murray, Linda, 79–80, 81, 83

Nash, Peggy: advice for new activists, 272; and Armstrong, 71–2; on bargaining units, 128–31; and Canadian Airlines, 160–2; on Canadian UAW split, 73–4; on Cashin, 92; on Chernecki, 129–30; childcare, 84–5; as director of women's programs, 105, 108; on gun control, 201; human rights, 78–9, 80; motherhood and CAW, 76–7; and obstacles, 245–6; on OWW, 28; and Payne, 96; as politician, 246, *246*; and

Quebec council, 230; "Solidarity in Diversity" slogan, 108–10; Starbucks collective agreement, 144; and B. White, 105, 108; and J. White, 181
National Action Committee on the Status of Women, 73
national executive board (NEB): Baker, 163, 200–1, 243–4; and childcare, 114, 115–16; Kryzaniwsky, 163; and Phillips's leadership bid, 248; J. White, 163
National Labour Relations Act (1935), 5
neo-liberalism, 61–2
Neron, Paule Ange, 230, 231–2
New Deal, 5
New Democratic Party (NDP), 104–5, 119, 146, 173–4, 182
Newfoundland and Labrador Federation of Labour, 96
newspapers, 3
Nickerson, Barb, *31*, 41
Nickerson, Bob: affirmative action at GM, 59; biography, 282; on men allies, 35; and Moses, 23; and Nash, 78; and Phillips, 69; and Phillips' mother, 68; and women's issues, 21, 29–31
9/11, 173
No Frills, 259
Nortel, 185–6, 187
North American Free Trade Agreement (NAFTA), 126
Northern Electric, 22, 27, 39, 179

Obama, Barak, 174
obstacles overview, 242–52, 253
OFL women's committee, 28, *31*, 55, 61
O'Neil, Jim, 68, 245
Ontario Federation of Labour (OFL), 28–30, *31*, 34, 55, 61
Ontario Human Rights Code, 20, 86
Ontario Provincial Police (OPP), 37–9, 41
Organized Working Women (OWW), 27–9, 30, 40

Pacific Western Airlines, 76
paid education leave program (PEL): and Pride Conference, 197; and *Tough Guise* video, 200; and union negotiators, 46; and J. White, 177–8; for women, 91; and women activists programs, 120; women/LGBT issues, 124
Parent, Madeleine, 44, 148–9, 269
parental benefits, 150
part time work, 139–40, 175
pattern bargaining, 258–9, 261
pay equity. *See* equal pay
Payne, Lana, *260*; overview, 93–6, 255–6, 259, 261, 262–7; advice for new activists, 269; biography, 282; and equal pay, 240; and D. Ford, 257–8; and Ford Motor Company, 260, 262; on front line workers, 258; on Metro workers, 258; as national secretary treasurer, xvi; running for presidency, xvi–xix; strike solidarity, *256*; winning presidency, *xviii*
PC World, 153
Phillips, Carol: overview, 67–9; advice for new activists, 269; affirmative action, 59; biography, 282; and Brophy, 124; and Bryden, 168; as director of public appointments, 105; at

GM rally, *251*; human rights and CAW, 80–1; and Kryzaniwsky, 116; leaving union, 246–52; OFL women's committee, *31*; on Payne, 265; secretary treasurer bid, 92
Piercey, Fran, 37, 38
Pilkey, Cliff, *17*, 20, 30, 263
Pilkey, Vi, 89
pinups, 17, 47, 81, 88, 89, 191
police, 36, 37–9, 41, 153
Possuns, Jack, 52
pregnancy, 51, 68, 74, 111, 140–1. *See also* maternity leave
Pretty, Tina, 98–100, 282–3
pro-choice. *See* abortion; Abortion Caravan
protests, 173, *225*. *See also* strikes
Pryce, Ruth, 224–6, *225*, 283
punching out, 86–7

Quebec, 230–4, *256*
Québec City 2001, 173

racialized workers: and changing culture, 252; at Chryslers, 220; and CIO, 7; committee, 219; education centre, 119, 121; employment equity law, 127; Equality in Employment commission, 126; and ESL, 144–5, 149; as isolated, 229; obstacles overview, 251; PC World, 153; in railway work, 226; on staff, 216. *See also individual workers*
racism: overview, 215–16; Diggs's experiences, 193; Hampden's experiences, 226; McMorris's experiences, 221, 223–4; in 1970s, 18; Pryce's experiences, 224, 225; as tool of division, 79–80. *See also* anti-racism; human rights
Rae, Bob, 104–5, 126–7, 162
Rand, Ivan, 15
Rand formula: overview, 15–16; as abstract, 45; as compulsory, 36, 41; and Fleck, 37; testing of, 33–4
Reagan, Ronald, 54–5
Rebick, Judy, 34, 60–1
recession, 126–7. *See also* Great Depression
Red Book actions, 134
Red Scare, 7
regrets, 52
representatives/stewards, 8–9, 13, 15
reproductive health. *See* abortion; Abortion Caravan
Retail, Wholesale and Department Store Union (RWSDU), 175
Reuther, Victor, 249
Reuther, Walter, 7
Richard, Mary Lou, 36, 37
Riche, Nancy, 69–70
Riddell, Jack, 39
Ritchie, Dave, 161–2
Ritchie, Laurell, xvii, 148–50, 271, 283
Rivera, 224–5
Robert's Rules of Order, 89
Robinson, Svend, 185
Roosevelt, Franklin D., 5
Rothman, Laurel, 85
Rowley, Kent, 148

safety, 146, 147–8, 210, 212
safety posters, 25
Sairanen, Sari, 209–12, 283
Sanghera, Bhupinder, 228–30, 283
satisfaction, 271–2
Saunders, Tom, 71–2, 110, 116

scabs, 16, 37–9
Schevinska, Sue, 162
schools, 4
Schultz, Pat, 54
second wave feminism, 19, 64, 252
Second World War: CIO, 33; constitutional amendment, 13; passing memories of, 28; and union membership, 5–7; women's post-war goals, 14
segregation, 18, 22–3
self employment, 104
seniority lists: overview, 17–20, 23, 234; Can Fab, 57; Chryslers, 48; GM, 88–9; and Labaj, 86; 3M, 177
September 11 attacks (2001), 173
Service, Office and Retail Workers Union of Canada (SORWUC), 289Ch.5n2
Service Employees International Union (SEIU), 174, 175
service sector, 142–3
servicing staff, 24–5
sexism/misogyny: at CAMI Automotive, 206–7, 208–9; at education centre, 227; education on, 124; at Fleck, 24; at Ford Motor Company, 59; as informal, 13; and leadership, 241; man caves, 86; of managers, 25; in meetings, 77–8; Montreal Massacre, 103–4; seniority lists, 17–18, 20; strippers at union hall, 196, 209; as tool of division, 79–80; and women's compliance, 242. *See also* equal pay; harassment; human rights; obstacles overview
sexual assault, 106. *See also* gender-based violence
Seymour, Al: biography, 283–4; and Fleck, 36–9, 40, 41, 42; on 2SLGBTQ+ rights, 186; and B. White, 60; and J. White, 181; and women's issues, 21
Seymour Barb, 41
Shields, Mike, 125, 249
shift work, 84–5, 87–8
shit-house meetings, 50
Shortall, Mary, 209
Shorten, Maurie, 19
Simpson, Sylvia, 144
Sisterhood, 273
Skinner, Mildred, 96–8, 97, 265, 284
Smitherman, George, 125
solidarity: Air Canada strike, 112; CAA, 237–8; CUPE, 257; defined, 83; and education, 123; enjoying, 269; Fleck strike, 40–1, 43–5; Ford strike blockade, 15; in formative years of UAW/CAW, 7; and harassment, 98–9; international women, 91; Northern Electric and Fleck strike, 39; OFL women's committee, 28; SACTU, 71; "Solidarity in Diversity" slogan, 108–10; women's lack of, 250, 252. *See also* men as allies
"Solidarity Forever" (Chaplin), 8
Solidarity in Diversity document, 175
South African Congress of Trade Unions (SACTU), 71
special accommodation, 55. *See also* maternity leave
Spencer, Greg, 110–11
spousal benefits, 187, 198
staff, 61, 116
Standard Automotive, 192

Stanford, Jim, 161
Starbucks, 144
Stelco, 15
Stellantis, 260, 261
Stephenson, Bette, 39–40
stewards, 8–9, 13, 15
St-Hubert, 232
strategic voting, 248
strike mandate,
General Motors, 260
strikes: Air Canada, 73–4, *73*, 110–11, 155; Beech Grove Golf and Country Club, 238–9; CAA, 237–8; CAMI Automotive, 198; and childcare, 111; Chrysler, 60; CIBC Visa, *75*; Credit Union, 165–6; CUPE, 257; De Havilland Aircraft, 67; fines, 257; Fleck Manufacturing, 36–45, *42*; Ford Motor Company, 10–11, 15–16, 59; General Motors, 6–7, 18, 60; Metro, 258–9; OFL women's committee, 28; Pacific Western Airlines, 76; and pay, 15; PC World, 153; recent auto industry, 261; Starbucks, 144; 3M, 176, 181; White Spot, 144; Windsor Casino, 52; Winnipeg General Strike, 5
strippers, 196, 209
Succamore, Jess, 272
Sugiman, Pam, 18
Summit of the Americas, 173

tampons, 50
taxes, 8
temporary work, 47, 139–40
"'That Wall's Comin' Down'" (Sugiman), 18
Theatre Passe Muraille, 44
Third Summit of the Americas, 173
Thompson, Ruth, 13
3M, 21, 176–7, 181, 185–6, 187
Tough Guise (video), 200
Trade Unions Act (1872), 5
Trades and Labour Congress (TLC), 7
trailblazers, 227–8
Transportation and Communications Union (TCU-Canada), 160
Travailleurs et Travailleuses de l'Automobile de Québec (TCA), 230
Trudeau, Pierre, 205
2SLGBTQ+ workers: overview, 185–94; benefits for partners, 185–6, 187–8, 198; caucuses, 191; courses for, 121; and Diggs, 190, 192–4, *194*; Fleck solidarity, 44; and Johnstone, 188–92; and Kelly, 186–8; and membership books, 158; national conference, 125, 189–90, 191, 193, 197; and PEL program, 124; pride, 190; and traditional culture, 252. *See also* human rights; *individual workers*

UN International Year of the Woman, 23, 27
unemployment, 5, 61, 126, 174
Unifor: overview, xix–xx, 259–60; elections 2022, xv–xix, *xviii*; formation of, 252–3; history of, 10; International Women's Day, 263–4; power of presidency, 264–5; strike solidarity, *256*; women's advocates, 131. *See also* Payne, Lana
union dues, 8, 15–16. *See also* Rand formula

Union Station, 153
unions overview: in mid-nineteenth century, 4–5, 33; and Rae, 105; structures of, 8–9, 24
United Aircraft, 16, 230
United Auto Workers (UAW): Canadian break from, 9–10, 59, 62–3, 73–4, 79 (*see also* Canadian Auto Workers); vs. CAW, 54–5; childcare, 55–6, 83–6 (*see also* childcare); education camp, 30–1; first woman organizer, 23–4; history of, 9; in 1940s, 3–4, 12–15; in 1950s, 16–17; in 1960s, 19, 22; in 1970s, 22–3, 30–1; in 1980s, 30–1; progress of, 29–31; structure of, 9, 287–8n7; women on staff, 43; women's committees, 45–6, 53–4; women's conferences, 54, 63. *See also specific workplaces*
United Food and Commercial Workers Union (UFCW), 92, 259
University of Toronto, 229

VIA Rail, 226–7
violence, 103–4, 105–10

wages. *See* equal pay
Wagner Act (1935), 5
Walker, Cathy, 145–8, 204–6, 209, 284
Walton, Laura, 257
washrooms, 49–50
websites, 133
Wells, Karin, 206
Weymouth, Terry, 141–2, 284–5
White, Bob: overview, 59–60; and affirmative action, 58–9; Air Canada strike, 112; and Bryden, 165; and CALEA, 73, 74; Canadian break from UAW, 9–10; CAW constitution, 63; as CAW president, 65–6; and challenge, 186; childcare poster, *85*; and Fleck strike, 40, 44; forming women's committee, 12, *54*; and Kirincic, 50, 52–3; and Kryzaniwsky, 113; as listener, 60–1; and mergers, 92; and Moses, 27; and Nash, 76, 105, 108; and 1988 election, 100–1; and Phillips, 71, 247, 249; and pro-choice position, 34; and Ritchie, 148; and Seymour, 36, 60; "Solidarity in Diversity" slogan, 108–10; as superstar, 59. *See also* Canadian Auto Workers
White, Elaine, 217–20, 265–6, 271, 284
White, Julie: overview, 120, 131, 176–84; advice for new activists, 273; gun control, 202–3, 204; International Women's Day, *183*; on national executive board, 163; and Payne, 96; and Phillips, 249, *251*; and 3M, 187; as "trouble," 244
White, Marilyne, 35, 60–1, 284
White Ribbon Campaign, 104
White Spot, 143
Why I March demonstration, *225*
wildcat strikes, 10–11, 59
Wilson, Gord, 26
Windsor Casino, 195
Winnipeg General Strike, 5
women activists course, *125*; overview, 122–4; and Dunphy, 199–200; and Hampden, 226; and Quebec workers, 231, 232, 233; and E. White, 218–19

women in skilled trades and technology awareness (WSTTA) program, 141–2
Women Unite! poster, *133*, *136*
women-only activities, 4, 107, 122–4
women's auxiliaries, 4
women's caucuses, 200–3, 233
women's committees: CAW, 105, 179–82; CLC, 35; and gun control, 182–3; and Johnson, 21; and McCloskey, 15–16, 19; in 1940s, 12, 13–14; in 1960s, 19; OFL, 28–30, *31*, 55, 61; UAW, 45–6, *54*; Unifor, 261; and E. White, 220
women's conferences: overview, 127–8; CALEA, 72; CAW, 91, 106–8, 179, 196; CLC, 69–70; and diversity, 225; and Phillips, 249; UAW, 16, 19, 63, 89; and J. White, 181; World Women Conference, 134. *See also specific conferences*
Women's March (2000), 91–2
World March of Women in the Year 2000, 135, *137*
World War II. *See* Second World War
World Women Conference, 134
World Women's March, 230

Yardy, Kim, 206, 249

Peggy Nash is the executive director of the Canadian Centre for Policy Alternatives. She was the former senior negotiator in the Canadian Auto Workers (CAW), where she had the privilege of working with many groundbreaking union women from the 1980s to 2011. She led the CAW's women's department for many years and initiated innovative leadership programs. She was the first labour woman to lead national auto bargaining. Nash later became an NDP member of parliament, a lecturer in politics at Toronto Metropolitan University, and an author. Nash was named to the Order of Canada for her work in the union and was awarded an honorary doctorate of laws from Brock University. She lives in Toronto, Ontario.

Julie White is the former long-time director of the CAW-Unifor women's department. She held many leadership positions in her local union including becoming the first woman president of CAW Local 27. She was elected to the union's national executive board and was later appointed director of the CAW women's department. In this role, White was responsible for the union's equity campaigns, education, mobilization, and workplace advocacy. She advocated for reproductive rights, childcare, the need for gun control legislation, and other measures to end gender-based violence. She lives in London, Ontario.